"Have we expected too much of 'liberation' in our
Has liberation theology fallen captive to the compe
for the most oppressed? In the most comprehensi
Michel Foucault and liberation theology to date, th
builds on Foucault's micro-politics of resistance to ....p .....in ascetic
practice not as the renunciation of sexuality, desire, and the body, but a
constant process of self-transformation."

—**Marcus Pound**, Durham University

"When Liberation Theology gets indecent then the dualism of freedom and
resistance comes to the fore. *Toward a Micro-Political Theology* introduces
the reader to a fresh and non-Western reading of Foucault."

—**Michael Hoelzl**, University of Manchester

"Chen's book brings Foucault into conversations with liberation theologies, showing the ways Foucault's analyses of power relations, sexuality,
and subjectification can correct liberation theologies' blind spots. *Toward
a Micro-Political Theology* opens new avenues for thinking about social
change and everyday resistance. I recommend it enthusiastically."

—**Kwok Pui-lan**, Candler School of Theology

"In this sharp review and analysis, Yin-An Chen separates the Foucauldian
wheat from the faux-liberation tares, showing us what genuine resistance
entails and how Foucault helps us imagine it. Full of fine distinctions, and
the unsparing critiques that come with them, *Toward a Micro-Political
Theology* first clears the ground of so much detritus piling up in Foucault's
wake and then recovers from the ashes something (self)transformative, a
political spirituality."

—**Jonathan Tran**, Baylor University

"In this highly insightful book, Yin-An Chen offers a rich micro-political
theology that poses hard challenges to extant theologies of liberation. He
shows that, to become most effective, liberation theologies should reflect
on how subject-selves are constructed via spiritual practice, as a mode of
resistance to capitalist accounts of subjectivity. Chen's call for the development of individual yet simultaneously non-privatized subjectivity, through
the dual lenses of resistance and desire, is original and compelling."

—**Susannah Cornwall**, University of Exeter

Toward a Micro-Political Theology

Toward a Micro-Political Theology

A Dialogue between Michel Foucault and Liberation Theologies

Yin-An Chen

FOREWORD BY
Jeremy Carrette

PICKWICK *Publications* · Eugene, Oregon

TOWARD A MICRO-POLITICAL THEOLOGY
A Dialogue between Michel Foucault and Liberation Theologies

Pickwick Publications
An Imprint of Wipf and Stock Publishers
199 W. 8th Ave., Suite 3
Eugene, OR 97401

www.wipfandstock.com

PAPERBACK ISBN: 978-1-7252-9490-5
HARDCOVER ISBN: 978-1-7252-9491-2
EBOOK ISBN: 978-1-7252-9492-9

Cataloguing-in-Publication data:

Names: Chen, Yin-An, author. | Carrette, Jeremy R., foreword.

Title: Toward a micro-political theology : a dialogue between Michel Foucault and liberation theologies / by Yin-An Chen ; foreword by Jeremy Carrette.

Description: Eugene, OR : Pickwick Publications, 2022 | Includes bibliographical references.

Identifiers: ISBN 978-1-7252-9490-5 (paperback) | ISBN 978-1-7252-9491-2 (hardcover) | ISBN 978-1-7252-9492-9 (ebook)

Subjects: LCSH: Political theology. | Foucault, Michel, 1926-1984. | Liberation theology—Political aspects.

Classification: BT83.59 .C45 2022 (print) | BT83.59 .C45 (ebook)

09/09/22

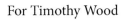

For Timothy Wood

Contents

Foreword by Jeremy Carrette | ix
Acknowledgments | xv

Introduction | 1
1 The Betrayal of Social Movements and Revolutions | 15
2 The Failure of Liberation Theologies | 28
3 Doing Liberation Theology with Foucault | 58
4 The Critiques of Political Theologies of Sexuality and Desire | 96
5 Prayer, Asceticism, and Subjectification as Resistance | 132
Concluding Reflection: Toward a Micro-Political Theology | 164

Bibliography | 175

The Many Sides of Foucault's Transformation

SINCE THE 1970S, MICHEL Foucault's searching analysis of knowledge, power and subjectivity has resulted in a transformation of thinking in the social sciences and humanities. The force of that transformation reflects not only how his work offers the capacity to rethink the hidden assumptions of knowledge, but the diversity of ideas within his critical project. This diversity is one that provides opportunity for readers to position Foucault in numerous ways and to frame different dimensions for specific purposes. Many of the presentations of Foucault isolate features of his work and some perpetuate a particular rendition of his thinking as it arrives through the different translation of works and popularizations. However, closer readers of Foucault will always wish to understand this diversity and the underlying complexity of his thinking through the various decades of work, playing with the nuances of his ideas over time. Each period of Foucault's thinking, for example, shows the experiments in thought, the evolution of a problematic and the developing methods: from early archaeology, through his Nietzschean genealogy to the techniques of the self and the arts of existence of the late works. What this demonstrates is that there are many parts to Foucault's thinking, which require a patient appreciation of someone engaging in a complex set of philosophical-historical exercises.

We might also recognize—against simple categorizations—that Foucault was comfortable associating himself with the critical project of Kant and the Enlightenment. In his essay on the Enlightenment in 1984, he was concerned with developing a philosophical attitude or ethos that was far from rejecting truth in any simple form.[1] He clearly held a commitment to strong normative positions on social justice—from political refugees, education and prison reform, Solidarity in Poland and gay rights—and sought to bring

1. Foucault, "What Is Enlightenment?," 32–50.

about a change in institutional practices. This is not to deny the ruptures that his philosophical critique created, but to appreciate the layers of his thinking across his life and the dynamics of reception and interpretation.

In addition, we find a layered complexity in Foucault scholarship through the various waves of publication: first, through the foundational texts during his lifetime; second, through the gathering of his wider papers in *Dits et écrits*[2] (selectively gathered in translation); third, through the extensive publication of the Collége de France lectures; and, finally, through the much awaited posthumous emergence of *Confessions of the Flesh*.[3] All these evolving scholarly episodes make for a more nuanced Michel Foucault than is found in textbook positioning. It is not surprising that Foucault resisted any simple positioning; he tried to escape the idea of "structuralist" in the 1960s and questioned the idea of the "postmodern" towards the end of his life. It is important, therefore, to question any attempt to reduce his thinking into one dimension or external framework, especially for a thinker who is seeking to hold a dynamic and evolving set of relationships in thought and practice. Pushing back against one particular reductive interpretation of his work, Foucault stated in 1978: "I never presumed that 'power' was something that could explain everything."[4] Power, like knowledge and subjectivity, are key parts of his analysis, but we cannot assume his thinking is limited to those dimensions in isolation or seek to essentialize one aspect over another.

As Foucault recognized, he had been "situated in most of the squares on the political checkerboard," but what fascinated him about this was what the multiplicity of attempts meant and what they revealed.[5] However, the range of positions depended as much on the reader and, as Foucault conceded in 1978, one could not demand how to be read:

> I believe that someone who writes has not got the right to demand to be understood as he had wished to be when he was writing. . . . A discourse is a reality which can be transformed infinitely. Thus, he who writes has not got the right to give orders as to the use of his writings.[6]

The range of readings was in part created by the way Foucault tried to generate a sense of the movement in thought and his own thinking; a

2. Foucault, *Dits et écrits*.
3. Foucault, *History of Sexuality*.
4. Foucault, *Remarks on Marx*, 148.
5. Foucault, "Polemics, Politics, and Problematizations," 111–19.
6. Foucault, "Michel Foucault and Zen," 111.

series of moves—as he suggested—like judo, with responses and tactical maneuvers.[7] To echo the terms of his 1969 *The Archeology of Knowledge*, subjects of knowledge are no longer isolated blocks of truth, but mobile formations, dynamic relations, operating in shifting fields of use.[8] Foucault can be seen in these transitions. In the mobility of these ideas we find the different analytic forms and critical approaches to knowledge he offered through his specific historical interventions.

To read the world through Foucault's analytic is to redefine the world in terms of understanding how different embodied groups benefit or suffer from shifting discourses that are perpetuated through institutional and social structures. It is to recognize that all forms of discourse shape the living practices and the mechanisms of inclusion and exclusion. It is to understand how individual subjects are formed through techniques of self-formation. It is to see how the body and its desires cannot be isolated from the social fabric. It is to see how different historical moments reveal the conditions for speaking and thinking in different ways and to see that there are choices and limits across time. In short, the many readings of Foucault show the rich resources he provides for examining a "positive unconscious of knowledge," the silenced and marginalized.[9]

It is within this multivalent context of Foucault's writings and the diversity of readings that theology found a new critical voice as part of that transformation of knowledge in the arts and humanities. Theology was opened up to a cultural analysis and a philosophical-historical critique that would offer new opportunities for insight. Since James Bernauer's early engagements in the late 1980s, the use of Foucault in theology and the study of religion has largely been defined by two distinct—though not mutually exclusive—forms: first, an exegesis of the theological and religious tropes in Foucault's texts and, second, an application of the broad methods and concepts applied to theological ideas and practices. The former studies have provided many fascinating excavations of Foucault's works: the historical accounts of the religious imagination, the archaeological openings of theological knowledge, the "contest with more than one round"[10] between "man" and God in the 1960s; the layered theological architecture of penal history and the pastoral formation of the sexual body in the 1970s; the ethical formation of the self in the church of late antiquity in the late 1970s and early 1980s. All such ideas were then reworked through the posthumous publication of the explorative

7. Foucault, "Interview with Michel Foucault," 1.
8. Foucault, *Archeology of Knowledge*, 73–74.
9. Foucault, *Archeology of Knowledge*, xi.
10. Foucault, *Order of Things*, 385.

Collège de France lectures and the publication of *Confessions of the Flesh*. These texts reveal the details of Christian spiritual practices for Foucault's understanding of Western subjectivity and the formation of the self. They provide us with a deeper textual appreciation of the place and significance of religious ideas and the nature of Foucault's understanding of spirituality. We also have a strong sense not only of the place of Christianity in Foucault's life, but also of his distinct selective choices and style in bringing questions and issues of the past into the present.

The second set of engagements between theologians and Foucault has produced an equally rich set of interventions. In many ways, the spirit of Foucault to bring about changes in practice drives these readings and applications. It is the potential of Foucault's methods and concepts to reinterpret the economy of pastoral practices, to uncover the inequalities within lived communities, to affirm the centrality of the body and desire and to reveal the significance of theological language in shaping the subject that shows the value of theological engagements. These works return us to the underlying normative commitments that Foucault's work offers in the struggle for justice. It is that struggle that provides Yin-An Chen opportunity to read Foucault and liberation theology in new and challenging ways.

Yin-An Chen is one of those voices that presents theology with a radically new opportunity to rethink the assumptions of liberation. His work seeks to address the neglect of sexual desire within the theological project of emancipation. What Yin-An Chen shows us is the necessity of the ongoing Christian commitment to transformation and the need for a constant re-examination of our ethical and spiritual life. He shows how the promises of revolutions and social movements always require the disruption of a prophetic voice. In so doing, he does not dismiss liberation theology, but rather takes us into a deeper understanding of the conversation between Marx and Foucault, a conversation between social structure and subjectification (the processes through which the individual is made into a subject).

Yin-An Chen's reading of Foucault carries forward the same normative commitment we identified in Foucault's work, the constant wish to overcome oppressive practices through different strategic interventions. This work combines careful exposition of Foucault's texts with the lived engagement of embodied theological worlds. Understanding the links between the sexual subject and the political apparatus drives this text in important ways—it helps us to rethink liberation.

Yin-An Chen's study develops and extends the liberation projects of Marcella Althaus-Reid and Jung Mo Sung by holding the fluidity of the theological project of sexual liberation. Liberation and freedom are not, as Foucault understood, fixed places. They are constant movements and reactions, which Yin-An Chen's thinking demonstrates through the "changing strategies of resistance." It shows that power is not fixed but is a set of relations, constantly moving and changing. Just as Foucault wanted to escape the framing of his work, so Yin-An Chen wants to develop the practices of escape in theological life. As Foucault pointed out in 1984: "We are prisoners of certain conceptions about ourselves and our behavior. We have to liberate our own subjectivity, our own relation to ourselves."[11] Such a liberation, as Yin-An Chen reveals, is a constant reactivation of our ethical commitments and our faith in making such change.

Jeremy Carrette[12]

---

11. Foucault, "Truth Is in the Future," 298.

12. Jeremy Carrette is professor of philosophy, religion and culture at the University of Kent, UK. He is the author of numerous works on Foucault, including *Foucault and Religion: Spiritual Corporality and Political Spirituality* (London: Routledge, 2000) and, with James Bernauer, editor of *Michel Foucault and Theology: The Politics of Religious Experience* (London: Ashgate, 2004).

Acknowledgments

THIS RESEARCH PROJECT HAS taken me about five years to complete, from the initial idea for my PhD project to the publication of this book. On the way, I moved from Durham University to the University of Kent and began exploring the possibility of ordained ministry in the Church of England (in the Dioceses of Canterbury and Southwark). These stages of my journey culminated in me doing my priesthood training in Cambridge. The completion of this book would not have been possible without friendships along the way, as well as the grace of God and the power of prayer.

First of all, I must thank Professor Jeremy Carrette for supporting me in my exploration of Foucault. I owe him a huge debt of gratitude for seeing the value of the idea for my PhD from the beginning when I simply wanted to develop queer political theology from my study at Durham and re-evaluate indecent theology through the lens of Foucault. Jeremy guided me to delve deeper, constantly challenging my readings and commentaries. I kept denying that I had become a "Foucauldian" but in the end, Foucault became one of my most important "keywords"! When I was down, frustrated and felt as though I had lost my bearings in academic life and my life vocation, Jeremy gave me strong encouragement and support, for which I shall always be grateful.

Secondly, I wish to thank Dr. Anna Strahan, my second supervisor, for encouraging me to go back to my earlier studies in anthropology to reconsider the contemporary discussion of anthropology of ethics. Thanks are also due to colleagues from the SECL at Kent, particularly Dr. Aina Marti-Balcells, Dr. Ben Conway, and Dr. Taylor Weaver, whose companionship along the way I have greatly appreciated.

My thanks also go to Dr. Ward Blanton and Professor Susannah Cornwall as my examiners. To them I owe gratitude for helping me to recognize the academic contribution of this project and for the encouragement they gave to me to publish it.

During my time studying for the priesthood at Westcott House, Cambridge, Professor Philip Sheldrake encouraged me to explore Ignatian spirituality. His support has proved invaluable, particularly when planning and writing chapter 5 of this book. I am deeply grateful.

I am also grateful to the many friends and fellow theologians who have given me feedback and advice concerning the many different incarnations of the book's sections. Special thanks are due to longstanding friends in SST, as well as friends on whom I tried out draft chapters—Rev. Jenny Walpole, Dr. Jenny Leith, Dr. Ip Pui Him, Kristi Stewart Elliott, and Tan Siek Leng.

Outside the academic and theological communities, I am grateful to have a group of friends who have always listened to the challenges and difficulties I have faced. They are: Isaac, Bo-Yi, Ming-Der, Tan-Chi, Hui-Chun, Alwyn and Ryan, Geoff, Dr. Roger Shuff, Fr. Giles Goddard, Fr. John Seymore, Harvey Howlett, Fr. Thomas Sharp, Fr. Harry Ching, Carrie Tseng, Iuyin and Xin-Che, James Newbury, Hiokhu, Patrick McGlinchey, Szu-Hui and Jenny, Jung Chen, and Westcott ordinands (Ben and Tash, Jack and Chrissy, Graham and Anouk, Wim, Sarah). I also give my thanks to my family, Jenna and Li-Yuan.

Finally, completion of this book would not have been possible without my partner, Tim. Thank you not only for your advice on language and writing, but also—and much more importantly—for your loving support of my ministry work and academic research on my vocational journey. And for cups of strong, brown English tea to sustain me during writing sessions!

Yin-An Chen
Fulbourn and the Wilbrahams

Introduction

Do We Still Need Liberation Theology?

THIS BOOK IS AN exploration of a micro-political theology. It begins with some questions. Do we still need liberation theology if we are living in a democratic society and enjoying its freedoms? What kind of liberation theology might be suitable in our context? Is there one liberation theology whose *method* can be applied to different contexts though they have been introduced to address different issues? What shall we do *if* liberation theologies no longer offer the best solutions?

These questions are all relevant to my personal context—but not limited to my East Asian background. I was born in the transitional time that followed the lifting of martial law in Taiwan in 1987. Opposition political parties were legally permitted, and restrictions on freedom of speech, assembly, and the press were gradually eased. The lifting of martial law also stimulated the repeal of the special law, the *Temporary Provisions against the Communist Rebellion*, in 1991. The repeal of this law was the signal that the "Cold War" had ended, as the threat of Communist China was no longer an "excuse" to tighten up national security and abuse the civil rights of the people.[1] But it also paved the way toward the full practice of democracy in Taiwan, including the first direct presidential election in 1996 and the first transition of power in 2000. The progress of democracy in Taiwan was rapid and strong. Social movements for indigenous people, for women, for workers, for LGBT people, and against housing injustice blossomed. And I was part of the generation that witnessed this rapid journey from an authoritarian country to a democratic country, and also part of the first generation to take civil rights and freedom for granted.

---

1. It remains a question whether the "Cold War" is finished in East Asia. Further discussions can be found in Chen, *Asia as Method.*

On the other hand, my generation suddenly realized that many social issues and oppressions could not be changed simply by changing the government and incumbent political party. It was naïve to suppose that throwing out an authoritarian government was the solution for everything and that a democratic government would always support equality and freedom. (Ironically, when a simple majority vote dominates a mechanism for parliamentary mechanisms and procedures, the voice of minorities is always traded off by politicians and the people.) The people gradually learned the lesson that changes of government could not guarantee freedom because democratic governments could also abuse their power and manipulate the people—just in a more open way than the former dictator did. So the question arose: What did the transition to democracy achieve? Could the people keep the fruits achieved by former revolutionaries and social activists?

Even more uncomfortably, when the government is taken over by the political party that was the "symbol" of progressive social value and used to be allied with other political and social movements, what should the new wave of social movements do in the continued pursuit of liberation? In Taiwan, after the change of government, social movements had been in an "ice age," since the biggest enemy had finally been defeated. It might have been expected that social reformations would progress their agendas within governmental institutions and through a parliamentary process. In such a context, how can social movements keep their energy? Who, now, is the "enemy" that needs to be defeated?

Of course, one important lesson to be learned is that those who fight for freedom and further liberation through revolutions and social movements should never cease campaigning. But even more significant than this is the understanding that the change and dynamic of power relationships should be the focus going forward, rather than a simple political structure. A change of government does not bring about a magical transformation. That being the case, how about other changes in social structures and the legal system? Are these social changes sustainable? Indeed, many social reformations and changes have been achieved in a short-burst period. But soon comes the realization that these movements not only need to be continued but also need to recognize a continuous change in the context. This journey is not a continuous one in which people just keep walking in the same direction toward an unchanged destination. Instead, the journey is tortuous and confusing, with a lot of challenges needing to be faced. (This is the main theme of chapter 1 of this book.)

These questions about social and political participation have perplexed Christian theologians too. Liberation theologians from the Presbyterian Church in Taiwan have been heavily involved in political reformation and democratization, have fought against government-by-*diktat*, and have sought the self-identity and self-determination of Taiwanese people. Cho-an-Seng Song was one of the key leading theologians to propose nation-building and the freeing of the voice of the oppressed Taiwanese people.[2] His theological perspective of Asian theology found special resonance with Minjung theology in South Korea.[3] However, in the light of political liberation and the successful democratization, what is the next step for liberation theologians in Taiwan, and indeed in other countries?

When Taiwan was governed by an authoritarian government, liberation theologians collaborated effectively with social activists fighting for different forms of social justice and values. Liberation theologians cared about feminism, labor rights, indigenous rights, and marginalized groups since they all stood together to fight against the oppressive structure—which was the government. They were all in solidarity with each other as they were all marginalized structurally and repressed by the state. However, when society and government become more democratized, do theologians in the younger generation still care about "liberation theology"? The democratizing of Taiwan saw an end to the solidarity between the church and other minority groups. Lacking the common enemy of a repressive government that they fought together to subvert, liberation theologians lost their vision and mission of political action and social participation. Did they still need to join feminist or LGBT movements? Did they want to stand for environmental issues? When the social structure that they had attempted to subvert had been successfully subverted, what form of structural oppression should they turn their attention to next?

If society has been democratized and the church can influence the legal system within the government structure, do we still need liberation theologians *in the street*? An obvious turning point arrived just prior to 2020 when political theologians in Taiwan and Hong Kong began to take a greater interest in the North American trend of public theology (such as Max Stackhouse, Stanley Hauerwas, and Miroslav Volf).[4] Marxism-influenced liberation theology was gradually played down by the church in its political agenda. The church and theologians looked for a new relationship with the government, no longer using confrontational tactics such as picket lines and

2. See: Song, *Tears of Lady Meng*, and Song, *Third-Eye Theology*.

3. See: Park, "Minjung Theology," 1–11.

4. For example, the Chinese version of *The Peaceable Kingdom: A Primer in Christian Ethics* (Stanley Hauerwas) was published in Hong Kong in 2010. The Chinese version of *A Public Faith: How Followers of Christ Should Serve the Common Good* (Miroslav Volf) in Taiwan in 2014. Their works have caught the attention of the Christian communities.

demonstrations to challenge policies. This implied that liberation theology—which always demands extra-governmental actions and is never in compliance with government—no longer meets the needs of the new context. It seemingly implies a truth that the birth of a democratic society is the end of liberation theology and that liberation theology is merely a strategy that is used when the government does not listen to the people.

Do democratic societies such as the UK, the USA, France, Germany, Taiwan, South Korea, and Japan need "liberation theology"? This question implies that liberation theology is *for* "Third-World" countries alone. Liberation theology is not needed in a "normal" and "functional" democratic society because its proposed action of subverting the government is no longer a necessary pathway to appeal for justice. (Even arguably subverting the government is not "democratic" at all.) If true, we do not need to continue liberation theology because its mission is done. However, viewed realistically, it may surely be agreed by all that political reformation never ends. Likewise, even when anti-racist, feminist, and LGBT movements have successfully subverted the long-standing structure of oppression, we all know that such liberation remains unachieved.

But what is the next step? After repressive legal systems, structures, and governments that have been responsible for supporting oppression have been discarded, continuous liberation movements need to deal with new structures that are established by themselves. While liberation movements keep in progress, we will face the reality that the structure that is constructed by revolutionaries, activists, and liberation theologians, can in the end be oppressive too. We cannot expect that fruits of our liberation movements will always be fresh and will not go rotten. (The related discussions shape chapter 2 of this book.)

Although my questions began as reflections on the fast growth of democracy in Taiwan, this book attempts to explore the future of liberation theology in democratic societies more generally. Is liberation theology still needed in societies that have achieved a certain level of freedom?

Foucault and Political Theory of Sovereignty

The exploration of the future of liberation theology opens up fundamental discussions about how social structures, power, oppression, domination, liberation, and freedom are analyzed. Michel Foucault (1926-1984) is one of the key philosophers in conversation with Marxism, existentialism, and (post-)structuralism. He also opened up queer studies as a discipline. His strong impact on disciplines across humanities and social sciences raises a lot of questions about sexuality, sexual liberation, body discipline, power relationship, and subjectification (or subjectivity). Foucault brings the idea of power and power relationships into the hot academic debates about contemporary thought and political theory—especially his idea of *biopower* or so-called *bio-politics*. Foucault's idea of bio-politics is important for my proposed micro-political theology because he seriously considers power and oppression in relation to the human body and sexuality. (Further discussion and analysis of this will be presented in chapter 3.)

Instead of the term "biopolitical theology," I prefer to use the term *micro-political theology* to avoid the confusion of terminology in recent applications of Giorgio Agamben (1942-). In his *Homo Sacer: Sovereign Power and Bare Life* (1998),[5] Agamben disagrees with Foucault's assertion that biopower, as a new technique of power in modern society, is a sign of transition from sovereign power to biopower. He argues instead that biopower has existed since ancient times. The distinctiveness of modern society and government is how sovereign power and biopower are strongly integrated and how biopower paves the way for the sovereignty of the state.[6] In contrast to Foucault's focus on life (sustained by sexuality and reproduction), Agamben gloomily draws attention to sovereign violence that holds the power of death through fostering or disallowing life.[7]

Agamben goes along with Carl Schmitt on the question of the exceptionalization of sovereignty, becoming "hysterical" about the supreme power of the state and its manipulation of the life of the people. Perhaps it will not, therefore, come as a surprise that, during the Covid-19 pandemic, Agamben has blamed the media and the authorities for spreading a state of panic.[8] The Covid-19 pandemic, in Agamben's view, was invented as an "exceptional" condition (in Schmitt's words), allowing the state to expand its sovereignty and power. Social distancing policy and lockdown are typical tricks of the state to manipulate people's lives rather than a caring policy intended to protect the people. Agamben's biopolitics puts a lot of effort into examining the power on *biological* bodies and attempting to restrain the state sovereignty from extending its unlimited power.

My micro-political theology regards Agamben's biopolitics as being pessimistic about political resistance, leading to a *nihilistic* viewpoint of power relationships. This is the exact opposite of what Foucault thinks,

5. Agamben, *Homo Sacer*.

6. Agamben, *Homo Sacer*, 6.

7. Agamben, *Homo Sacer*, 88.

8. Agamben, "L'invenzione di Un'epidemia." See the English translation in: Foucault et al., "Coronavirus and Philosophers."

because Foucault has faith in political resistance, though he considers that it must be as nuanced and flexible as the deployments of power relationships. Foucault analyzes various forms of dominance and oppression for exploring a possibility of resistance—instead of disappointing us by trying different kinds of resistance. For Foucault, it is powerful and exciting to recognize that the omnipresence of power implies the omnipresence of resistance. And this is something Agamben cannot imagine in his hysterical theory of biopolitics.

On the other hand, Agamben merges Foucault's biopower into his interest in sovereignty. But this is contradictory to Foucault's inclination since—through having dialogues with Marxism, especially with Althusser—Foucault is no longer interested in sovereignty and repressive apparatuses. As Katia Genel argues:

> Foucault abandons the theory of sovereignty and law in order to study the technologies of power which are no longer presented exclusively internal to a code of legality or sovereignty, codes which in fact mask the new modes of the exercise of power.[9]

For Foucault, power deployments are more than something that is from the state, or higher. In this sense, Foucault may criticize Agamben's biopolitics because the latter misleads the way to understand power—particularly, that power is seen as an unbeatable monster that can manipulate people without any restraints. In comparison to Agamben, we can recognize why Foucault turns to focus on a subject and the process of becoming a subject (subjectification). This is because the analysis of subjectification shows the trajectory of power relationships; that is, it actualizes how power exerts itself on the subject by constructing their desire and sexuality.

Bearing in mind the difference between Foucault's and Agamben's biopolitics, we can understand why I keep Agamben's biopolitics at a distance and why I use the term "micro-political theology," instead of "biopolitical theology." In fact, for Foucault, the concern with biological life is not important for his biopolitics at all. He is concerned above all with desire. Foucault's analysis of power in micro-politics demonstrates how desire and sexuality are incorporated into power deployments for serving capitalism. Here my micro-political theology is closer to Heike Schotten's proposal of *Queer Terror* (2018). Schotten sharply points out that:

> The problem with sovereignty is not its exceptionalizing of "bare life," as Agamben suggests, but rather its ideological construal of "life" as the highest value via a futurist temporalization

9. Genel, "Question of Biopower," 47–48.

of desire that, in Edelman's language, "queer" all those who think or act otherwise.[10]

Schotten puts her emphasis on *anti-moralism* and *dissidence*. It means to embrace precisely what is determined to be unembraceable, unthinkable, unreasonable, or immoral.[11] Resonating with *Queer Terror*, my micro-political theology advocates disobedience to what we are taught as "morality," which merely sustains the stability of power and the given condition of society. My micro-political theology requires redirecting of our subjectification and reshaping of our desire and sexuality so that we can orientate our desire in counter-directions against power relationships.

Following Foucault's suggestion, my micro-political theology looks for freedom within power relationships, rather than a power-free zone of liberation, because it is impossible to find a place without any involvement of power. Political resistance is based on the practice of the self in which individuals reject being incorporated into the task of reproducing and consolidating social structures. In comparison with Agamben's obsession with power and sovereignty, Foucault turns to the analysis of the subjectification to find his strategy of resistance. These questions will be expanded in chapter 3.

Foucault in Theology

My micro-political theology is a political theology that is built with Foucault's insights into power, domination, and freedom. This is not the first project to incorporate Foucault's thoughts into theological construction, or to read Foucault "theologically" or "religiously." Although we cannot deny the fact that Foucault's interest in Christianity increases in his final years of life, he has no interest in Christian doctrine at all. What draws his attention is the techniques and practices of Christianity rather than belief and faith in Christianity. Hence, I insist that we cannot make a theological conclusion based on Foucault's reading of Christianity—but we can still listen to what Foucault may tell us about his exploration of power relationships, or at least allow him to present his findings of domination and oppression. In my view, what Foucault can contribute to theology is not his thought in itself but his insights.

James Bernauer is a prominent Jesuit theologian who attempts to theologize Foucault and ambitiously explores the work of the "final Foucault,"

10. Schotten, *Queer Terror*, xix–xx.
11. Schotten, *Queer Terror*, 59, 161.

expounding what he considers to be Foucault's great enthusiasm for Christianity in the 1980s and 1990s.[12] Bernauer even regards Foucault's postmodern thought against modernity as an expression of negative theology. For example, when Foucault declares the death of human beings, this is human liberation—challenging the contemporary power of culture that attempts to determine self-identity.[13]

In comparison with Bernauer's way of reading (which has been criticized for reductionism), Jeremy Carrette takes another approach to the relationship between Foucault and theology. Carrette recognizes that "religious theme" or mainly "Christian theme" takes an important role in Foucault's writings, but he rejects any translation of them into theological arguments. Carrette carefully analyzes what the spiritual or religious *means* for Foucault concerning the body and the modern emergence of sexuality.[14] He then makes a distinction of Foucault's religious theme between *spiritual corporality* and *political spirituality*. The former emphasizes the social embodiment of religious faith (spiritual) whereas the emphasis of the latter is on the religious practice itself as political action. I argue that this distinction can be paralleled with the difference between liberation theologies and my micro-political theology. (This will be further discussed in chapter 5.)

Taking Foucault's religious theme as a key topic, Carrette's analysis is a cogent explanation of how Foucault's thoughts are rooted in the connection of the body, sexuality, and subjectification. Similarly, Mark Jordan also observes that the theme of religion and Christianity takes an important role in Foucault's writings. In particular, Foucault is fascinated by ritual practices and ceremonies of Christianity in relation to bodily discipline. Jordan notices that Foucault uses religion as rhetoric to examine how religious languages and speeches articulate and form bodies and how bodies are "uttered" by speeches.[15] On the other hand, through rituals and speeches convulsing, these bodies are "straining to be antisocial, to escape control, and to transgress the boundary."[16] Based on Jordan's delicate commentary on Foucault's writings, we can see how religious speeches and rituals are deeply connected with power, disciplines, and bodies. But Jordan does not construct more theology based on his commentary on Foucault.

---

12. See: Bernauer and Keenan, "Works of Michel Foucault," 119–58.

13. Bernauer, "Prisons of Man," 378.

14. Carrette, *Foucault and Religion*, 44–84.

15. Jordan, *Convulsing Bodies*, 10.

16. Jordan, *Convulsing Bodies*, 38.

In *Foucault and Theology* (2011), Jonathan Tran worked on Foucault and his theological application.[17] Rather than analyzing Foucault's theme on religion and Christianity, Tran shows how Foucault shares his insight on the analysis of power and how Foucault can teach theologians about Christian faithfulness, particularly in the face of capitalist power.[18] Tran pays attention to the care of the self, considering it to be Foucault's response to the omnipresence of power and his indication toward Christian eschatological hope. Tran expands the idea of *resistance* into a broader sense of Christian *witness* in resonance with Hauerwas's ecclesiology of the "Church" as church-by-worship.[19] In Tran's viewpoint, Foucault seems to reach the limitation of secular philosophy, meaning that he fails to offer or reveal a real hope for human beings even though he may well disclose the complexity of power and oppression. Following Foucault's exploration of Christian practices in early Christianity, Tran draws his attention to the care of the self and regards it as an important technique for constituting a Christian subject "within and against worldly relations of power."[20] For Christians, this is a central practice of *resistance-as-witness*—which aims at letting the world know why and how to worship God rather than money.

My micro-political theology and Tran's theology of *resistance-as-witness* share some insights from our reading of Foucault's philosophy. For example, I agree with him that Foucault's analysis of the omnipresence of power leads him to explore the techniques of self-care; hence, subjectification (the practice of the self) can be considered as resistance. Tran does not go through an exegetical reading on Foucault. As a Christian theologian who has a specialism in early Christian history, Tran promptly recognizes how Foucault's fresh viewpoint on self-care as resistance—from outside theological academy and without obligation to Christian doctrine—links with Christian witness in the world. Tran's theological application of Foucault is creative and inspirational.

But Tran's reading cannot appreciate why Foucault pays attention to the "precarious" state of power relationships and why Foucault is tirelessly exploring his analysis of power instead of satisfying any theory of power. Foucault's power analysis should not be reduced to a statement that "power is everywhere." And my micro-political theology attempts to take the complexity of power relationships seriously, as this is the strategy for coping with power—particularly if we do not stubbornly regard what

---

17. Tran, *Foucault and Theology.*
18. Tran, *Foucault and Theology*, 3.
19. Tran, *Foucault and Theology*, 4.
20. Tran, *Foucault and Theology*, 123.

Foucault reveals as a theory of power but as *an analysis of power* in history. In other words, the complexity and dynamic of power relationships should be regarded as the nuance of power analysis. But Tran's movement towards eschatological hope goes too fast to catch this point. It may explain why he cannot recognize the practice of care of the self as *political* resistance in itself and why resistance has been "depoliticized" to Christian witnesses in Tran's proposal. (In chapter 4, there is a related discussion about the balance between ontology and ethics, alongside an analysis of theological proposals from liberation theology and the Radical Orthodoxy movement.)

Asceticism and Resistance

It may be clear that, as Tran firmly insists, "Foucault's philosophy does not make possible Christian witness, but it can make Christian witness slightly more visible."[21] Resonating with my micro-political theology, Tran also emphasizes reading Foucault's interest in asceticism in the early Church Fathers and considers it the treasure of understanding the power of Christian practices in witness to God's power and authority. Tran enthusiastically expands Foucault's initial exploration of asceticism into his proposed idea of the self. The self of the ascetic Christians is "a self given to self-giving rather than self-possession."[22] It is "embodied most fully in the martyrs, one gives of self not to achieve the self, but rather to reclaim it."[23] For Tran, this reclamation of the self in the ascetic practice of denunciation and self-denial is the best alternative to the capitalist idea of the self—which is achieved by taking, gaining, and possession. The practice of "Christian asceticism," in this sense, is the practical guidance of self-care—which helps Christians understand that suffering "may be one of many paths traversed on the way to soul's salvation."[24] And this practice of self-care in asceticism should cultivate Christians to witness God's power and authority.

Here Tran smoothly and successfully transfers Foucault's exploration to his theological construction as he sees the end of Foucault's philosophy as the beginning of theology. In his interpretation, Foucault's notion of "asceticism" is removed from his context and is then essentialized as the identical practice of "Christian asceticism." Tran ignores how Foucault explores different techniques of the self from the modern sexual liberation movement to Greco-Roman culture and, in the end, Christian asceticism. This implies

21. Tran, *Foucault and Theology*, 12.
22. Tran, *Foucault and Theology*, 14.
23. Tran, *Foucault and Theology*, 120.
24. Tran, *Foucault and Theology*, 138.

that there is a journey of conversion, at the end of which Foucault finally turns to Christianity and finds his way to the salvation of the self and subjectification. As John McSweeney's book review points out:

> [Tran leaves] the reader with the impression that Foucault's main analysis of practices of the self lay with the Christians rather than the Greeks and Romans, with the former more important.[25]

My micro-political theology argues that Tran's interpretation misses the point—that whether this practice of asceticism can be resistive fully depends on its relationship with power. Not all ascetic practices are subversive or resistive. Not all renunciation of the self is liberating. We cannot simplistically regard Christian asceticism as resistance and witness to God any more than we should adopt the naïve belief that sexual liberation can always bring about liberation. In Foucault's exploration, "Christian asceticism" becomes resistive under the circumstance that sexual liberation turns to be repressive and dominant over human sexuality.

Cautiously maintaining this uneasy balance between asceticism and sexual liberation, my micro-political theology argues that the kernel of Foucault's asceticism is indifference and detachment (in the Ignatian sense) rather than a specific form of Christian asceticism—which is narrowly defined as self-denial, renunciation, and self-giving. We need to search for an understanding of asceticism which is different from the repression of sexuality and desire. (This will be discussed in chapter 5, together with Ignatian spirituality as a practice of subjectification.)

There is an urgent call to save the practice of asceticism from the repressive renunciation of sexuality and desire. Christian asceticism (if following Tran's theology to the extreme) may run the risk of dragging us back to the oppression of self-identity and demonization of sexuality and desire. For example, such renunciation may structurally deny the self-identity of LGBT people, as they have been taught for decades to renounce their "ungodly" desire. On the other hand, Christian asceticism may also distract us from serious recognition of human desire and from coping with these convoluted drives—as they may not only lead us to rejoice in human nature but also drag us into vicious darkness in sexual abuse and power manipulation. Foucault cares about power as well as sexuality, desire, and the body.

Here we come to the foundation of my micro-political theology—which is the theology of sexuality, desire, and the body. Unfortunately, this has been generally forgotten by theologians who are interested in Foucault or power and politics, so that we can rarely find a political theology that is

---

25. McSweeney, "Book Review: *Foucault and Theology*," 215.

actively engaged with the theology of sexuality, desire, and the body. (In chapter 4, I will set out my critiques of the related theologies of Marcella Althaus-Reid, Jung Mo Sung, and Daniel Bell and explain why their considerations cannot be politically subversive.)

My micro-political theology calls for reconsidering *a political theology of sexuality, desire, and the body*—based on Foucault's thought. This is because I believe that the political battle over dominance and resistance is situated in the battle of our desire. I share Sarah Coakley's insight in her project *The New Asceticism* (2015).[26] Coakley sharply points out that *a training of desire* is the key issue, as well as a choice concerning "what the *final* telos of one's desire is."[27] Inspired by Gregory of Nyssa, Coakley further argues that "virginity" does not mean "sexlessness"—but the "withdrawal from *worldly* interests" (including the building up of families, status, and honor).[28] This idea of virginity is exactly what asceticism means for my micro-political theology, as I will identify the (re-)orientation of our desire as the most important part of the practice of the self.

Christian writings in asceticism help us *reimagine* our desire. Learning from their wisdom, we may *train* and *orientate* our desire to take the opposite direction from that to which the world and power manipulate us into. This kind of ascetic practice is always *queer* as it always rebels against what we are forced to be, become, and act. This way of practicing asceticism is different from reading Christian asceticism as an ancient instruction book which teaches us to cope with the contemporary crisis of sexuality and desire through renouncing and repressing desire and sexuality. On the contrary, what this ascetic wisdom teaches us is to denounce what the world forces us to desire and love. When the world and its relationship with us keep changing, we need to constantly change our strategy of resistance to them.

Book Chapters

In chapter 1, I will review the extent to which the aims of political revolutions and social movements have been achieved. At the same time, I will evaluate the extent to which the fruits of success have been secured and maintained. Thanks to the manifesto and viewpoint of Marxism, I believe that these different levels of revolution may bring about freedom and liberation. Hence, revolutionaries and activists have put all their efforts into throwing out oppressive structures. However, taking a pessimistic view,

26. Coakley, *New Asceticism*.
27. Coakley, *New Asceticism*, 30.
28. Coakley, *New Asceticism*, 50.

and based on history and our empirical experiences, although it is the case that some liberation and structural changes have been achieved, their fruits did not last long, failing to maintain hard-won freedoms. This is not about the failure of these movements to complete the process of revolution or to complete it thoroughly. The issue is that the fruits of revolutions and social movements have been stolen and the promises of revolutionaries and social activists have been broken. Here my micro-political theology does not deny the great success of revolutions and social movements. But a big question remains: How can we secure our achievements?

In chapter 2, I will survey how liberation theologians in the church parallel the works of revolutionaries and social activists in the world. By means of reading different trends of liberation theologies together, we can recognize how they learn from each other and attempt to revise their mistakes and weaknesses. However, I will show that, in the end, different liberation theologies fall into an unhelpful game of competing with each other, claiming that a specific group they speak for is the *most* oppressed group. This results from an over-reliance on the analysis of social structures—which is used to define the social position of the oppressed group but never pays enough attention to the involvement of the subject and their experience. Thus, liberation theologies, being obsessed with the analysis and description of these structures, have failed to recognize how oppressive systems *work on* individuals.

In chapter 3, after recognizing the failures of liberation theologies, I will introduce Michel Foucault into the conversation, as a sincere thought-explorer of dominance and freedom, setting out the conclusions he came to in his lifetime. Firstly, Foucault pricks the utopian bubble that believes in a power-free zone. There exists no place where power is not engaged, as it is power relationships that hold society together. Secondly, Foucault is more concerned with resistance than with liberation. His attention then focuses on the constitution of sexuality and desire and he attempts to find his strategy of resistance in the practice of the self. He challenges almost all of our assumptions about freedom and oppression, as inherited from Marxism and liberation theologies, and his insights will be the foundation of my micro-political theology.

Foucault having shown us in chapter 3 that political theology should turn to a consideration of sexuality and desire, I will examine in chapter 4 how sexuality and desire have been engaged by three political theologians (Marcella Althaus-Reid, Jung Mo Sung, and Daniel Bell). My micro-political theology will argue that their theologies cannot do the job as they optimistically anticipated because all of them failed to recognize subjectification— that the subject is not given but is constructed within power relationships.

For example, Althaus-Reid is too naïve to recognize how perversion is involved in power relationships and that subversion may not come simply from the embrace of the margins. Through reading Sung and Bell together, I will show why they should work together as ethical actions and how ontological transformation should collaborate inseparably. My micro-political theology, based on Foucault's view of subjectification as resistance, argues that political resistance must start from the transformation of the self in sexuality and desire, which is about the practice of the self.

In chapter 5, I will bring an analytical study of Foucault into the conversation to calibrate the direction of my micro-political theology. It is inspirational to carefully interpret Foucault's attitude toward religion, particularly the Iranian Revolution, because Foucault indicates a pathway toward *political spirituality*, which shows how religious practices themselves can be political—in comparison with spiritual corporality (the idea that religion is political through engaging with politics). Extraordinarily, even incomprehensibly, Foucault turns to explore the practice of asceticism in the context of searching for his response to sexual liberation. Furthermore, in the second part of the chapter, I will exemplify Ignatian spirituality of indifference as an ascetic practice of political resistance. The kernel of asceticism for Foucault and my micro-political theology is the practice of *constant detachment* from power relationships, which manipulate and guide the orientation of desire and sexuality, rather than merely the renunciation of the self.

1

The Betrayal of Social Movements
and Revolution

IN THIS CHAPTER, I will show how, from the perspective of empirical studies, social movements and revolutions have failed to fulfill what they have promised. From that same perspective, I will analyze how these movements have struggled against various new forms of oppression. Before we move on to that discussion, however, there is a need to clarify that the purpose of showing the limitations of these social movements and revolutions is to explore the further response of political theology to the real situation. This is a necessary first step towards the examination of liberation theologies (which I will explore in chapter 2). To be perfectly clear at the outset, I do not believe in any nihilistic view of social and political change.

Why Revolution?

Revolution, or a riot by the people, as a way of forcing political authorities to change or to give up their power is nothing new in human history. Its purpose is to show the people's dissatisfaction with the *status quo* and propose change. As someone who regarded social and political revolution as the only way to set the oppressed free—as set out in *The Communist Manifesto* of 1848[1]—Karl Marx is unquestionably one of the most prominent revolutionary figures in history. In Marx's view, history is in progress through the continuing class struggles between the owners of the means of production (the bourgeoisie) and the workers (the proletariat).[2] This

1. Marx, *Communist Manifesto*.

2. Here Marx and Engel were influenced by the concept of the Darwinian revolution. They even sent a copy of *Das Kapital* to Darwin, who thanked them politely but then cut the first 105 of its 122 pages. Moreover, the emergence of the place of humanity was not just process, but progress: "lower forms . . . gave way to higher ones." Worsley, *Marx and Marxism*, 66.

conflict between social classes drives the development of human society in revolution. Marx believed that the world will come to an end by social and political revolution when all the proletariat stand together to fight for their lives and bring an end to exploitation.[3] The revolution—which is a struggle against exploitation by the bourgeoisie—will create a new and equal society by means of destroying class division and empowering the proletariat. The state will henceforth take an important role in concentrating all production and distributing it equally and justly.[4]

Thus, Marxists believe that the revolution of the proletariat—who represent the oppressed—will bring about social liberation and freedom. They yearn for a time when the oppressed eventually resolve to be in solidarity with each other when all the societal benefits that have been stripped away from the oppressed will go to those who deserve them. They believe the revolution will make society more equal by removing the divide between the proletariat and the bourgeoisie. The proletariat contribute their physical labor, which is exploited by the bourgeoisie due to the fact that the proletariat lack the means of production. Both proletariat and bourgeoisie should labor equally to gain what they want to gain. The proletariat will not only be liberated from the slavery of laboring for the benefit of the bourgeoisie, they will also be free from exploitation. For Marxists, the ultimate goal of revolution is to create equal and fair conditions for both the proletariat and the bourgeoisie. In the end, revolution benefits all humanity.[5] Revolution is the only way to achieve liberation and freedom.

Marxist thinking brought about a huge change in politics in the twentieth century. In the arena of international politics, communist activists (arguably inspired by Marxism) strove for a new society that respected human dignity and equality. During the Cold War an alliance of communist countries, including the Warsaw Pact in Eastern Europe and certain East Asian nations, came into being.[6] Communist revolutionaries achieved great success in 1922 when the Union of Soviet Socialist Republics was established. By the late 1940s, there existed significant tension between the ideologically opposed liberal democracies of "the West" and the Warsaw Pact countries and their allies.

Although Marx's attitude toward nationalism was ambiguous (perhaps reflecting the conflicting interests of nationalism and proletarian internationalism), revolution-triggering Marxist theory played an important role in the

---

3. Marx, *Communist Manifesto*, 86.

4. Marx, *Communist Manifesto*, 75, 86.

5. Worsley, *Marx and Marxism*, 78.

6. See: Service, *Comrades!*.

wave of national independence movements in the Third World during the twentieth century.[7] This is because Marxists have recognized how capitalism has worked with imperialism to exploit and manipulate colonial territories for the benefit of empires. The imperial system serves the capitalist system—in which the relationship between the bourgeoisie and the proletariat is no different from the relationship between empire and colony. National independence movements are perceived as the first step to freedom from exploitative colonialism. In such a context revolution is the path to independence from the colonizer and the right to self-determination.

Changing and Reforming Legal Systems

Not all social movements are influenced by Marxist-triggered revolution. Nevertheless, it is undeniable that Marxism has played an important role in the relationship between revolution and liberation. For example, in the United States, although neither the Civil Rights Movement of the 1950s and 1960s nor the Stonewall Riots of 1969 were associated with any communist revolutionary movement, both these movements strove for equality of the marginalized and the oppressed.

In the Civil Rights Movement, Martin Luther King called for a non-violent social revolution against racial segregation policy. Targeting a specific unequal law, the movement successfully put pressure on the government, resulting in the passing of the Civil Rights Act of 1964, which abolished racially discriminatory policies and continues to protect the equal civil rights of African Americans.[8] Later, in South Africa, the US Civil Rights Movement was both the inspiration and the motivation for the bilateral negotiations between 1987 and 1993 that achieved the release of Nelson Mandela and brought an end to apartheid. The Civil Rights Movement thus provided a template for later non-violent revolutions.

The Stonewall riots were the trigger for a series of violent demonstrations against discriminatory laws and led to conflict with the government. Although the violence of the Stonewall demonstrations stands in contrast to the peaceful process of the Civil Rights Movement they nevertheless

7. In his short article, Eric Weitz shows how the concept of "self-determination" appears in Marxism from Immanuel Kant and Johann Gottlieb Fichte to Karl Marx and then to Otto Bauer and V. I. Lenin. See: Weitz, "Self-Determination," 462–96.

8. The firsthand history of African-American grassroots movements can be seen: Chafe, *Civilities and Civil Rights*. Also, considering the broader context such as political Cold War background, and the black winner at the 1968 Olympic Games, see: Joseph, *Waiting 'Til the Midnight Hour*.

helped to bring gay culture into the public eye.[9] The resulting change in the social and cultural environment encouraged more sexual minorities to come out, to express their identity freely, and to challenge the stigmas arising from misunderstanding and ignorance of homosexuality.[10] The drive to recognize discrimination against homosexuals and the stigmatization of homosexuality eventually brought about legislation to de-criminalize homosexual acts in countries across the world—the UK's Sexual Offences Act of 1967 being one such example.

After the Stonewall riots, as part of a strategy of liberation, sexual minorities were encouraged to "come out" to make homosexuals more visible, tolerated, and generally better understood by the general public. Some years later, gay people coming-out also played a part in relieving the stigmatic association between HIV/AIDS and the gay community.[11] The coming-out movement has also helped build the community of LGBT people, overcoming various geographical, social, and racial barriers, and breaking down the social and psychological isolation of LGBT people.[12] In 1970, on the first anniversary of the riots, the first Gay Pride called on sexual minorities to stand up and speak out for equal rights. The spirit of Gay Pride, continuing the spirit of the Stonewall riots across the world, is far from being merely a festive carnival—it is a political parade that aggressively and subversively challenges the mainstream social values of heterosexuality.

Both the Civil Rights Movement and the campaign for LGBT rights targeted legal systems that discriminated against the oppressed and the marginalized. Their strategy was first to flout the old unjust law and then to demand the implementation of new equality laws. They did not challenge the existence of government, but instead put their efforts into adjusting the oppressive legal system. They instigated cultural change rather than created a new foundation for the state. What they achieved—and continue to achieve—asserts passively that equality and freedom are goals that can be attained by social movements that aim at reforming the system instead of renouncing it. Violent revolutions such as those that have overthrown oppressive regimes and replaced them with communist ones have not been necessary.

---

9. About the history of a series of Stonewall riots, see: Carter, *Stonewall.* For some discussions about gay rights (particularly of marriage equality) and its movement in the United States, from the legalistic perspective, see: Frank, *Law and the Gay Rights Story.*

10. Jones, "LGBT Identification Rises."

11. Weeks, *Coming Out*; Cass, "Homosexual Identity Formation," 219–35.

12. Eliason, "Identity Formation," 31–58. Also, coming-out has a positive impact on mental health and the development of the self, see: Rosario et al., "Coming-Out Process," 133–60.

The Long Struggle of the Feminist Movement

The Women's liberation movement, or feminist movement, is another typical example. As Engels has prophetically argued, the exploitation of women is part of the exploitation of labor because women have traditionally been regarded as the property of men.[13] Although the struggle for legal, cultural, and social equality has lasted for centuries, women are still a long way from receiving equal treatment with men in the workplace. In wartime America in 1943, an iconic milestone was achieved, the symbol of which is popularly known as "Rosie the Riveter." "Rosie" was the depiction in a poster campaign of a woman in a role normally reserved for men—that of a riveter in an armaments factory. The caption read "We Can Do It!" and the intention was to call on women to step up and take jobs in an industry that would normally be reserved for men, while the men were serving in the armed forces. The poster propagated the idea that women could work in industrial manufacturing roles just as well as men could.[14]

"Rosie the Riveter," with her sleeve rolled up to reveal a muscled arm, was the embodiment of female equality with men in tough manufacturing jobs and became in due course a powerful political symbol of the women's liberation movement. No longer were women to be confined to their traditional roles, including that of the housewife—here was a woman who could compete with men in an occupation previously thought to be suitable only for members of the male sex.[15] Seventy years later, "Rosie the Riveter," with her "girl power" stance, is still used by celebrities (such as Beyoncé) and by politicians to advocate equality and autonomy. Loudly and clearly, "Rosie" is saying to other women: "We can do what they can do."[16]

The "Rosie" poster campaign was the backdrop to the release of women from their traditional domestic role and into the manufacturing

13. Engels' account, based on evolutionary anthropology of L. H. Morgan, demonstrates the relationship between family form and class. He argues that the unequal relationship between husband and wife is the material foundation of the bourgeois family and that wife and monogamy support the transmission of property. Engels, *Origin of the Family*. Also, Marx calls for the abolition of the family in Marx, *Communist Manifesto*.

14. Frank et al., "Rosie the Riveter," 75–78; Gluck, *Rosie the Riveter Revisited*. Cited from Santana, "From Empowerment to Domesticity," 1–2.

15. For example, "Women laid off in 1945 at the Ford plant in Highland Park, Mich., fight back against the company's discrimination." In the photo from National Archives, female demonstrators hold various placards saying, "Stop Discrimination because of Sex," "Ford Hires New Help We Walk the Streets," "How Come No Work for Women." Frank et al., "Rosie the Riveter," 78.

16. This Instagram post has been "loved" by more than one million people and also raised many criticisms and discussions about whether this icon is a feminist icon. See: Winson, "Sorry Beyoncé"; Orr, "Bey Can Do It."

industry at a time when labor policy discouraged most women from working at all, especially if they were married.[17] The poster campaign was highly successful in encouraging women into industry at a time when the demands of the armed forces had denuded the factories of male workers. But it went even further than merely recruiting women into "blue-collar" manual worker positions—women also began to rise into professional/managerial positions, substantially crowding-out their male counterparts, as Bellou and Cardia point out.[18]

For some women, their experiences in the wartime manufacturing industry were not just about gaining a position where they could earn money, but also a way to empower the self. Betty Jeanne Boggs, a riveter working in a plane factory at age seventeen, described her experience: "I worked on a war plant (. . .) and it had been an enjoyable experience. Even today, I am very proud of that (war) job. I can always say, 'Hey, I was a riveter during World War II.'"[19]

Opening up opportunities for women to work in factories not only shows the breakdown of the separation of domestic women from industrial men but also empowers women to leave their homes to work in the industry. It is like a call for a silent revolution, which challenges the stereotypical family values that confine women to domestic chores. It is a sign of women's liberation from domesticity and of their newfound freedom to choose their careers. (More on the women's liberation movement in theology will be discussed in chapter 2.)

Here the shared faith of activists in these examples is that an unequal social environment and discriminatory legal system can be successfully challenged by political revolutions and social movements, regardless of whether their methods are violent or non-violent. Targeting the unjust system and changing it is *the* way to liberate the oppressed from exploitative conditions. The action of calling for social movements or political revolution assumes and shows, at various levels, skepticism about the prospect of change in itself. For example, revolutionaries in particular recognize the impossibility of equality and opportunity for the oppressed in the current structure. To subvert and disobey social rules and regulation is the only path to the future. Total despair about the prospect for change and the existing social structure turns out to be the hope and the motivation for revolution.

---

17. Goldin, "Role of World War II." Cited from Bellou and Cardia, "Occupations after WWII," 124–25.

18. Bellou and Cardia, "Occupations after WWII," 126.

19. Gluck, *Rosie the Riveter Revisited.*

Social Movements' Betrayal of the Oppressed

Do these political revolutions and social movements fulfill their promise to the oppressed? What I attempt to do here is to highlight the limits of these movements, despite the significant achievements they have made historically, to open up the discussion about liberation and freedom. I will then argue that, in the end, these revolutions and social movements do not achieve their goal. In the final analysis, they fail to liberate the oppressed because the fruits of revolutions and social movements are temporary and are not permanently retained. The long-term success of these revolutions and social movements should prompt us to consider whether revolutions and social movements are still the best and most assured pathway to liberation and freedom of the oppressed. Will the oppressed never be liberated? How can we understand the predicaments of the oppressed and the disappointing outcomes of revolutions and social movements that have transpired after their initial "victorious" achievements of liberation and freedom? In what ways have revolutions and social movements betrayed the oppressed?

The Defeat of the Communist Revolution

The fall of the Berlin Wall in 1989 and the dissolution of the Soviet Union in 1991 gradually ruined the dream of communist solidarity. This is because these events dramatically signified the end of communist revolutions and symbolized the triumph of capitalism and liberalism. As the American political scientist Francis Fukuyama has pointed out, democracy will finally win the whole world, because democracy is the most reasonable political system for humanity.[20] (Ironically, he also uses the Marxist term *the end of history*, even though he argues that history will not end with the arrival of communism.) All humans, Fukuyama assumes, are driven by their desire as calculative economic beings, and the drive to satisfy this desire directs human history, which will result in the market economy.[21]

Fukuyama's prediction creates a mindset in the West that there will be no more communist countries, that Marxist theory will not save the world and that economic liberalism will justify itself as the Truth. For example, the development of social democracy and Tony Blair's and Bill Clinton's use of the term the "Third Way" can be seen as part of a sea-change in attitudes to communism and socialism in Western societies.[22] This serves

---

20. Fukuyama, *End of History*.
21. Fukuyama, *End of History*, 135, 338.
22. This wave is supported strongly by Anthony Giddens, a famous British

to deepen the disappointment with communism and related faith in Marxism, and prompts us to question: Shall we keep our faith in Marxism to liberate the oppressed even though history tells us that revolution might not be the pathway to liberation?

The Unfinished Business of Racial Discrimination

Racial discrimination has not ended in the USA, South Africa, or indeed anywhere else. One recent horrifying example of this has been the Charlottesville Rally in Virginia in 2017, which was a clear manifestation of hatred against non-white people.[23] The death of George Floyd in 2020 stimulated another wave of the Black Lives Matter Movement and demands for something to be done about continuing racial injustice and police brutality.

In 2020 and 2021, as the fear of COVID-19 has risen, Asian people and their businesses have been subjected to attacks and have been accused of spreading coronavirus. Two women attacked Chinese students in Australia, punching and kicking one of them and yelling 'Go back to China' and 'you fucking immigrants.'[24] As the pandemic has progressed it has become increasingly apparent in both the UK and the USA that failure to dismantle historical structural racism has severely hampered efforts to bring the virus under control. Based on medical statistics, people of black ethnicity in the UK have had the highest diagnosis rates and, by May 2020, 25% of patients requiring intensive care support were of black or Asian background, due to segregation and living in deprived neighborhoods with poor public health provision.[25] The spread of COVID-19 will not be contained before

---

sociologist. See: Giddens, *Third Way*. Other scholars such as Noam Chomsky also tried to combine liberalism with socialism. Chomsky argues that a libertarian socialist vision is "the proper and natural extension of classical liberalism into the era of advanced industrial society." This is because "the classical liberal ideals as expressed and developed in their libertarian socialist form are achievable. But if so, only by a popular revolutionary movement, rooted in wide strata of the population and committed to the elimination of repressive and authoritarian institutions, state and private." See: Chomsky, *Government in the Future*, 67.

23. After the Civil Rights Movement, many scholars continued to reflect on what "racism" is and what kind of action constitutes racism. Scholars prefer to consider racism in the context of racialization so that racism becomes a thing in itself, a social relation. In this sense, we can recognize how a new racism was born in the 1960s in the US. See: Bonilla-Silva, *White Supremacy*; DiAngelo, *White Fragility*.

I am also surprised to discover that "White supremacy" is not a new term in the US and South Africa. One of the most important works was published to analyze it in the 1980s: Fredrickson, *White Supremacy*.

24. "Covid-19 Fueling Anti-Asian Racism," para. 9.

25. Razai et al., "Mitigating Ethnic Disparities."

the UK government recognizes that structural racism impedes the equal distribution of public health resources. The American sociologist, Eduardo Bonilla-Silva, also points out that the pandemic reveals that the color-blind racism in the process of policy-making cannot cope with structural issues such as "class and racial inequalities, the lack of a proper safety net, and the need for universal health care."[26]

In another less-publicized (though no less controversial) example of racial discrimination, Asian American students sued Harvard University for negatively considering their racial background in their admission procedures when compared to other racial groups.[27] Harvard was forced to concede that their admissions committee "consistently rated Asian-American applicants lower than others on traits like 'positive personality', likability, courage, kindness and being 'widely respected.'"[28] This meant that Asian applicants were required to show higher marks than students from other ethnicities, including white people, leading to discriminatory exclusions of Asian candidates for admission. Bizarrely, this was done in the name of diversity policy—a policy supposedly designed for the protection of racial minorities and the disadvantaged. In this complex case, Asian students ceased to benefit from their protected minority status. But this is not the only recent example of racism against Asian people. Jane Hyun proposes a new phrase—the "bamboo ceiling"—to point out how cultural and organizational factors create barriers that Asians must overcome when rising to leadership roles.[29]

These new challenges of racial equality show that forms of racial discrimination have become more complex and frequently less obvious. They are nonetheless reminders that racism has not been defeated and is never far away. But these cases also prompt us to question: What was the political victory of equality and civil rights if racial discrimination has not been defeated? What more can be done to liberate people of all races after discriminatory laws have been abolished?

26. Bonilla-Silva, "Color-Blind Racism."

27. Jaschik, "Numbers and the Arguments." Also, another "typical" discussion about anti-Asian American stereotype and discrimination can be seen: Chou, *Myth of the Model Minority.*

28. Hartocollis, "Harvard Rated Asian-American Applicants."

29. Hyun, *Breaking the Bamboo Ceiling.*

The Hijack of Queer Politics

London Pride has lost the spirit of the Stonewall "riots" since a large multi-national bank (Barclays) sponsors the event. That an economically privileged group has become the leading sponsor of Gay Pride means the death of the subversiveness of the LGBT resistance movement.[30] Meanwhile, as LGBT people in Britain have become less legally oppressed in overall terms, gay culture has become more and more "mainstream" in public and popular culture. Mainstream values, including capitalism, patriarchy, and heteronormativity, are incorporated, embraced, and even reproduced in the development of "pink capitalism."[31]

Commerce has been quick to recognize the potential profit to be made from the LGBT community (the "pink money"), as they are often high-spending and voracious consumers of luxury goods. The identity of queer politics ends up helping the market mechanism to target their customers to increase their profit—a typical process of market segmentation.[32] This new festive experience of gay pride is contrary to the spirit of the original Gay Pride, which was against social mainstream values, such as capitalism, and which expressed solidarity with other oppressed people. An example of this is the LGBT group "Lesbians and Gays Support the Miners," which supported striking miners in their bitter national dispute with the government of Margaret Thatcher in the 1980s.[33]

On the other hand, stereotypical "gay" images invented and shaped by marketing have returned to shape the identity of individual gay people. This is well represented by the well-known American TV series, *Queer Eye for the Straight Guy*, in which five fashionable gay men (called the "Fab Five") "rescue" the "masculinity" of male straight men in terms of fashion, social skills, lifestyle, and cultural taste. Thanks to the TV series, gay men have become stuck in a new stereotype of so-called "metrosexuality" or "customer masculinity."[34] This not only misrepresents homosexual men who are not white, urban, or middle-class, but it also excludes other members of the queer community (especially lesbian and transgender).

---

30. Clews, *Gay in the 80s*, 116–24.

31. Sears, "Queer Anti-Capitalism," 92–112; Gluckman and Reed, *Homo Economics*.

32. Gluckman and Reed, *Gay Marketing Moment*; Peñaloza, "We're Here, We're Queer," 9–41.

33. Perrigo, "Gender Struggles," 407–17. This article about the misogynist culture of the British Labor Party in 1979 before LGSM can be a comparative study to understand the masculine culture in Labor Party. More discussions about LGSM can be seen: Kelliher, *Solidarity and Sexuality*.

34. Hart, "We're Here, We're Queer," 241–53; Clarkson, "Contesting Masculinity's Makeover," 235–55.

Identity politics, which is used by LGBT activists to build up the queer community and set the victims of homophobia free, initially aimed to bear and share the suffering of excluded and stigmatized sexual minorities. Their further aim was even to empower the marginalized—going beyond the group of minorities in terms of sexual orientation and gender identity—to subvert social norms and order. Ironically, the identity of LGBT people has been appropriated by consumerism and pink capitalism, to stimulate profit-taking, shaping the desire to consume, and forming the customer identity. The LGBT community now supports pushing up sales volumes rather than empowering the weak and other minorities.[35] This prompts us to question: What have the Stonewall riots given to the oppressed? Do identity politics still work for the marginalized?

Women's Bodies in Capitalism

Does the "legend" of Rosie the Riveter truly transform and change the employment situation of women? Although the gender pay gap has been gradually lowered, it still exists and the gap remains shockingly large in some industries, particularly in higher-paid jobs. According to the UK's statistics in 2020 (not hugely impacted by the pandemic), "the 90-percentile male employee (who earns more than 90% compared to other male employees, but less than 10%) earns substantially more than the equivalent woman employee. The difference in pay, expressed in gender pay gap terms, is 16.7% for full-time employees."[36] In the field of business and financial project management professionals, women hold 36% of these jobs and earn 17.3% less than men. For medical practitioners, women earn 12.6% less than men though they hold almost half of these jobs (48%).[37] In the half-century since Rosie the Riveter, women have gained the right to access jobs they would not previously have been able to take while their pay remains unequal to that of men in similar jobs.

An additional but largely ignored fact behind the iconography of Rosie the Riveter is that these women, who had a patriotic passion for their work, were still needed to do their household chores and child-care functions after work. They did not work less than men in the same paid employment, but they bore additional responsibilities of unpaid work at

35. Although same-sex marriage is not recognized in China, its "Pink economy" is currently valued at $300 billion to $500 billion per annum (globally, the LGBT community is estimated to spend more than £2 trillion each year.) See: Taylor, "With 'Pink Yuan' Ads."

36. "Gender Pay Gap in the UK: 2020."

37. "Gender Pay Gap in the UK: 2020."

home.[38] In fact, women were doubly exploited by capitalist industry and the householder. Susan Willis criticizes the work that women were doing in factories as being just like doing a gym workout in a nautilus machine. This is because "nothing is produced but the body itself."[39] The body of a woman becomes a labor force and is appropriated and controlled by the needs of capitalism and war even though exploited women were proud of their achievement and contribution.

On the other hand, as Engels foresaw, unpaid domestic labor underpinned the fact that women were merely victims of capitalist exploitation.[40] Outside their regular paid occupation, women continue to bear the bulk of responsibilities in domestic work. The patriotic vocation of female labor discreetly forces women to be overexposed to capitalist exploitation, including the owners of factories and machines, and the nation-state that supports the capitalist system.[41] A propaganda poster, produced by the Office of War Information and the War Manpower Commission, shows a soldier cajoling a man and a woman into working and says, "I can't win without you. STAY ON THE JOB and FINISH THE JOB."[42] This propaganda explains why women were encouraged to keep production high, in disregard of their non-negotiable domestic work.

Due to the double exploitation of women, capitalism can increase its profit from men (who traditionally are not distracted by housework) and women (who now work in factories). The idea that women have become liberated from their household is just a fantasy—women have been forced to become more directly exposed and vulnerable to the exploitative capitalist system. It prompts us to question: What ultimately does the legend of Rosie the Riveter contribute to the women's liberation movement? Did women, really achieve their liberation in the freedom of working in a factory industry or indeed any other occupation?

A Summary

In this chapter, I have reviewed different revolutions and social movements, from full-scale communist revolution to various lower-scale movements

---

38. Frank et al., "Rosie the Riveter."

39. Willis, "Work(ing) Out," 1-18.

40. Engels, *The Origin of the Family.*

41. Two classic books have pointed out how women are exploited by capitalism and their domestic responsibilities. See: Dalla Costa and James, *Power of Women*; Abbott et al., *Introduction to Sociology.*

42. The poster can be found in Frank et al., "Rosie the Riveter," 76.

for civil rights, such as LGBT rights and women's rights (especially the right to work). For revolutionaries, the entire system is corrupt, so they prefer to revolt against it and replace it with a new system. Social activists, by contrast, believe it is possible to effect change without overthrowing the current system. By means of non-violent or riotous actions, they hope to achieve legal and cultural change in society. In my view, revolutionaries and social activists are similar but they expect different levels of change. Otherwise, they all believe that the oppressed and the marginalized should recognize the system or the structure that causes inequality and oppression. For communist revolutionaries, that system is the system of economic liberalism. For the Civil Rights Movement in the 1960s, it was the battle over the 13th Amendment to the U.S. Constitution. For LGBT activists in England and Wales, it was about passing the Sexual Offences Act 1967. For women during wartime, success meant being positively accepted as a "labor" of production. These revolutions and social movements have all achieved great success in the last hundred years.

However, I am more concerned with the question of whether the fruits of these revolutions and social movements have been maintained. I argue that, as history and empirical experience have shown, these revolutions and social movements do not bring about a *permanent* state of liberation and freedom for the oppressed, even though they temporarily achieved their purposes and made big steps forward. Since the fall of the Berlin Wall, Communist revolution seems to have been under a sentence of death. In terms of the achievements of social movements, the situation is even more complicated if we recognize the fact that oppression has not yet been eliminated. Racism still exists, appearing in different forms. The LGBT movement has been hijacked by pink capitalism and undermines the diverse identities of the queer community. Feminist liberation merely allowed women to be doubly exploited. Revolutions and social movements lost their fruits after declaring their great victories over oppression in society and politics and the legal system.

In other words, these revolutions and social movements can bring about a dramatic change to liberate the oppressed from a specific oppressive condition, but they cannot provide the oppressed with freedom forever, or even "sustained" liberation. Eventually, the oppressed are captured again by another new form of oppression. If it is true that liberation and freedom from oppression cannot be maintained, can we say that these revolutions and social movements were successful?

2

The Failure of Liberation Theologies

IN CHAPTER 1, FROM the perspective of history and empirical experiences, we have already reviewed the success of revolutions and social movements and their failure to maintain the fruits of liberation and freedom. The concept and method of revolutionaries and social activists are also shared by liberation theologies. Most liberation theologians are themselves revolutionaries or social activists. In this chapter, I will further explore how freedom and liberation have been received in liberation theologies by political revolutionaries and social activists. I believe that reading the history and empirical experience of revolution and social movements with the text of liberation theologies can help us understand how liberation theologies might fail to bring about liberation and freedom to the oppressed. I will then show how liberation theologies have reproduced the same assumptions and strategies proposed by revolutionists and social activists so that they fall into the same trap, failing to maintain the liberation and freedom of oppressed people.

I will scrutinize how the concept of liberation and freedom has been introduced into the methodology of liberation theologies without any critical examination. From Latin American Liberation theologians to feminist theologians to womanist theologians, all try to improve the model of liberation theologies by means of slightly adjusting the methodology. But I will argue that their revision does not bring about a huge change from what revolutionaries and social activists have proposed. They merely replicate a narrow understanding of power relationships and oppression, over-rely on structural analysis, and lack a vigilant consideration of subjectification within the development of liberation theologies as a whole. This will bring us to Michel Foucault, whom I will discuss in chapter 3.

I will begin with Latin American Liberation Theology, which offers a systemic basis for the methodology of liberation theologies, and then see how feminist theology responds to it. I will then introduce womanist theology—which has been concerned with multi-oppression in terms of race, gender, class, and religion—to see whether this revision can save the methodological model.

The Foundation: Latin American Liberation Theology

Latin American Liberation Theology sets the founding stone for liberation theologies in general. It systematizes the theological methodology of liberation and freedom. There are four contributions of Latin American Liberation Theology to the so-called new political theology—in contrast to old political theology in the German tradition (such as Schmitt). The four contributions are:

1. An ecclesiological concern

2. The action in the present context

3. The focus of human experience

4. The prioritization of the poor

An ecclesiological concern is an important insight for political theologians. It means that the church is the body that takes political action, doing political theology for herself. This concern came originally from a contextual response in Latin America. This is because the churches in Latin America did not sufficiently respond to their oppressive context in politics, economy, and global marginalization, although Christianity is the majority religion and assumes to hold more social and cultural power.[1] Liberation theologians were surprised that the church, especially the Roman Catholic Church, only took a spiritual role and regarded herself as a spiritual organization. This self-identification of the church resulted in narrowing her mission merely to saving people's souls after death, through offering "spiritual" bread. Such a theology ignored the significance of the church's mission—which is to serve as a real bread for feeding people's physical bodies.

The theology of the spiritual bread—irrelevant to our physical body—was popular in Latin American because of the impact of imperialism. It was the consequence of unconditional acceptance of the theory of secularization which was invented in European academia to *describe* the phenomenon of rationality and the decline of religious authority. But in Latin America, the secularization theory became normative and directed the churches to keep away from the secular sphere. This agenda served the preferred specific

---

1. Christian Smith, a sociologist, offers a good introduction to and analysis of the relationship between the development of liberation and its historical context since 1930 via Vatican II council in 1960s. See, Smith, *Emergence of Liberation Theology.*

political purpose of authority, which was that the churches should not be involved in politics. As Kee and Sugirtharajah criticize, this reproduction of the theology from imperialist Europe leaves the churches in Latin America powerless and tame in the oppressed situation.[2]

William Cavanaugh, a Roman Catholic theologian of "Eucharistic politics," gives the example of the church system in Chile—which lacked the power to challenge the oppressive political—by showing the relationship between political torture and the dysfunction of the Eucharistic body.[3] He argues that when the Pinochet regime forced its dominance on the people by abuse, terror, and torture, the church did not stand up for the people or fight against the dictatorship. This is because the church as the Body of Christ was so "handicapped" by the secular state that she lost her body—which the church embodies and functions.[4] Cavanaugh furthermore explains that this inclination towards the dysfunctional Body of Christ resulted from the theology of Jacques Maritain, which was the most popular and mainstream Catholic theology at that time. In the view of Maritain, the church exercises an indirect power over the temporal only in the form of "counsels" or "direction," specifically as a director of morality and a saver of spirits and souls.[5]

Cavanaugh's theology provides us with the background knowledge necessary to understand why Latin American liberation theology needs an ecclesiological concern, which means that the church, as the Body of Christ, should be an active agent of political theology and action. The church became powerless because she was under the yoke of the state to such an extent that she was not concerned with physical bodies experiencing pain, hunger, and cold. On the other hand, taking advantage of the church's powerlessness, the state had a chance to slide into the replacement of God, by claiming itself as the omnipotent governor of the world—whose all-powerful omnipresence can be displayed in its use, control, manipulation, and torture of the people.

2. The church in Latin America has an inseparable relationship with European colonists since its development worked with the expansion of imperialism and colonialism. The theology being taught in Latin American churches inherited the European theological tradition of the colonists. This critique has been noticed by Althaus-Reid who strongly criticizes the influence of colonialism in Mariology. This point will be discussed in chapter 4. Also, Kee and Sugirtharajah criticize that liberation theology is insufficiently aware of colonialism, which is the root of Latin American liberation theology. Sugirtharajah, *Bible and the Third World*; Kee, *Marx and the Failure of Liberation Theology*.

3. Cavanaugh, *Torture and Eucharist*.

4. Cavanaugh, *Torture and Eucharist*, 21–71.

5. Cavanaugh, *Torture and Eucharist*, 161; Maritain, *Things That Are Not Caesar's*.

Overemphasis on the spiritual body of the church—its big failure—has been considered by many Latin American liberation theologians, particularly Roman Catholic theologians, such as Rafael Avila, who are more interested in the sacramental practice. Avila emphasizes that the nature of the church is the *Body* of Christ, which is a real body that can function, be a live presence, and freely act in society.[6]

Here we can see the deeper purpose of Latin American Liberation Theology's ecclesiological concern, which is resistance against secular power's attempts to silence the voice of the church, separate her from politics and society, and restrain her from her subjectivity of being the Body of Christ. This ecclesiological concern encourages the political participation of the church to respond to contextual issues because, in the Eucharistic celebration, the ecclesiological Body of Christ is instituted and participated in in the world.

Action in the present context is the second contribution to liberation theologies. Raul Vidales, a Mexican liberation theologian, points out that Liberation Theology "conducts a hermeneutic process regarding the present from within the context of the present, ever remaining open to the future as it does so."[7] Giving it the term "praxis-based" paradigm, Liberation Theology has shifted its focus from a doctrine-oriented and doctrine-constructed paradigm to one that is practice-oriented.

European and Northern American academic theology is criticized for being obsessed with the interpretation of transcendental God and creating God in philosophical doctrine.[8] This philosophizing of God, in the eyes of liberation theologians, is problematic. This kind of understanding of God can find its support in a theological inclination of Thomism toward philosophically systematizing Christian doctrine.[9] As Stephen Bevans argues, it is also characterized by the thought of Descartes and especially Kant in the

---

6. The body of Christ manifests in the Eucharistic body of Christ and in the body of the church. For further reading about the Eucharistic body of Christ in the world see: Avila, *Worship and Politics*. He argues that the Eucharist itself is political "in itself" and occurs necessarily in a political context in the context of Latin America (in the book's chapter 3).

7. Vidales, "Methodological Issues," 36.

8. See, Petrella, *Latin American Liberation Theology*.

9. For example, systematic theology and philosophical theology are subjects in European faculties of theology. This is what *Christian Theology: An Introduction* (updated five times as the bestselling theological textbook in English-speaking areas), mentions when it refers to the architecture of theology including Biblical studies, *systematic* theology, *philosophical* theology, historical theology, pastoral theology, and spirituality or mystical theology. See, McGrath, *Christian Theology*, 104–10.

development of Western modernity.[10] Through introducing a set of concepts (such as rationality and subjective responsibility), these academic theologies from Europe and Northern America construct themselves in an abstract and theoretical way—which is remote from people's daily life.[11]

When Latin American liberation theologians criticize academic theology, they argue that "rationality or intellectual knowledge was not enough to constitute genuine knowledge."[12] In the process of theological reflection, they emphasize *praxis*—an action connecting what we believe with what we practice. As Vidales points out, doing theology has to be involved with taking action, because truth "is not simply something that can be known or talked about but something that must be acted upon and realized in deeds."[13] Liberation Theology then challenges any theology that lives in an ivory tower and is distant from the reality of human life.

Here we can conclude that, for Latin American Liberation Theology, *doing* theology is not merely about the interpretation of God. It is about *change*. This statement is rephrased from Marx's critique of Feuerbach that "the philosophers have only *interpreted* the world in various ways; the point is to *change* it."[14] Doing theology always involves the action of changing the present situation.

A focus on suffering is the third contribution of Latin American Liberation Theology. As Vidales argues, recognizing the experience of human suffering is a tool for making theological reflection more contextual. It is also a strategy for rejecting abstract theological thinking.[15] It is worth clarifying that doing theology from below, from human experience, is not meant to be anthropocentric or to prioritize human beings over God. On the contrary, it means, through recognizing human experience, that the space of a "dialectical relationship" between human experience and the word of God is open.[16] In this view, theology can be perceived as a process of knowing God and God's action when God's people keep reading the word of God interactively and encountering God in person. Knowing God is not to accept what we are

10. Bevans, *Models of Contextual Theology*, 64.

11. For example, in the field of Christian ethics, Banner criticizes this kind of abstract moral theology, so he proposes "everyday ethics" or "the ethics of everyday life," considering the real context of moral decisions. See, Banner, *Ethics of Everyday Life*.

12. Bevans, *Models of Contextual Theology*, 65.

13. Vidales, "Methodological Issues," 38.

14. Cited from Bevans, *Models of Contextual Theology*, 65.

15. Vidales, "Methodological Issues," 43.

16. Vidales, "Methodological Issues," 44.

taught to believe, which is a one-way revelation from God, and which makes God so objective, so indifferent and so absolute.[17]

However, for Latin American liberation theologians, the focus on the experience of human suffering is not a behavior of self-pity or rationalization of suffering and adversity. Instead, it means to listen to the voice of sufferers. In his book *On Job*, Gustavo Gutierrez highlights that Job was a righteous person, so it was reasonable for him to dispute all reasons that were given by his friends to rationalize and justify his suffering. Job straightforwardly refused to repent for his undone sins. Gutierrez believes that this experience of Job, which is shared by all sufferers, encourages them insistently to "make a plea" to God the Judge.[18] It is a paradox that the sufferers encounter God in person when they keep questioning and asking why they suffer and why they need to experience misfortune.

This paradox, then, is the first step in doing theology. As Job responded to God, "I had heard of you by the hearing of the ear, but now my eye sees you" (Job 42:5). Job met and saw God in person when he questioned God and made his pleas and complaints, instead of tamely bearing his suffering. The story of Job teaches Latin American liberation theologians that the recognition of the experience of suffering opens up a space for listening to sufferers and for observing the real situation of sufferers as it happens. The focus on the experience of suffering draws theological attention not only to the reality of human life but also to the ongoing conversation between God and God's people.

When we talk about the focus on human suffering, it does not mean that we should take a sentimental approach—merely showing sympathy and compassion to the sufferers. Conversely, for Latin American liberation theologians, the method of recognizing human suffering is by analyzing an oppressive system to find the cause of oppression. They assume that a social structure—in which all human beings are situated—exists and that it is the cause of the suffering. For example, economic dependency theory has been widely used in Latin American Liberation Theology to analyze the socio-economic reality of Latin America.[19] As Gutierrez argues, "it made possible

17. This criticism has been well developed by John A. T. Robinson in his controversial book, *Honest to God*. He rejects thinking of God as "up there" and argues that we need to think about God through our existence and the culture in which we are situated. God continues to reveal God-self but not necessarily in religion or the church. See, Robinson, *Honest to God*.

18. Gutiérrez, *On Job*.

19. "An initial wave of dependency thinking was triggered by the work of the Argentine economist Raúl Prebisch (1901–86). He introduced the idea of an industrial, hegemonic center and an agrarian, dependent periphery as a framework for understanding the emerging international division of labor between North and South. Prebisch argued

a structural analysis of the evils present in this reality, and suggested courses for remedying them."[20] Initially, social structural analysis is a supportive tool for understanding human experience. It further helps liberation theologians to grasp a broad picture of the context that explains why people suffer. Here we see that social structural analysis becomes a default characteristic and basic method of doing Latin American Liberation Theology.

The prioritization of the poor is the fourth contribution to liberation theologies. This contribution comes from a fundamental question: who suffers the most? For Latin American Liberation Theology, the answer is "it is poor people, especially those who are in economic poverty." They point out that in the Beatitudes, Jesus has already given clear and simple teaching: "Blessed are the poor in spirit, for theirs is the kingdom of heaven."[21] God preferentially blesses the poor and reveals God-self within them.[22]

Latin American Liberation Theology criticizes earlier theology (particularly European and North American academic theology)—which has lost its privilege to accept and recognize the simple teaching to the poor. As Christopher Rowland concludes, theology must be "rooted in ordinary people's everyday experience of poverty."[23] If, as Gutierrez argues, theology cannot give up the privilege it inherited from European colonialism, and listen to the voice of the sufferers, it will never be able to approach God and understand God's teaching. This is because God is revealed in the cry of the sufferers.[24] Even though educated expert theologians and church elites may

---

that the wealth of poor nations tended to decrease when that of rich nations increased due to an unequal exchange of industrial versus agricultural goods in the North-South trading relationship." Darity, "Dependency Theory," 300.

20. Gutiérrez, "Task and Content," 22.

21. Matthew 5:3. Also, liberation theologians prove that the poor have privilege according to the Bible. The related discussions can be seen: Gottwald, *Bible and Liberation*.

22. I prefer using the term "God-self" over "Himself" in order to avoid the masculine pronoun for God and to reject imposing sexuality on God. The term, "God-self," has been adopted in the liturgy of some inclusive churches. For example, since 1981, *Metropolitan Community Churches (MCC) Inclusive Language Policy and Guidelines* has declared: "Where possible, replace pronouns with non-gendered nouns, or use balanced gendered pronouns or words such as 'who,' 'whom,' 'one,' and 'God-self.'"

However, this term is not always perfect. For example, Nancy A. Hardesty pointed out that the word God-self works in a sentence such as "God made us for Godself." It does not work as well in a sentence like "God himself is at work in our lives." Therefore, she proposed that "one suggestion here is to adopt the language of Scripture and creed to say "God, very God, is at work in our lives." Or one can achieve the same emphasis by doubling the names of God as in "God Almighty is at work in our lives." Hardesty, *Inclusive Language*, 57–58.

23. Rowland, "Introduction," 1–2.

24. The meaning of poverty is amplified to include at least three concepts in 1967:

read the Bible in Greek or Hebrew, the encounter with God is based on our deep experience—which leads us to see God in despair—rather than our intellectual knowledge. In this sense, we can understand Gutierrez's provocative insistence: "What runs like a thread through all liberation theology is a commitment based on contemplation of God in the suffering Christ whose presence is hidden in the poor."[25] It is in the presence of the poor that the understanding of a hidden God has been concealed.

Furthermore, this prioritization of the experience of the poor is not knowledge that leads to action. It is the knowledge that comes *from* our actions. No action, no knowledge. Latin American Liberation Theology rejects proposing a theological methodology, like academic theology, which initiates intellectual philosophical thinking. Instead, theological knowledge is based on the reflection on people's action in society and politics.

The first and primary step of doing theology is to be in solidarity with the poor—action is prior to thinking, and praxis is prior to theory. One such example is that Latin American liberation theologians do not "conceptualize" the doctrine of sin, but regard sin as segregation in society and between God and all creatures.[26] As Gutierrez argues:

> [Sin is] the break in our friendships with God and in our fra-
> ternity with humans (. . .) the refusal to accept another as
> a brother and sister, in oppressive structures built up for the
> benefit of a few, in the despoliation of peoples, races, cultures
> and social classes.[27]

Theologically, the action of being in solidarity with the poor is the action of salvation, redeeming the poor from sin. It allows the poor to vocalize their experience. It also requires theologians and the church to hear their voices. For Gutierrez, through freely sharing the suffering in poverty in society and the people of God, theology finds its foundation to become an *authentic* theology of liberation.[28] As Rebecca Chopp comments, doing Liberation Theology is to "guide the transformation of all human beings into new ways of being human."[29] The prioritization of the experience of

---

material poverty, spiritual poverty and poverty as a commitment to be assumed by all Christians. And this amplified understanding of poverty is accepted by Gustavo Gutiérrez too. See, Gutiérrez, "Task and Content," 25–26.

25. Gutiérrez, *Truth Shall Make You Free*, 3.

26. This concept of salvation regarding sin as isolation is developed by queer theology in liberation agendas. See, Cheng, *From Sin to Amazing Grace*.

27. Gutierrez, "Faith as Freedom," 48–49.

28. Gutierrez, "Faith as Freedom," 51–52.

29. Chopp, "Latin American Liberation Theology," 174.

the poor leads to participation in social transformation, through being in solidarity with the poor. This listening to the cry of the sufferers is the starting point for bringing about change.

The Critiques of Latin American Liberation Theology

I would like to raise two critiques of Latin American Liberation Theology in terms of its theological methodology, which may also be inherited by other liberation theologies.

Firstly, although Latin American liberation theology has pinpointed how academic elites control the power to construct theology, it does not elucidate the issue of *the power of interpretation* well. Who exactly owns the power to interpret the experience of the poor? Liberation theologians claim to prioritize the suffering of the poor, especially those who are illiterate or uneducated. But can these poor people tell their own stories? Or do the elites and theologians still get involved in the process of interpreting, or at least translating, the experience of the poor?[30] This is not an issue of whether the poor are "allowed" to speak, but of *how* educated and academic theologians can truly understand and learn from the situation and story of the poor.

Liberation theologians have made efforts to organize "Christian Base Communities," which are sharing groups where theologians and poor people can read and reflect on the Bible together. However, this does not mean the gap between the poor and theologians is removed.[31] There still exists a *process* of producing theology—from the experience of the poor to the new materials that are "used" and "appropriated" by theologians. It is undeniable that the cry of the poor starts to be heard, but this cry still requires mediation and translation by theologians to "serve" and "present" in the academic circle. In other words, in terms of the power of interpretation, the poor are "alienated" from their story and experience.[32] The

30. Thistlethwaite has a similar observation and critique. See, Thistlethwaite, "On Becoming a Traitor," 25.

31. Christian Base Communities established themselves in different countries in Latin America to gather people to read the Bible together and think about how to act in everyday life. This kind of gathering and organization has fostered the development of democracy in Brazil and Chile, see Cavendish, "Christian Base Communities," 179–95.

32. Here, I use the term "alienation" to criticize how Marxist-influenced liberation theologians alienate the experience of the poor. In Marx's thought, alienation occurs when laborers are separated from what they produce so that a product will not belong to its producer anymore. That is, capitalism reduces the labor of the worker to a commercial commodity to trade it in the market. See, Marx, *Economic and Philosophic Manuscripts*. In this sense, Latin American liberation theologians also grab the experience of the poor and separate the poor from their experience to "trade" them in their

experience of the poor is perceived by academic theologians as a theology of "the other"—which is still something of a novelty.

In fact, the poor turn out to be those who need to be listened to, instead of writers to be read. This is because they are generally not able to write about their suffering. When the experience of the poor is alienated through the intervention of translation and interpretation, their experience is deemed to be treated as an "objectified text"—whose authors are assumed to die but whose readers are actively alive. The poor then can never be the authors of their own story. In other words, the narrated experience of the poor remains, but the poor, as real human beings themselves, are invisible. Latin American Liberation Theologians seemingly care about the "experience" of the poor much more than the poor themselves.

Along with the disappearance of the poor themselves, Latin American Liberation Theology has been obsessed with *explaining* why the poor have the experience of suffering by introducing the analysis of political-economic structure. I argue that, when the aim of liberation theologians in listening to the stories and experiences of the poor is to "prove" the validity of economic dependency theory, something is lost, however enthusiastic and sincere the processes they use might be. The result is that the experience of the poor is trimmed to fit the theory. Thus, it contradicts the methodology proposed by Latin American Liberation Theology by prioritizing a theory over human experience. Listening to the experience of the poor does not matter anymore. But their experience remains "useful" to challenge unjust social structures. Ironically, in the name of bringing liberation and freedom to the poor, Latin American theologians regain the power to construct their theology *of* the poor through interpreting the experience of the poor. The poor become objectified as "useful" and "valuable" others.

A second critique is *the neglect of the diverse experience of the poor*. In Latin American Liberation Theology, there is only one experience of the poor, defined by their position within a political-economic structure. On the one hand, structural analysis helps to define and recognize how oppression exists and functions within social structures. On the other hand, it simplifies and generalizes all individual experiences into one model, which is easier for social activists and revolutionaries to be in solidarity with. For example, the diverse experiences of the poor in Mexico or Brazil, or even in India, are no longer important for Latin American liberation theologians because they all are under the same umbrella category—the poor.

The term "the poor" means those who share the same structural position—they are all in peripheral and underdeveloped countries, where they

academic market.

are exploited by the wealthy core countries (in the sense of economic dependency theory). The experience of the poor can now clearly be described in terms of their structural position. In the name of being in solidarity with "all the poor," different groups of poor people become one group. This kind of generalization of diverse experiences becomes "acceptable," regardless of race, religion, sexuality, and nationality. Ivan Petrella (who also attempts to bridge his context in North America with the context of Latin American Liberation Theology) argues that poverty and economic oppression are far from unique to Latin America. Poverty is a shared phenomenon all over the world, as the world is a zone of social abandonment.[33] We cannot, therefore, define "the poor" as a specific group of people in the developing countries, who are disconnected from the poor in the developed countries.

Precisely when the term "the poor" first came to be constructed and defined as a collective subject in Latin American Liberation Theology is debatable. It may be understandable that the new collective subject is created for global solidarity, but this overemphasis on the "universal" experience of the poor has heavily influenced the development of future liberation theologies. An example of this is the debate between feminist theology and womanist theology.

A Challenge: (White) Feminist Theology

Feminist theology poses a challenge to Latin American liberation theologians in the debate over the representation of the sufferer. Latin American liberation theologians believe that the experience of the poor is the most representative of the sufferer in general. However, feminist theologians, like Elisabeth Schüssler Fiorenza, insist that sexism is the most fundamental and primary oppression in human history. Women, they argue, suffer the most.[34]

In common with many feminist theologians, Mary Daly feels powerless while reading the Bible. In contrast to the poor—who can empower themselves through reclaiming and re-discovering the Biblical texts in the Gospels, in Job, in Exodus, and in landless Israel—what can women find in the Bible and Christian tradition? The suffering of women is even less discernible than that of the poor because women are oppressed even by their religious faith and spirituality. Daly criticizes the church for having normalized sexism and patriarchy for centuries "under the guise of the name of God." The Bible and the formation of church tradition are entirely

33. Petrella, *Beyond Liberation Theology*, 5–45.
34. Schüssler Fiorenza, "Critical Feminist the*Logy of Liberation," 27.

misogynist.[35] The authors of the Bible were too biased to see the valuable participation of women close to Jesus. They even attempted to conceal the glorious presence of women and rewrite the stories about them. For example, Mary Magdalene's role as the first witness of Jesus' Resurrection and as the first Apostle sent by Jesus to proclaim the good news, is not given the prominence it deserves.[36]

Here we can see how the Bible and church tradition have been accomplices in sexism—silencing the voice of women and continually forbidding women to articulate their suffering and disclose their oppression. More fundamentally, when Christian theology is constructed based on the experience of men to replace the position of God, and when images of God are almost exclusively male, where can women find a God who is not their oppressor?[37] In this sense, feminist theology challenges Latin American Liberation Theologians' assumption about poverty, as well as their economic definition of "the poor" because they cannot recognize women as the most oppressed group. Feminist theologians sharply point out how the situation of women is not even "comprehensible" to men when they are ignored and humiliated by the Bible and by church tradition.

Feminist theologians further criticize Latin American liberation theologians for their blindness to sexism and its patriarchal basis, which results in them being unable to bring about redemption and liberation to women. As Marcella Althaus-Reid argues, Latin American Liberation Theology is too obsessed with political-economical liberation to recognize that the "privilege" of the poor is in a male image.[38] This kind of theology—that benefits from sexism—kicks the ladder of liberation away from other oppressed groups, especially women. Although Latin American Liberation Theology claims to be concerned with the experience of the poor alone, it excludes the suffering of women in poverty. It does not consider women to be "the poor," confining the experience of the poor to the experience of men. What feminist theologians want to raise awareness of is that women are doomed to submit to the authority of men and to be manipulated by men's power—unless the distortion of the theological tradition can be subverted.

---

35. See, Daly, *Beyond God the Father.*

36. Mary Magdalene was the first witness of Jesus' Resurrection. Hippolytus of Rome referred "to the women at the tomb of Jesus as "apostles," which developed into Mary Magdalene often being called the *apostola apostolorum.* Yet others like Celsus, Renan, and in our own time even a staunchly orthodox writer like Ricciotti have downplayed her importance." O'Collins and Kendall, "Mary Magdalene," 632.

37. Ruether, *Sexism and God-Talk.*

38. Althaus-Reid, *From Feminist Theology to Indecent Theology,* 1–15.

Through launching a challenge to Latin American Liberation Theology, there are two contributions of feminist theology to liberation theologies: (1) Deconstruction of the patriarchal structure, and (2) the building of an inclusive community.

Deconstruction of the patriarchal structure is the first and most important contribution of feminist theology. Early in the nineteenth century, Elizabeth Cady Stanton suggested re-reading the Bible from a women's perspective. In *The Woman's Bible*, she offers a fresh perspective and a complete rethink on the canonical history of the Bible. She insists that the Bible is not a neutral text expressing and recording God's oral revelation but a text that has been constrained by, and is written in, patriarchal ideology.[39]

Elisabeth Schüssler Fiorenza, a Biblical scholar of the twentieth century, taking up the mission of reading the Bible from a female perspective, names this patriarchal ideology "kyriarchy"—which means "rule of the lord, master, father, and husband"—to include various relationships of masculine domination.[40]

> [Kyriarchy is] an analytic category in order to be able to articulate a more comprehensive systemic analysis, to underscore the complex interstructuring of domination, and to locate sexism and misogyny in the political matrix or, better, patrix of a broader range of oppressions.[41]

Like Latin American Liberation Theology, which claims that rich and elite Christianity cannot understand God, feminist theology asserts that androcentric Christianity—which has been shaped and formed by a misogynist context of ancient culture—cannot reveal the image of God or correctly interpret the Word of God. In this sense, the mission of doing feminist theology is to recognize how the male-dominant structure disorientates Christian faith, and how women can become free from that misogynist tradition.

Feminist theologians highlight the significance of *reconstructing* the understanding of the origin of Christianity to see the nature of the church community which Jesus built up in his time. This reconstruction is a journey of *uncovering* because the whole church tradition which we experience and participate in has been hijacked by kyriarchy. Most women's stories, then, are obscured by the male-dominant narrative.[42] This uncovering of women's experience, especially in early Christianity, is an act of resistance to

---

39. Stanton, *Woman's Bible*.
40. Schüssler Fiorenza, *Rhetoric and Ethic*, 5.
41. Schüssler Fiorenza, *Rhetoric and Ethic*, 5.
42. Schüssler Fiorenza, *In Memory of Her*.

kyriarchy, which is imposed on women by men to support male dominance. This uncovering of the original reality also means *restoration* of the presence of "patristic" women—breaking down male-constructed mythology and undermining the justification for the male representation of God.

Phyllis Trible is another feminist theologian who is determined to restore the silenced voice of women in the Bible. She points out that there are plenty of voiceless women hidden in unnoticed narratives of the Hebrew Bible—such as the exiled slave woman Hagar, the raped princess Tamar, the young, sacrificed daughter Jephthah, and the raped and murdered nameless concubine.[43] These oppressed, silenced, and suffering women are required to be liberated from the misogynist and male-dominated Bible. The liberation will begin with the re-interpretation of the Bible in a way that restores the value and presence of women.

For example, by forensically analyzing the Biblical text, Trible pieces together the facts about Miriam that she was honored and respected by the people of Israel and that she was perceived as a female prophet in the journey of the exodus. However, in the end, the written-down narrative of Miriam is distorted and misrepresented. She has been described as a woman who disobeyed male authority in the person of Moses, thereby receiving God's punishment. More significantly, the narrative implies that she disobeyed "a man." The credit for Miriam's devotion and leadership is stolen by Moses—in order to strengthen his power, sustain his authority, and justify the exclusively male tradition of prophets.[44] It is in "terror" (in Trible's words) that these Biblical texts attempt to repress women. For feminist theologians, if the interpretation of the Bible cannot be subverted and the original situation of Christianity cannot be restored, women certainly cannot be redeemed.

Thus, the demand is that the formation of church tradition is scrutinized to liberate women. Church tradition is usually accepted without any criticism because it is regarded as the protection of God's revelation, and the unique expression and continuation of it.[45] Therefore, what feminist theologians do in exploring church tradition is like an *excavation* of the acts of women in the "covered" tradition. This survey is done by asking where women were in Jesus' time, whether their voices were inaudible, or were silenced in history, or how

43. Trible, *Texts of Terror*; Crenshaw, *Whirlpool of Torment*.

44. Trible, 如何和聖經摔跤; Brenner-Idan, *Israelite Woman*.

45. Ratzinger, who went on to become Pope Benedict XVI, for example, maintains that Tradition "is ultimately based on the fact that the Christ event cannot be limited to the age of the historical Jesus, but continues in the presence of the Spirit." See, Ratzinger, "Dogmatic Constitution on Divine Revelation." Cited from Hilkert, "Experience and Tradition," 68.

their presence was erased from the church memory.[46] Anne Carr calls this excavation the "historical experience" of women.[47]

But these findings do not serve only to expand our understanding of Christian tradition. By disclosing how the Bible and tradition have been formed by male perspective and power, the findings of the "historical experience" of women themselves shake the patriarchal authority of the Christian faith. They also undermine the authority of men, justifying their power. As Susan Frank Parsons argues, "to give attention to women's experience" is "to throw open to question the unchallenged assumption that men's experiences speak for everyone and are thus, by default, normative for all."[48] This questioning of the invisibility of women is the subversion of patriarchal culture in the church.

The church tradition that we have followed for thousands of years (which we call "apostolic tradition") is the product of androcentrism—which selects, interprets, and edits what Jesus taught. But in fact, it also welcomed and embraced women.[49] In this sense, the voice and experience of women are placed by feminist theology "at the center rather than the periphery so that their speech and presence become normative."[50] This is the strategy adopted by feminist theologians for ending the exclusion of women—the deconstruction of the patriarchal structure, the restoration of women's experience in tradition, and the fair presentation of the voice of women in the Bible.

The construction of an inclusive community in the church is the second contribution of feminist theology. Although feminist theologians put their emphasis on the situation of women, they have voiced concern about the experience of *all human beings*. This is because, as Mary Catherine Hilkert says, "God is to be discovered in human experience."[51] Catherine LaCugna also declares that feminist theology "draws its strength of conviction from women whose experience tells them that the kingdom of

46. Not all feminist theologians maintain their respect for church tradition; Mary Daly and Daphne Hampson are two such figures. Daly was from a Catholic theological background but, in her later life, she thought that the church tradition was hopelessly patriarchal and misogynist, leading her to abandon the theology. See: Daly, *Church and the Second Sex.*

47. Carr, "New Vision," 23.

48. Parsons, "Feminist Theology as Dogmatic Theology," 116.

49. Schüssler Fiorenza, *In Memory of Her*, 56.

50. Carr, "New Vision," 17.

51. Hilkert, "Experience and Tradition," 60.

God preached by Jesus promises a different order of relationship among persons than what prevails today."[52]

Based on these affirmations, feminist theologians go beyond securing their own interest as women and aspire to build up an inclusive community—which is for everyone instead of exclusively for women or the poor. Anne Carr is aware of the danger of feminist theology that merely reverses the order but reproduces the sexual hierarchy. She calls for a fundamental transformation in creating a new relationship:

> The goal of feminist theology cannot be simply to reverse the distortion by making men or certain classes and races or non-human creation subordinate. Rather, feminist theology must search for a new mode of relation that is inclusive of all.[53]

In this sense, we can conclude that the liberating agenda of feminist theology is not the construction of a female-dominant society (which turns the structure of gender discrimination upside down). Its goal is to embrace all creation into the community of God. It should avoid putting up barriers—which may exclude anyone from their relationship with God, in terms of their social class, gender, race, and sexuality.[54] This eschatological hope of an inclusive community is ultimately for the whole ecology and environment, not only for men and women.[55]

Feminist theology should not, therefore, be considered as a theology *for* women, or a theology *of* women. It is a theological project based on women's experience, which is aimed at pursuing the rights and equality of all human beings—a theology that represents the primary and fundamental oppression in human history. Here we see how feminist theology attempts to avoid the same trap that the male-dominant theology has fallen into—namely, that "the (male) experience" represents the whole of humanity and neglects the experience of women, the other half of human beings. Ann Loades makes a fair conclusion:

> We require a radical reconstructing of thought and analysis which comes to terms with the reality that humanity consists of women and men; that "the experiences, thoughts, and insights of both sexes must be represented in every generalization that is made about human beings." In other words, only half the story

52. LaCugna, "Introduction," 2.

53. Carr, "New Vision," 14.

54. The concept of inclusiveness is well developed in queer theology. For example, Cheng points out that the inclusiveness showing God's radical love is a main spirit of queer theology. See, Cheng, *Radical Love*.

55. Ruether, *Sexism and God-Talk*.

has been told. The half that now needs to be given prominence concerns women.[56]

Loades's conclusion is an important one, and worth highlighting. She argues that a theological reflection based on the voice and experience of women is not a theology for women alone, but for *both* women and men. In a way, it is similar to Latin American Liberation Theology because they both want to reflect on human experiences for their own liberation agenda (leaving the possible bias of representation aside). However, in order not to reproduce the failure of Latin American Liberation Theology in constructing an exclusive community only for "the poor," feminist theology *resources* the experience of women for constructing theology rather than *normalizes* it.[57]

Realistically, as Fiorenza has recognized, this idea of an inclusive community for all creation is still far from our reality at present, so it directs feminist theologians to a more eschatological perspective of inclusivity. The term for church in the New Testament—*ekklesia*—is integrated by Fiorenza as meaning "the actual assembly of free citizens gathering for deciding their own spiritual-political affairs."[58] It is believed that, by placing women's experience and voice at the center, the *ekklesia* of women may transform the relationship between women and men. But this *ekklesia* will come only when the structural-patriarchal dualism is overcome.[59]

The Critiques of Feminist Theology

The abstraction of experience is the first critique of feminist theology. This is because the methodology of feminist theology is intended to provide a unique *standpoint* of thinking and reflection from the perspective of women. The methodology of feminist theology fully echoes the feminist epistemology of "standpoint theory." As Sandra Harding says, standpoint theory has its root in Marxism and its purpose is to offer knowledge for the oppressed through revealing knowledge that is socially situated.[60]

> Standpoint theory's focus on the historical and social locatedness of knowledge projects and on the way collective political and intellectual work can transform a source of oppression into a source of knowledge and potential liberation, makes

56. Loades, "Introduction," 2.

57. Carr, "New Vision," 21.

58. Schüssler Fiorenza, *In Memory of Her*, 344.

59. Schüssler Fiorenza, *In Memory of Her*, 343–51.

60. Harding, "Introduction," 8–10.

a distinctive contribution to social justice projects as well as to our understanding of preconditions for the production of knowledge.[61]

Feminist standpoint theory may ask this question: How can women offer a different knowledge from the male-dominant one? They can, because they occupy a specific social position that allows them to see something that cannot be seen by men. This revealing of their social situatedness and their position within the social structure is what women can distinctively offer. Like feminist standpoint theory, feminist theology necessarily relies on the social position, which defines women and recognizes their experience.

In this light, I argue that "the experience" (to which feminist theologians claim to pay attention) is a misleading term because standpoint theory considers what women *think* rather than what they feel. Examining what women think about their social position offers feminist theology "knowledge" in mind, which is detached from the female body. Due to its prioritization of the exploration of women's standpoint, feminist theology neglects a proper concern about the real and even "physical," experience of women's suffering. All women's experiences that are heard have been transferred into the construction of feminist knowledge, to find a *shared* experience of all women.

Elisabeth Moltmann-Wendel also raises her concern over the disappearance of real women's experience and the neglect of women's bodies—due to feminist theologians' attempts to access the experience of women by establishing a "standpoint." But the body that is neglected is a real physical and experiential body through which people feel suffering.[62] Moltmann-Wendel further points out that Jesus' message is always related to our physical condition and his salvation is about our whole person socially, spiritually, and physically.[63] If women were to lose their body—their media to God and the world—due to it being stigmatized for its relationship with sin, how could they encounter God and receive God's healing? What Moltmann-Wendel attempts to achieve in her theology of embodiment is the retrieval of our body so that our experience and suffering can be revisited.

Women's experience should not be translated into epistemological knowledge—which is too distant from women's suffering in daily life. The

61. Harding, "Introduction," 10.

62. Elisabeth Moltmann-Wendel has noticed the significance of the body in constructing theology. She argues that "If the body begins to stop functioning, we make those around us insecure. And in such crises, we have another experience, namely we *are* bodies. The instrument which copes with life and gives pleasure in life gives us another experience: that is our prison." Moltmann-Wendel, *I Am My Body*, 1.

63. Moltmann-Wendel, *I Am My Body*, 37.

abstraction of women's experience causes feminist theologians to be deaf
to what women truly feel in their bodies—and blind to what these women
look like in the flesh and where they come from. When feminist theologians over-rely on defining women by their structural position and social
locatedness, thereby abstracting their experience, they will no longer listen
attentively to women's experiential suffering.

The homogeneity of women's experience is the second critique. It is the
repetition of the failure of Latin American Liberation Theology, whereby diverse experiences are generalized into "one experience"—which is defined as
a specific category of "the poor." Feminist theologians do not avoid falling into
this trap of generalization, and of confining the difference between women's
stories and "the" model of feminist standpoint—identified as the standpoint
of "white" women. And the failure to recognize the difference between women
has also troubled (white and Western) standpoint theory.[64]

In the first critique, I pointed out that feminist theology—using
standpoint theory to abstract the experience—has lost its concern with
the real suffering of women. More accurately, due to feminist standpoint
theory, feminist theology relies on the concept of social structure—and
where women are situated in the structure—to analyze how sexism works.
The result is that the subjectivity of women and their experience is restricted to their social position.

It cannot be denied that this structural analysis discloses structural
oppression efficiently and that this finding may build up greater solidarity
amongst women as a whole, irrespective of social position. However, the
price of such analysis is that *all* women become the same and are assumed to
share the *same* experience of suffering, which is oppressed by the universal
system of sexism and patriarchal structure. In this sense, for feminist theologians, it is also unnecessary to spend time hearing different experiences
of suffering from individual women, because they are all assumed to be
the same and are defined by the same social structure. Analyzing systemic
oppression and social structure becomes the replacement for listening to
sufferers and understanding their suffering. Treating women as one homogenous group obscures their individuality.

In response to this homogeneity of women-as-a-whole, Linda Hogan
insists that the concern with *difference* has to be incorporated into the basic
methodology of feminist theology. She then proposes a feminist methodology, which she calls the "hermeneutic of difference." Hogan recognizes the
danger of the sameness of women's experience becoming taken over by the
image of white women, and she sees that the experience of white women

64. Harding, "Introduction," 7.

has become accepted as the norm for all women. White feminist theologians should therefore examine the way in which the white female standpoint is applied becomes the projection of the image of white women, how it claims to be the experience of all women, and how it homogenizes the sameness of women's experience. At this point, we may therefore conclude that, although feminist theology attempts to subvert the prioritization and generalization of the poor in Latin American Liberation Theology, it ends up repeating the same failure, by overemphasizing the shared identity of all women and marginalizing the experiences of women of color.[65]

Pamela Sue Anderson suggests that "we need to articulate the interplay of bodily, material, and social differences using a revisable conception of the sex-gender distinction."[66] Indeed, it is good to analyze women's experiences in relation to social position, but feminist theologians should not allow structural analysis to take over the whole discussion. Women are socially constructed but are not a social product alone. Feminist theologians should not overemphasize gender (constructed socially) and forget sex (body in material). In this view, Anderson calls for a balancing perspective that rethinks the identity of gender "and" sex. She then argues that the understanding of the factors of sex-gender should include "sexual, gender, racial, class, ethnic, and religious orientations."[67] This will enable feminist theology to become more realistic and to analyze women's daily lives in a more down-to-earth fashion, as well as acknowledge the diversity of women's images and experiences. Anderson's proposal leads us on to womanist theology.

A Response: Womanist Theology from the Third World

Womanist theology draws on the voices of women's experiences and stories from the Third World. The usage of the term "womanist" is still debatable in contrast to "feminist." But following the definition of Alice Walker, who is an African-American social activist, I simply define womanist theology as a Black feminist theology or a feminist theology of color.[68] As Walker asserts, African-American women have different experiences from white women. This recognition of the difference merely emphasizes different dimensions of women rather than distinguishes or divides women by their race.[69]

65. Hogan, *From Women's Experience*, 166–67.
66. Anderson, "Feminist Theology," 47.
67. Anderson, "Feminist Theology," 47–48.
68. Walker, *In Search of Our Mothers' Gardens*, xi.
69. Walker, *In Search of Our Mothers' Gardens*, xi; Junior, *Introduction*, xi–xxv.

In this sense, womanist theology can be considered a response to Latin American Liberation Theology and white feminist theology, as it brings together the concern with poverty and political-economic oppression and the concern with sexism. It is different from feminist theology, which has been regarded as a theology of educated white women in North America and Europe.[70] Womanist theologians assert that feminist theology is too "white," and too Eurocentric, to empathize fully with the suffering of non-White women; that is, feminist theology excludes the context of non-White women.[71] For example, Audre Lorde criticizes Mary Daly in her so-called "radical feminism" project for failing to include black women's heritage so that she cannot articulate the racism and separation between women. This is because Daly retains the assumption that "non-white women and our [black] histories are noteworthy only as decorations, or examples of female victimization."[72] In Lorde's view, Daly has not only failed to build up a real solidarity of all women, but has also caused infighting. She then says:

> To imply that all women suffer the same oppression simply because we are women is to lose sight of the many varied tools of patriarchy. It is to ignore how those tools are used by women without awareness against each other.[73]

To redeem feminist theology from the generalization of women's experience, their movement is strongly supported by women from African and Asian backgrounds, (even though some feminist theologians have taken part in and have received nourishment from the movement too).[74] Here I will point out three contributions by womanist theology to liberation theologies: (1) The attention to multi-oppressions, (2) the formation of women's experience, and (3) the expression of sufferings. I highlight especially the works of

70. Feminist/womanist theologians from the Third World identify themselves in different ways. For example, Kwok Pui-lan, a Hong Kongese female theologian, still prefers to use the term "feminist theology" in her writing. But in order to avoid confusion, I prefer to call feminist/womanist theologians from the Third World "womanist theologians," in contrast to feminist theologians who are White and in North America and Europe. It is not to say that the two have not learned from each other.

71. Further see, King, *Feminist Theology*. This book collects articles from many feminist theologians representing the voices of women in Africa, Asia, and Latin America as well as those working among minorities in places such as Israel, the USA, and the Pacific.

72. Lorde, "Open Letter to Mary Daly," 96.

73. Lorde, "Open Letter to Mary Daly," 95.

74. Asian theology and African theology are defined by the ethnic identity of individual theologians rather than by geographical differences. Here, it is not necessary to differentiate African-American theology from the theology in the African Continent.

two theologians: Delores S. Williams, an African-American womanist theologian, and Chung Hyun Kyung, a Korean womanist theologian.

The attention to multi-oppressions is the first contribution. Womanist theology does not see the issue of oppression as being confined to only *one* social group (whether social class, poverty, sexuality, or race). The experience of African-American women has shown that they suffer from multi-oppressions of social class *and* of sexuality from white and black men and "white women." African-American women are betrayed both by black men (shared race) and by white women (shared sexuality).

For example, the voices of black women are erased in the history of black liberation.[75] Black male theologians placed their masculine experience of slavery at the center of re-reading and interpreting the Bible. They claimed that the experience of black men and women, rather than white missionaries who taught them theology, were best placed to foster understanding of the story of Israel's liberation. The exodus event was identical to the story of God leading the black community from being slaves to becoming free "men." As Cecil Cone, a black male theologian, says, "what [the Old Testament's Almighty Sovereign] God did for the children of Israel was in harmony with the slaves' own understanding of the divine."[76] Black women, who denied their gender identity, were called to be in solidarity with other black men against racial oppression.

Paralleling their liberation narratives with the Biblical exodus, Black (male) theology copies and shares the methodology of Latin American Liberation Theology. The only difference is that for black (male) theologians, black slaves are especially privileged when it comes to taking the position of the Israelites, who were enslaved in Egypt. The identification of black slaves with Israel in Egypt creates a convincing Biblical narrative of Black Liberation Theology.

However, Delores Williams criticizes this kind of narrative of black enslavement for excluding the stories of black women. Her objection is to the reproduction of a system of masculine and violent language.[77] This is why Williams suggests replacing the exodus narrative with the *wilderness* experience, which she considers a better fit with the black experience and community (both women and men) and the African-American existence in North America.[78] For Williams, African-American women have lost their identity when they participate in Black Liberation Theology—a movement

75. See, Hopkins, *Introducing Black Theology.*
76. Cone, *Identity Crisis*, 36.
77. Williams, *Sisters in the Wilderness*, 133–36.
78. Williams, *Sisters in the Wilderness*, 141–43.

that is dominated by black men, and which excludes women and family. If Black theology is for all black people, she proposes that:

> Any aspect of African-American people's experience and of African cultural sources used to shape resistance doctrine must be "de-coded" of all androcentric, gender, homophobic, class, and color bias.[79]

In this light, Williams insists that black theology should not focus solely on the challenge of white dominance. The subversive project of the de-construction of male-dominant ideology that oppresses black women must be incorporated, because the previous agenda of Black Liberation Theology was still too androcentric to include sexual liberation. For Williams, if black women cannot be liberated from sexist oppression, this black liberation will be far from complete.

On the other hand, African-American women have difficulty in sharing the identity and experience of white women, including (white) feminist theologians. This is because white females were traditionally part of the system of oppression—white women were the masters and black women were their slaves. The oppression suffered by African-American women reveals the facts: Firstly, women can be oppressors. Secondly, the suffering of black women has already proved that their experience, life, body, freedom, and rights are dominated and manipulated by their female masters. It is not evident that all women (regardless of race) suffer in the same way.

In response to the long history of discussing patriarchy in (white) feminist theology, Williams enlarges its definition "as a term to describe black women's relation to the white (male and female) dominated social and economic system governing their lives."[80] When patriarchy is criticized, womanist theologians insist that we should not forget the participation of white women. We should not simplify the system of oppression which can be more than one-dimensional. We should not be so naïve as to believe that black women would not be oppressed by black men (themselves the victims of racism), or by white women (the victims of sexism). Oppression does not function in a binary or one-dimensional way.[81] Williams's understanding of patriarchy sets a new direction for liberation theologies—one that insists that sexual liberation must work hand in hand with other liberations, including the liberation of race and social class.

79. Williams, *Sisters in the Wilderness*, 192.

80. Williams, *Sisters in the Wilderness*, 164; Williams, "Color of Feminism," 42–58.

81. Kelly Brown Douglas also points out "the need for a multi-dimensional and bifocal analysis that confronts all that oppresses the Black community as it impinges upon the community or is harbored within." Douglas, *Black Christ*, 109.

The formation of women's experience is the second contribution of womanist theology. This says that the purpose of constructing womanist theology is to *form* and *transform* women's experience, instead of merely interpreting God's story from the feminist standpoint. The experiences of other women are not "other" stories (which should be heard in Latin American Liberation Theology and feminist theology), but stories to which we can all relate (in womanist theology)—so that we all can be formed by these stories of God and women. Delores Williams takes the story of Hagar as an example of one that is sympathetic to African-American women's experiences. Both face the same predicament of "poverty, sexual and economic exploitation, surrogacy, domestic violence, homelessness, rape, motherhood, single-parenting, ethnicity and meeting with God."[82] As the subject of slave oppression and abuse by her male master (Abram) and her female master (Sarai), Hagar becomes the key symbolic figure of African-American womanist theology.

In addition, in contrast to the emphasis on the exodus event, Hagar went into the wilderness and encountered God there. Williams regards this wilderness as an open space—in which black women are displaced but encounter God in their darkness and their suffering. (Unlike the Promised Land or the exodus event from Egypt, the wilderness is the place where the oppressed, the sufferers and the displaced meet God *in person*.)[83] Here we can see that womanist theology is not about picking up a glorious Biblical story to which women can transfer their oppressed position—one *to* which and *with* which they can identify. Hagar is certainly not a glamorous character. But more importantly, Hagar's experience shows how God initiates God-self sympathy and empathy to meet those who are in despair and who are totally powerless in person.

What, then, is the significance of Hagar's encounter with God? Firstly, instead of pointing towards a hermeneutical process of understanding God, the encounter is intimate and directly empowers women. But controversially, when Hagar first leaves for the wilderness, God sends her back home! As Williams notes, Hagar was not liberated from oppression at that time but was given an opportunity to survive and enjoy *quality of life*.[84]

82. Williams, *Sisters in the Wilderness*, 5.

83. Grant argues that the story of exodus is not enough to identify with black women's experience, so she proposes that black women identify with Jesus as a divine co-sufferer. This is because they both were persecuted and forced to suffer. See: Grant, *White Women's Christ*; Coleman, *Making a Way*, 14.

84. Williams, *Sisters in the Wilderness*, 175. I believe that the World Health Organization's definition of quality of life explains about Williams's idea well: Quality of Life is defined "as an individual's perception of their position in life in the context of the

Hagar did not receive an immediate liberation, but she was empowered by the encounter. This is fully about life-saving and direct empowerment. Secondly, the encounter provides reassurance. Hagar and African-American women both bear the responsibility for rearing their children on their own. This can be difficult, especially when they are in poverty, in the wilderness, and homelessness. The encounter offers reassurance that God will support them on their journey.[85] Wilderness becomes a place "in which God gives personal direction to the believer and thereby helps her make a way out of what she thought was no way."[86]

What Williams attempts to point out is that the empowerment of the oppressed will not be achieved by interpreting the Bible, or by the oppressed knowing that God understands their suffering and predicaments. Oppressed women—and the oppressed generally—will not be empowered by opening the Bible. On the contrary, women are empowered through a real encounter with God—who sides with them and opens a way for them.

In other words, when womanist theology reads the Bible, the first step is to re-tell the story. The second step is to understand their suffering from the viewpoint of the retold story. The third step is to allow the story to form and transform us while seeing and encountering God in the story. In the example of Williams, by retelling the story of Hagar (rather than Sarai), African-American women *throw themselves into* the narrative, so that they can be formed and transformed by the story of Hagar.[87] This womanist method of reading the Bible is the reverse of the method used by their partners in liberation theologies: The first step is to define the experience of the oppressed, in terms of the standpoint. The Bible is then interpreted and understood from the perspective of the experience of the oppressed.

The formation of the experience also has another dimension—which is *discipleship*. As Monica Coleman suggests, black women should pattern their lives as disciples, this being "a way to combat the sin of servanthood." Coleman adds: "Understanding discipleship as salvation implies that

culture and value systems in which they live and in relation to their goals, expectations, standards and concerns." See: "WHOQOL: Measuring Quality of Life."

85. Williams, *Sisters in the Wilderness*, 31.

86. Williams, *Sisters in the Wilderness*, 96.

87. I appreciate Monica Coleman's review of salvation in womanist theology, she uses the term—vision—to describe this way of reading the Bible. The womanist way of reading the Bible is allow God to draw the oppressed and women into the participation of the story and the recognition of the vision of the ministry. "Jesus saves because of what he does. Jesus teaches, heals, condemns evil, prays, and loves. [Dolore] Williams believes that God is acting through Jesus to invite humans to participate in this ministerial vision. Salvation comes from this *vision* we see in the life of Jesus." Coleman, *Making a Way*, 23.

salvation is an ongoing process. It is a model for life."[88] The experience of suffering turns out to be something we can *work on*, rather than a source of self-pity. In discipleship, the experience of suffering is formed and transformed to live *within* that suffering. The formation of the experience enables us to recognize God, who has accompanied us and has opened a way in the dark wilderness. This is the reason why Williams comments critically on feminist theology, saying:

> While some feminist theologians claim the prophetic tradition significant for the biblical foundations of feminist theology, they give little or no attention to the way in which the wilderness figures into the work of *making* the prophet and *making* a people.[89]

This is about making "a people"! The experience of women's suffering itself is an answer to the oppression. Knowing how women are oppressed cannot set them free but shaping and forming the oppressed people of God can.

The expression of individual suffering is the third contribution to liberation theologies. As discussed in the last section, our experience is not a resource of seeking liberation but something we can work on, and I will show that womanist theology offers a space for the sufferers to express their experience and feeling of suffering. This theology is confidently expounded by Chung Hyun Kyung, a Korean-American womanist theologian.

Chung points out that Korean women suffer from multi-oppressions of Confucianism, colonialism, patriarchy, poverty, domestic abuse, sexual inequality, and labor exploitation. The burden of these sufferings is so intolerable that nursing a grudge may take over many Korean women's entire lives, including Chung's mother. The fate of Korean women is driven by hatred (*han* in Korean). Under such circumstances, she affirms: "I want to do theology in solidarity with and in love for my mother so as to resurrect crucified persons—like her—by giving voice to their hurts and pains."[90]

For this purpose, doing womanist theology is to give these hopeless women—who are silenced and living without a voice—the means of expression. It is also to offer an escape from feelings of outrage, hatred, and hurt. In this light, being in solidarity with the oppressed means helping *them* to articulate their experience of oppression and speak of their feeling in suffering (rather than to enable theologians to construct theology based on their testimony). Womanist theology does not just shape the experience of the oppressed by forging the wilderness experience through

---

88. Coleman, *Making a Way*, 17.

89. Williams, *Sisters in the Wilderness*, 142. The emphasis is mine.

90. Chung, *Struggle to Be the Sun Again*, 5.

which God encounters God's people. It also creates a liberating space for the oppressed—by enabling them to articulate their anger and to accept their feeling of hatred.

Instead of sticking to the limited resource of Western Christianity, Chung controversially employs a ritual from Korean Shamanism, known as *kut*.[91] *Kut* is only practiced by women. The rite of *kut* allows silenced ghosts to come to articulate their *han* and encourages women to speak aloud their feeling and experience of hatred and suffering. When these hatreds of oppression can be heard by being articulated, they are eventually released. Chung further explains that this release of hatred, called *han-pu-ri*, can be understood as the liberating power of Jesus who frees oppressed women from injustice and suffering.[92] For Chung, the end of injustice comes from the action of verbally naming and defining oppressors, and exposing their experience and feeling of suffering.[93] Peace may only come spiritually, psychologically, or even physically when hatred and injustice are named.

Chung's womanist theology gives a voice to the oppressed. But it is different from other liberation theologians' attempt to translate the experience of the oppressed into a theological language. Chung's womanist theology simply allows the oppressed to speak out. What theologians can do here is not to translate, write down or analyze the suffering—but to *create a space* that has been limited and repressed by oppressive systems.

These oppressive systems have already encompassed different layers of oppression and repression. For example, women are not allowed to speak (sexism). Poor women are incapable of expressing themselves and telling their suffering (poverty). Asian women do not receive empathy from their white sisters, or even from their African sisters (racial division). Korean women regard obedience and silence as their virtues (cultural sexual oppression from Confucianism). Christian Korean women are not allowed to use "pagan" liturgy to verbally share their suffering with other women (repression from the orthodoxy of imperialist Western Christianity).

---

91. Some Western theologians have noticed that Asian theology is rooted in multi-religious and less Christian-influenced influential area, meaning that Asian theology has to deal with its relationship with other religions or naturally appropriates some resources from other religions. Moltmann, "Political," 10. On the other hand, in the journey of fighting for gender equality, Asian womanist theologians need to recognize the complexity of cross-cultural and inter-religious contexts. For example, Kwok Pui-lan points out how religions "have influenced gender construction [that] will help Asian womanist theologians to understand in a nuanced way the religious and cultural legitimation of patriarchy." Kwok, *Introducing Asian Feminist Theology*, 49.

92. Chung, "Han-Pu-Ri," 145.

93. Chung, "Han-Ru-Ri," 143.

Giving space for women to speak "directly" and "without any media-tor," the ritual of *kut* breaks all taboos and subverts multi-oppressions that attempt to keep women in silence. This truly empowers the oppressed to discern and reflect on what they suffer. Oppressed women do not need theologians telling them how to define their suffering and why they suffer. In womanist theology, the experiences, stories, and feelings of the oppressed themselves become the *focus* rather than tools of social analysis or theologi-cal interpretation. They do not need to serve any theologians but have their *status quo* value and meaning. They are not reducible and should not be reduced to any abstract theological concept.

In the case of Chung's *han-pu-ri*, womanist theology proposes a new methodology to deal with the experience of oppressed women—those whose sufferings will not end immediately. It does not mean that womanist theology does not care about liberation anymore, but it shows that, realisti-cally, liberation will come in a gradual process. When womanist theology comes to the experience of the oppressed women, the primary task is no longer analyzing the social structure by listening to their stories. This is be-cause, by allowing the oppressed to speak, they can be truly empowered and can build up the basis for liberation. Seeking liberation has become about paying attention to each *individual* who suffers structural oppression. Thus, liberation should begin with their experience.

Also, in womanist theology, when different feelings and experiences are kept as they are and not reduced to any social analysis, more experienc-es—which may be inconsistent with the model of liberation theologies—can be recognized. Womanist theologians, especially Chung, challenge the intention of trimming all experiences of suffering to fit a certain category of knowledge. This is echoed by Chandra Talpade Mohanty, an Indian woman-ist theologian. She reminds us that even the experience of the "Third World Woman" is not "a singular monolithic subject."[94]

Womanist theology directs liberation theologies back to serious con-cern with what oppressed women *experience* and attempts to find liberation and freedom from there. What the oppressed experience in their suffering and oppression becomes the locus of doing liberation theology because the experience itself discloses the oppressive systems.

A Critical Review of Liberation Theologies

In this chapter, I began by reviewing Latin American Liberation Theology (which is the methodological foundation of liberation theologies), conversing

94. Mohanty, "Under Western Eyes," 333; Wong, *Poor Woman*, 129–30.

with feminist theology (which revises the methodology of Latin American Liberation Theology), and then womanist theology (which critically responds to feminist theology). Developing from Latin American Liberation Theology to womanist theology, liberation theologies make a huge effort to define and recognize the oppressed, and to engage with the experience of the oppressed. But on the opposite side of the coin, I conclude that liberation theologies have failed due to the two issues: (1) *The involvement of the subject* and (2) *the theological application of human experiences.*

The involvement of the subject is not seriously considered in liberation theologies. When the sufferers do not have the power to interpret their experiences and feelings, they are objectified and compartmentalized by liberation theologians—even though they may be situated within different oppressed situations. Ivan Petrella calls this phenomenon "monochromatism," which is obsessed with just "one," *either-or* scope of oppression. Critically evaluating Black Theology, he comments:

> [Monochromatism] dramatically limits the pool of resources they can draw upon to actually engage the task. In the end, color of memberships and membership in a professional guild takes priority over liberation from material blight."[95]

Due to the compartmentalization of monochromatism, every individual subject becomes unimportant. The social category that a subject belongs to, or in which a sufferer is situated, takes a primary role in defining the subject. The subject is alienated from their experiences, feelings, and even their bodies (through which they feel and experience).

The theological application of human experiences is overlooked. The individual experiences of the oppressed are over-ridden by a collective experience—which is abstract, theoretical, and homogeneous. The diversity of the experiences of oppressed sufferers have been underemphasized to demonstrate the theories of social analysis of liberation theologians.[96] When the experiences of the oppressed are merely heard and collected by theologians to support their social analysis, the experiences are eventually replaced with the conclusive statement of an analysis. This theological

95. Petrella, *Beyond Liberation Theology*, 84–85.

96. Petrella has a similar criticism of the application of social theory in liberation theologies. This overreliance on social theory is referred to as "gigantism," which has two type of deprivation: "abstraction" and "demonization." "In the former, the theologian identifies the cause of material poverty with such abstraction that they are impossible to tackle. Thus, the poor suffer from evils produced by "capitalism," "neoliberalism," or "globalization," terms that are used as place markers for the cause of oppression, but which are rarely carefully examined and concretely defined." Petrella, *Beyond Liberation Theology*, 102–3.

methodology abandons the initial purpose of concern with suffering so that the experiences of the oppressed are no longer prioritized as liberation theologians intended and claimed.[97]

These two issues point towards the problem which is fundamentally rooted in liberation theologies—that is the over-reliance on Marxism and its structural analysis. The problem can be observed in Marxist concern with poverty in Latin American Liberation Theology and standpoint theory in feminist theology. Even for womanist theology, it just makes the analysis *more delicate* in response to the context of Third World women. However, no matter how liberation theologies revise their application of the Marxist methodology, they continue to struggle to work out *the ways* in which these multi-oppressions are interwoven to propose *a further strategy* for seeking liberation and freedom.

Liberation theologies, in this light, must revisit their relationship with Marxism and their reliance on social analysis. As I have demonstrated in this chapter, they have not yet done enough to cope with multiple oppressions. As I have shown in chapter 1, their methodology has reached its limit in maintaining the fruits of revolution and social movements. Apart from sticking to social structures, liberation theologies have failed again and again to recognize how oppressive systems work on each individual victim, and how freedom can be achieved if all oppressive systems are inextricably intertwined. In chapter 3, I will introduce Michel Foucault with the aim of carrying out a thorough examination of how the oppressed suffer. This may explain why liberation theologies are not radical enough to maintain the fruit of social revolutions and avoid their failures.

97. Petrella uses the term "amnesia" to criticize how liberation theologians forget their purpose of fighting against poverty at the beginning of constructing the theology. Petrella, *Beyond Liberation Theology*, 93. He criticizes that the theologies of the color pay their attention to "ethnic identity" and they neglect the issue of poverty. However, I cannot entirely agree with his criticism because I argue that the birth and the context of the theologies of the color are for ethnicity rather than for poverty. This failure of seeking the priority is repeated in all liberation theologies.

3

Doing Liberation Theology with Foucault

IN THE PRECEDING CHAPTERS, I explored the difficulties encountered by revolutions and social movements, and by liberation theologies, as they inherited and responded in different ways to the theory of Marxism. However, based on empirical experience, what Marxism has so far brought to us has not been as great as it promised, or as we expected. In this chapter, I will invite Michel Foucault to join the conversation because I believe his philosophy will help *broaden* our understanding of oppression and domination. I argue that if liberation theologies want to bring about liberation and freedom, they need to build up our capacity to recognize that domination has been both produced and reproduced in a more complex and dynamic form. Learning from Foucault, our attention needs to be drawn to the practice of *political resistance*, rather than be obsessed with analysis of social structural alone.

This chapter has five sections in which Foucault's viewpoint of dominance, subjectification, and freedom is explored.

1. Foucault challenges the utopian expectation that a power-free society is achievable.

2. Foucault's idea of power relationships is developed alongside his conversation with Althusser and Marxism, and with Durkheim and Functionalism.

3. For Foucault, resistance is possible, though it does not mean "liberation." His critique of power is still related to his criticism of capitalism.

4. Foucault suggests taking the constitution of sexuality and desire with the birth of perversions into account in the analysis of power relationships.

5. For Foucault, subjectification, which means the practice of the self, is a resistive practice for dealing with governmentality.

A *Realistic* Recognition of No Power-Free Zone

Foucault differs from those who strive to find and build a society in which there is no injustice or oppression. He does not take this kind of utopian idea because he believes that no one can escape from power relationships. As his famous quote says in *The Will to Knowledge*:

> [The omnipresence of power] is produced from one moment to the next, at every point, or rather in every relation from one point to another. Power is everywhere; not because it embraces everything, but because it comes from everywhere.[1]

This quote can easily be interpreted in such a way as to accuse Foucault of supporting nihilistic political power: If we cannot escape from power relationships, if power is omnipresent, what is the point of seeking liberation and resistance? How can Foucault's concept of power and freedom work out? (It is important to clarify what Foucault does *not* mean before moving onto his theory of power relationships.)

Charles Taylor is one of those who struggles with getting his head around Foucault's view. Taylor's criticism is that Foucault is inconsistent when it comes to talking about the relationship between power and liberation. He argues that "power, in his [Foucault's] sense, does not make sense without at least the idea of liberation."[2] For Taylor, there must be a subject-object in domination—which means "something must be imposed on someone."[3] Thus he argues that it is impossible to bring about freedom, while passing by the idea of liberation. We may agree with Taylor's criticism that Foucault leads us into confusion. But here I argue that it is valuable to figure out why Foucault separate freedom from liberation—as this will help us figure out why liberation movements do not bring about freedom. Ironically, what Taylor considers confusion is the point that Foucault *exactly* wants to raise and proposes to get rid of. Taylor's criticism may be important. But if Taylor and other liberation believers are dead right, why do we still struggle to find what they call "freedom"?

Paul Patton introduces Isaiah Berlin's two concepts of liberty into the conversation to help clarify various concepts of freedom used by Taylor and Foucault.[4] Concerning positive freedom, both Patton and Berlin attempt to reach the ultimate goal of self-mastery. But they are on different tracks, in terms of their fundamental understanding of power and freedom. For

1. Foucault, *History of Sexuality*, 1:94.
2. Taylor, "Foucault on Freedom and Truth," 173.
3. Taylor, "Foucault on Freedom and Truth," 172.
4. Berlin, "Two Concepts of Liberty," 166–217.

Taylor, the freedom of the subject is "defined simply as the absence of external constraints upon action, then an opportunity concept is all that is
required."[5] Striving for freedom is striving for an environment—in which all
subjects are not restrained by external powers and are free internally, with
consciousness and autonomy.

But for Foucault, this is not enough. "His concern is with the external
support of the forms of social consciousness and being." This is why Foucault
"attempts to chart some of the institutions, practices, and bodies of knowledge which help to define and to maintain particular kinds of individuality."[6]
The condition of freedom and the concept of the subject are both put into
question in a more complicated situation. Unlike Taylor, Foucault does
not want to fall for the naïve belief that a *full* range of conditions setting *all*
people free can be found. If this is the reality, how can oppressed subjects get
rid of power (which has been considered as purely evil for Taylor, for other
liberation believers, and even for Jean-Paul Sartre)?

This significant question is what I will explore in the rest of this chapter. But I think it's worth briefly looking at Foucault's short response before
we move on to further discussion. In 1984 (the year of his death), Foucault
was asked to respond to Sartre's dictum that "power is evil." Foucault's
straightforward response was that Sartre's idea "has often been attributed
to me, which is very far from what I think. Power is not evil. Power is
strategic games."[7] On the other hand, he was asked about how truths can
be told if "the one who can formulate truths also has a power, the power of
being able to say the truth and to express it as he wishes" and how he may
sort out the problem of communication (in Jürgen Habermas's sense).[8]
Foucault promptly criticizes Habermas for assigning a "utopian" place to
relations of communication. He further explains:

> It is being blind to the fact that relations of power are not some-
> thing bad in themselves, from which one must free one's self. I
> don't believe there can be a society without relations of power.
> (. . .) The problem is not of trying to dissolve them in the utopia
> of a perfectly transparent communication.[9]

Here I think Foucault has explained without any ambiguity how he considers power and, more accurately, "power relationships." Foucault may

5. Patton, "Taylor and Foucault," 267.
6. Patton, "Taylor and Foucault," 264.
7. Foucault, "Ethic of Care for the Self," 18.
8. Foucault, "Ethic of Care for the Self," 17.
9. Foucault, "Ethic of Care for the Self," 18.

agree with the ultimate goal of seeking freedom, but he is dubious about any possibility of building a power-free zone for individual subjects, or for utopian relations of communication. In Foucault's view, a more *realistic* approach to liberation and dominance, concerning our understanding of power and freedom, must be taken!

Foucault's Concern with Power Relationships

Although it is debatable whether Foucault is a Marxist, I assume that understanding the conversation between Foucault and Marxism may help us figure out his concept of politics through recognizing what he inherits in his time and what he criticizes. The influence of Marxism in France was dominant, and Foucault himself admits that before the May Rebellion of 1968 everyone was a Marxist, a phenomenologist, or a structuralist. However, he also admits that his interests in psychiatry and the history of medicine were marginal and a niche topic alongside mainstream French thought.[10] It was impossible for Foucault not to inherit any Marxist thoughts, so the issue is how critically Foucault deals with his Marxist inheritance. He identifies himself as "neither an adversary nor a partisan of Marxism" but he "always asks politics what it had to say about the problems with which it was confronted."[11]

In particular, Foucault was inspired by the events of May 1968 to ask more questions—which were "derived more or less directly from Marxism"— which were "about women, the relations between the sexes, about medicine, about mental illness, about the environment, about minorities, about delinquency"[12] Like the motivation of this book chapter, Foucault's reconsideration of politics begins with his question about the Marxist concept of politics, and with his reflection on the political revolution and social movement of May 1968. I argue that Foucault does not entirely deny his conversation with Marxism, but he has recognized that these questions should be asked and that the political doctrine of Marxism is definitely not enough.

A Conversation with Althusser and Marxism

Étienne Balibar identifies that when Marxism has muddied the issue of the "juridical representation of power"—whether the exercise of power can go

10. Foucault, "Michel Foucault: An interview," 125.
11. Foucault, "Polemics, Politics and Problematization," 115.
12. Foucault, "Polemics, Politics and Problematization," 115.

beyond the rule of law—"Foucault himself suggests ways of getting out of this mirror relationship between law and the critique of law."[13] This is caused, Foucault argues, by the obsession of Marxism with criticism of the state. But more confusingly, Marxism cannot identify its role in dominance clearly, especially when it oscillates between "the idea of all powerfulness" and "the radical idea of its being without power."[14] The Marxist debate over the state just falls into an endless cycle of criticism of the state without leading to any conclusion. To enlarge the discussion of dominance and power, Foucault senses the need to reflect on the old theory of the state.

For Marxists, the key concern is how the external institutions of oppression can continue to function as the deployments of power, for the maintenance of any form of sovereignty, and the benefit of capitalism. These institutions—called "the apparatus of oppression"—include government, military, the church, and family. Louis Althusser (also a tutor of Foucault) defines two kinds of state apparatus: the "Repressive State Apparatus" and the "Ideological State Apparatus."[15] The former is displayed in the Government, the Administration, the Army, the Police, the Courts, the Prisons, etc., and uses violence and physical repression to dominate. The latter is deployed in religion, education, family, media and culture, etc.[16]

Althusser's model breaks down the traditional Marxist binary, based on determinism of the economic base, and incorporates various social dimensions to analyze how the state displays and deploys its power over the people. These different apparatuses continue to serve the state, so it is an extension of traditional theories of the state. Also, standing firmly in Marxism, Althusser asserts that "all Ideological State Apparatuses, whatever they are, contribute to the same result: the reproduction of the relations of production, i.e. of capitalist relations of exploitation."[17] (I will discuss Foucault's conversation with Marxism in terms of capitalism in the next section.)

Foucault is not satisfied with Althusser's extended theory of the state. Although he may agree with Althusser's rationale—which is that the traditional theories of the state were too descriptive to explain the complexity of power dominance[18]—the whole theory, for Foucault, is fundamentally wrong when it comes to the vision of dominance concerning the state. What is meant is that the relationship between the state and dominance

13. Balibar, "Foucault and Marx," 50-51.

14. Balibar, "Foucault and Marx," 50.

15. Althusser, "Ideology and Ideological State Apparatuses," 85–126.

16. Althusser, "Ideology and Ideological State Apparatuses," 142–45.

17. Althusser, "Ideology and Ideological State Apparatuses," 154.

18. Althusser, "Ideology and Ideological State Apparatuses," 141.

needs to be scrutinized, rather than the negation of the role of the state in dominance. As Bob Jessop observes, Foucault criticizes all these theories of the state for uncritically insisting on *a priori* assumptions about "its essential unity, its pre-given functions, its inherent tendency to expand through its own power dynamic, or its global strategic development by a master subject."[19] Foucault attempts to shift away from any *power-from-above* theories of the state that continues to attribute the dominant power to the state and government. His theory is a *power-from-below* theory of power—a power that is always present in relationships and that *comes from* all relationships, whether inside or outside apparatuses.[20] As Foucault posits:

> There is no binary and all-encompassing opposition between rulers and ruled at the root of *power relations* and serving as a general matrix—no such duality extending from the top down and reacting on more and more limited groups to the very depths of the social body.[21]

Foucault attempts to find a theory that covers not only the concern with the state but also the concern with other forms of dominance, whether they have been mentioned by Althusser. But more importantly, in Foucault's proposal, our understanding of oppression and dominance does not need to be measured in its relationship with the state. The state is not the center of the whole system of oppression. The state and all other state apparatuses are *part* of the system, like a matrix, which deploys and displays power without any central "government."

I argue that Foucault's proposed concern with the state is a more critical and fundamental way of actualizing Althusser's criticism of former theories of the state. This is because Foucault calls for a description of how the state is actualized and defined in the way it deploys its power and dominance. As Jessop argues, through its governmentalization of the state, instead of its institutional government, the state is recognized.[22] What Foucault requires us to see is how the state becomes the state with dominant power in the real context, instead of what the state is and how repressive the state can be. The state has not disappeared in Foucault's analysis. He believes instead that the

---

19. Jessop, "From Micro-Powers to Governmentality," 36.

20. The term "power-from-below" might be slightly misleading. What I mean here is to make a rhetorical contrast between Foucault's proposal and other theories of the state. In fact, Foucault's theory of power relationships shows that power is omnipresent and from everywhere, not only from above or from below.

21. Foucault, *History of Sexuality*, 1:94 (emphasis added).

22. Jessop, "From Micro-Powers to Governmentality," 38.

state comes alive only when it acts (with or without legitimacy) and when it functions as a state. As Jessop comments:

> The idea of government as strategic codification of power re-lations provides a bridge between micro-diversity and macro-necessity and, as Foucault argues, a focus on micro-powers is determined by scale but applies across all scales.[23]

This draws our attention to what Foucault means when he fundamentally challenges the theories of the state in the Marxist tradition. When Foucault gives up inheriting the theory of the state by means of deconstructing its given nature, he goes on to develop his understanding of power. Foucault asserts that "[power] is not to be defined because it does not exist."[24] These words seem to be very radical[25] but what Foucault meant here is no different from his proposal of the concern with the state—in which he emphasizes the complexity of all power working together, instead of any new definition of power. In the same interview, Foucault adds:

> I speak from the possibilities of intelligibility given by the analy-sis of mechanisms of power on the condition that one never speaks of *Power* but rather speaks of different instruments, tools, relations, techniques, etc., that allow for domination, sub-jectification, constraint, coercion, etc.[26]

Foucault calls for a deep understanding of deployment and display of power in relationships, in instruments, and indeed anywhere. We should not as-sume that power, like the state, has a given and a priori substance. If power can be recognized only when it exercises function, it is not abstract. If power exists independently, it can never be recognized, or the isolated existence of power is undefined or undefinable. If power only appears in all kinds of relationships, there is no "power" but "power relationship."

---

23. Jessop, "From Micro-Powers to Governmentality," 39.

24. Gordon et al., "Considerations on Marxism," 106.

25. In fact, Foucault's language was very strong in the interview, as he said, "I am the most radical enemy that one can imagine of the idea of power, and I don't ever speak about power." He also said, "I hate power, I hate the idea of power, and that is what people don't understand you get these completely naïve critiques that say "aha, he doesn't define power." Gordon et al., "Considerations on Marxism," 106.

26. Gordon et al., "Considerations on Marxism," 106 (emphasis in original).

A Conversation with Durkheim and Functionalism

Before moving on to the next section (in which I will explain power relationships in detail), it will first be helpful to reflect on the *purpose* of power relationships in Foucault's philosophy. I argue that Foucault attempts to offer a *holistic* perspective on power relationships to discern how society and different powers are related to each other. We should not be too surprised at Foucault's interest in proposing a "holistic" perspective if we consider that, in his time, French structuralism was mainstream, and Emile Durkheim and Marcel Mauss, through Claude Lévi-Strauss, were influential in French academia.

According to Foucault's biographic chronology,[27] in 1972 he began to give some attention to social controls and the system of punishment in nineteenth-century France. In 1975, he published *Surveiller et Punir: Naissance de la Prison* (English translation in 1977 *Discipline and Punish: The Birth of the Prison*). Interestingly, reading this book's structure alongside Durkheim's *The Division of Labor in Society* may help us recognize that Durkheim and Foucault both attempt to show two models of social order and their maintenance. Durkheim stresses the evolutionary progress of society—whose social bonds "evolve" from mechanical solidarity in primitive society to organic solidarity in industrial society. And these two models of social solidarity can be seen in their different systems of penalty, law, and social order.[28]

In *Discipline and Punish*, Foucault also shows how penal systems (tortures and punishments) and disciplines represent different kinds of social order and the mechanism of body control.[29] For Foucault, analyzing these models of body control in historical penal systems and prisons helps us recognize different models of power in modern society, even outside prison walls. They both recognize how institutions and legal systems represent social relationships and maintain social order.

It is not surprising that Foucault has some criticism of Durkheim. Foucault argues that Durkheim's analysis, like some structural functionalism, is inclined to generalize some specific social forms and assumes them to be universal situations (for the sake of their scientific epistemology). For Foucault, these changes in social order must have their historical contexts and their reasons to change but Durkheim neglects to observe and analyze them from the standpoint of "new tactics of power."[30] Foucault

27. Bernauer and Keenan, "Works of Michel Foucault," 163.
28. Durkheim, *Division of Labour in Society*.
29. Foucault, *Discipline and Punish*.
30. Turkel, "Michel Foucault," 181.

is not satisfied with the lack of historical and particular concern in Durkheim's "scientific" analysis.[31]

On the other hand, Foucault affirms that writing *Discipline and Punish* was inspired by his visit to Attica Prison in New York State. Following his visit, he began thinking about how prisons function in societal constitutions and to believe in "each society being able to function only on condition that a certain number of people are excluded from it."[32] Durkheim's structural functionalism prompts Foucault to analyze different forms of social order and power mechanisms of power and to question "how society can hold individuals together."

In Foucault's view, the focus of Durkheim and other structural-functionalism on the coherence of society is a narrow one. They both assume that society functions and is maintained in a harmonious, stable, and homogeneous way. But Foucault insists that the excluded should be involved because society cannot function or be maintained without them. He adds that "through what system of exclusion, by eliminating whom, by creating what division, through what game of negation and rejection can society begin to *function*?"[33] In this sense, Foucault does care about the function of society, but his focus is on exclusion, erasure, and denial, rather than the solidarity of collective consciousness. Foucault is more interested in these questions asked by structural functionalists than the theories to apply.

Recognition of Foucault's conversation with structural-functionalism helps us clarify why Foucault turns to power relationships and why he does not fall into a nihilistic view of power. As Neil Brenner has argued, if power is considered as a functional system, resistance (or things that are excluded and erased) can then be seen as a force of counter-functions that supports the function of this social system.[34] Unlike Durkheim, Foucault's discussion does not begin with the "assumption" that society functions as a singular whole unit, or that all social organizations function together to maintain society as an undivided unit. On the contrary, what Foucault is concerned with is *how* society can be a whole unit and what these mechanisms are in society.

Foucault attempts to analyze it from scratch without any theoretical assumptions. His analysis does not begin with assuming social organizations and then observing their relationships within society. Foucault's starting point is that these organizations exist only when they function and

---

31. Foucault's general criticism of science in psychology and sociology can be found in Foucault, "On the Archaeology of the Sciences," 297–334.

32. Foucault and Simon, "Michel Foucault," 27.

33. Foucault and Simon, "Michel Foucault," 28.

34. Brenner, "Foucault's New Functionalism," 679–709.

exercise; therefore, to define these elements, we must examine their process of formation. As Arnold Davidson points out:

> [Foucault's analysis] is characterized, first, by anti-atomism, by the idea that we should not analyze single or individual elements in isolation but that one must look at the systematic relations among elements; second, it is characterized by the idea that the relations between elements are coherent and transformable, that is, that the elements form a structure."[35]

Davidson's critique shows that Foucault explores a non-reductive and holistic approach to understand social life. Foucault's theory presents an image of society that is more dynamic, productive, and reproductive because they are all in the process of being formed and becoming part of society. This requires us to describe and analyze how they are related and connected instead of applying any theory of social structure.

Foucault's holistic approach also helps him to get away from reliance on the Marxist theory of totality. Foucault's theory of power relations enlarges such Marxist theories as determinism. As Foucault clarifies, "mechanisms of power" (to use his words) have been concerned with "extraordinarily varied fields of mechanisms of coercion, of domination, of exclusion, etc., the catalog is definite."[36] The interaction of power is no longer in a symmetrical form of dominants and the dominated, and oppressors and the oppressed—which are *point-to-point* relationships. (Foucault's response to economic determinism will be discussed in the next section.)

I argue that Foucault's proposal of power relationships draws us into an analysis of how various power forces are interconnected and how they cooperate ubiquitously within the whole of society. Power relationships resemble adhesives that glue different parts of society together as a whole unit. Ironically, Foucault's image of power relationships becomes ironically very systemic, like a neatly interwoven web, from which no single person or place can be free. All power relationships are seen in a cooperative and organic way because power is not steadily situated in institutions or apparatuses but is *diffused* in every relationship. The whole web of power relationships is constructed and maintained by all connected points of power. But we also need to notice Foucault's break away from Durkheim and structural functionalism—he does not believe that cooperation serves the coherence of society, although he still assumes that this cooperation works for some purposes (capitalism especially).

---

35. Davidson, *Foucault and his Interlocutors*, 11.
36. Gordon et al., "Considerations on Marxism," 105.

From the perspective of Foucault's holistic approach, the omnipresence of power means that power is produced at every point and results in making society *whole*. Foucault contends that "when I say that power, that relations of power are omnipotent, it means precisely the opposite of the affirmation that *power* is omnipotent."[37] Foucault rejects false interpretations which begin with regarding power as an autonomous and independent entity (commonly shared by the theories of the state). Foucault never indicates that there are innumerable individual institutions and power centers, so we should keep enlarging our list of identified power centers, like Althusser expands the list of State apparatuses. Foucault insists that the strategy of deploying power relations is *over-all* and *all-pervasive*.[38]

Power and Resistance

For Foucault, power and power relationships are not identical. If we are blind to recognize power relationships, we are also unable to see power itself. However, we might still struggle with accepting Foucault's over-all statement that "power is omnipresent." And some questions are commonly raised to challenge this statement: Is Foucault's assertion that power "relationships" are omnipresent just a 'typo'? Can we say that "power is everything" or "everything is power"? More importantly, is it possible for us to resist power?

There are three points that require consideration here.

Firstly, we must remember Foucault's basis—that no power can exist independently. I argue that the reason "power" can be omnipresent is that power appears in *all* of our relationships and we make relationships with the world and with objects, whether we intended to make them or not. Foucault prefers not to use the ambiguous and confusing term "power," because what he means by power does not rest on a focal point nor is it gathered in any center, as most people assume. Foucault rarely uses the term power, but when he does use it, he must be assuming that the power is located within the context of all our relationships. In this sense, power is omnipresent because our relationships with others are everywhere too.

Secondly, I argue that making these authoritative statements of absoluteness (like "everything is power" or "power is everything") is not Foucault's intention. He points out that "these relations [of power] would not have been established if power was omnipotent, or if there was such a thing as

---

37. Gordon et al., "Considerations on Marxism," 107 (emphasis in original).
38. Foucault, *History of Sexuality*, 1:99.

omnipotence."[39] Put simply, if power is everything or vice versa, power will be fully nihilistic and pointless because the recognition of this power does not mean or refer to anything. It is pointless when we try to use "everything is power" to explain things. For Foucault, it is not wordplay. Precisely to the extent that power is *not* everything, it is possible to recognize how powers are connected in relationships. Foucault invites us to analyze how power relationships can be "effectively found at each instant, in family relations, in sexual relations, in pedagogical relations, in relations of knowledge, etc."[40]

Based on these two points, we may begin to sense how Foucault thinks about resistance to power. He may promptly say, "yes we can," and add:

> Where there is power, there is resistance, and yet, or rather consequently, this resistance is never in a position of exteriority in relation to power (. . .) [The existence of power] depends on a multiplicity of points of resistance: these play the roles of adversary, target, support, or handles in power relations. These points of resistance are present everywhere in the power network.[41]

This paradoxical statement by Foucault reveals the truth that counter-power is part of power relationships, and that power and resistance exist for making society whole (in his holistic perspective). The existence of resistance is defined by its relationship with power. Therefore, when resistance is recognized, it must mean that there exists power—which is opposed *to* and *by* its resistance. Power cannot be defined, except by revelation of its relationship with the counter-power, or its resistance. That is, the interaction between power and resistance discloses the existence and location of power.

Thirdly, the coexistence of resistance and power has two implications. (1) In the epistemological sense, this presence of resistance reveals the *trajectory* of power—by showing the interaction between power and counter-power. (2) This trajectory of power also discloses its power relationship between power and resistance—because resistance defines and produces power which it defies. Resistance should be regarded as the cause rather than an effect or consequence of the presence of power. As Foucault said, "resistance comes first, and resistance remains superior to the other forces of the process; power relations are obliged to change with the resistance."[42] Resistance, in this sense, creates power since power is created to seize resistance and put it under dominated control.

39. Gordon et al., "Considerations on Marxism," 107.
40. Gordon et al., "Considerations on Marxism," 107.
41. Foucault, *History of Sexuality*, 1:95.
42. Foucault, "Sex, Power and the Politics," 167.

Moving on, if power is created by resistance, we should recognize that dominance from power is not the cause of resistance. In Foucault's logic, resistance underlines the need for power. Thinking from the holistic perspective, resistance should *not* be seen as a threat to destroy society and power, but strength created to maintain and construct the wholeness of society. Resistance should not be considered as a negative reaction to thwarting the dominance of power. Resistance, conversely, is an active and positive force to constitute power itself. As Foucault argues, "to resist is not simply a negation but a creative process: to create and recreate, to change the situation, actually to be an active member of that process."[43]

This is more confusing and even disturbing for utopian dreamers who crave resistance-for-change because Foucault implies that resistance is destined to fall under the control of power. But leading such a pessimistic and nihilistic understanding of power is not Foucault's intention. I argue that his reversal of the relationship between resistance and power reveals the strength of making a change—which is a "strategic" reflection on the resistance in the light of revolutions and social movements. Power is not and will not be eliminated by any form of resistance, whatever its scale. Foucault reminds us that both resistance and making a change are not in a straightforward relationship—if we have considered the permanent involvement of power. Foucault is not saying that resistance is impossible, or that resistance-for-a-change is not possible. He requires us to pay attention to that dynamic process of power relationships—in which power itself needs to change to dominate new resistance—so that the kind of resistance we create will change and create a new form of power. The form of resistance is in a corresponding relationship with its form of power. Resistance may bring a change by constituting new forms of power, rather than through its own effort.

Power Resistance without Liberation?

Foucault's critique of sexual liberation is the best example of how we may expect too much from liberation and misrecognize the dynamic relationship between power and resistance. *The Will to Knowledge* (1976) was misunderstood as a bible for sexual liberationists, although Foucault is very suspicious of propaganda about sexual repression (which claims that sexuality has been repressed in modern society, and therefore requires liberation). Foucault points out that these practices of sexual liberation have already been incorporated into the new system of power control.

43. Foucault, "Sex, Power and the Politics," 168.

As Foucault has repeatedly reminded us, power is not steadily sitting in an apparatus from which sexuality is liberated. Unsurprisingly, power deployments are active, flexible, and creative enough to enable themselves to quickly engage with sexual liberation and suddenly hijack the fruits of liberation movements. Foucault thinks that the questions about repression should be reframed in response to this rapidly changing context. He suggests asking "*why do we think* that we are repressed?" rather than "why *are* we repressed?"[44] This question helps us re-identify the power relationship between our so-called liberation and repression. Clearly, Foucault does not think that liberation and repression are separated into two sides in a fixed binary relationship. This relationship is not a permanent condition that can be achieved once and remain forever.

Foucault furthermore reveals how the action of sexual liberation fails to resist and how it is incorporated into power control. When sexual liberationists call for brave articulation of sexuality, they expect to break the silence of sexual taboos and subvert sexual repression. That probably achieved its liberation goal at the beginning, but it did not last for long. Foucault discovers that the articulation of sexuality has been encouraged to construct new medical knowledge of sexuality. The involvement of medical knowledge of sexuality becomes the way in which power identifies normality and abnormality.[45] The more we talk about sexuality, the more we are caught in these new power relationships that normalize certain kinds of sexuality and exclude those seen as homosexuals who cannot comply with normality.

Will Foucault destroy our hope in finding liberation? The situation, in which sexual liberation can be easily appropriated by other forms of power relationships, results from a narrow understanding of repression that gives us restraint, restriction, and confinement. Simultaneously, our understanding of liberation is limited to the achievement of removal of all restrictions and restraints. For Foucault, the more crucial question should be reframed: If we have misrecognized the deployments of power and the work of power relationships, how can we find the right way to liberation?

Foucault suggests that the binary dichotomy between repression and liberation should be discarded and the analysis should start with "polymorphous techniques of power."[46] I argue that there is no specific model of subverting power dominance in Foucault's theory. In the case of sexual

44. Foucault, *History of Sexuality*, 1:8–9 (emphasis added).

45. Foucault also makes use of the history of madness to demonstrate how medicine, particularly psychic knowledge, defines and excludes madness. See: Foucault, *Madness and Civilization*.

46. Foucault, *History of Sexuality*, 1:11.

liberation, Foucault draws our attention back to analyzing the trajectory
of power relationships—including where power is situated, how power is
changed when its relationship with resistance is changing, and what kind of
new power is created to manipulate resistance. Foucault then suggests:

> My main concern will be to locate the forms of power, the chan-
> nels it takes, and the discourses it permeates in order to reach
> the most tenuous and individual modes of behavior, the paths
> that give it access to the rare or scarcely perceivable forms of
> desire, how it penetrates and controls everyday pleasure.[47]

As there is no specific remedy for all situations, Foucault not only requires
us to diagnose the deployments of power relationships before prescribing
the drug and taking any medicine. He also points out that when we can
identify the various forms of power, we may also recognize how power gets
involved in our pleasure and desire—which have been below the radar of
those who fight for liberation in revolutions and social movements.

Controversially speaking, considering articulation of sexuality does
not help achieve freedom and liberation. Liberation for Foucault is not the
pathway to achieving any kind of freedom, though he is seen as a founder
of queer theory. Nor is sexuality something that needs to be liberated. In
writing *The Will to Knowledge*, Foucault knows that his purpose is not to
survey the knowledge of sexuality in history. He aims at understanding the
way that power relationships are deployed and how sexuality and desire are
manipulated. I will continue Foucault's discussion of sexuality and desire in
the latter part of this chapter, but before moving on I would like to briefly
explore the *teleology* of Foucault's concept of power relationships.

Does Capitalism Still Matter?

Before moving on to focus on the construction of sexuality and desire in
Foucault's thought, we should clarify a question: If, from a holistic perspective, power relationships are deployed to maintain the wholeness of society,
does it hold any other purpose? What does Foucault think about the teleology of society functioning as a unit?

We have recognized that Foucault has shifted his focus onto the
concern with *micro-power*—power relationships and discipline on the
docile body. He is not concerned with political-economic structures
of dominance. Foucault's shift should be considered as his engagement
with asymmetrical relationships to overcome the limitation of previous

47. Foucault, *History of Sexuality*, 1:11.

theories based on binary and symmetrical dichotomies—which separate micro-power from macro-power, and structure from agency. This will bring us to the next level of (and my last point on) the conversation between Foucault and Marxism: Does Foucault still care about economic exploitation in capitalism, as other Marxists do?

In *Capital: Critique of Political Economy*, Marx painted a picture of capitalism in terms of the cooperation of commodity, labor, and market. However, this portrait of capitalism is not Foucault's research interest. Foucault, when considered as a Marxist, does not hesitate to believe that capitalism has a decisive impact on modern society. He amplifies the Marxist concern with capitalism by recognizing the subtle involvement of capitalism. In *Discipline and Punish*, Foucault argues that the birth of prisons and the exploitation of wage labor are "historical twins." It is not that these two phenomena have a causal relation but rather that they are both shaped by the same cause—that is capitalism.[48]

Foucault notices that the commonly shared experience of being a prisoner and being a laborer is the management of time. Capitalism, in these contexts, enables time to be a measurable object—which is calculated, valued, and possessed—to support the function and the benefit of capitalism. In this view, the laborer's time is exchangeable with money. Time is no longer abstract and imperceptible but a *calculable* object.

The Marxist discussion of capitalism is expanded by Foucault when we figure out how time has become the exploited property of laborers. For traditional Marxists, proletariats have nothing but their physical labor; therefore, their physical labor is the only thing they can contribute in exchange for money. But in Foucault's eye, not only their labor but also their time should be regarded as exploited properties.[49] The use of time has been included in the calculation system of capitalism. And this is something Marx did not recognize.

Imprisonment as a punishment would make sense when we comprehend how and why the time measurement is applied in prisons to regulate the *property* of prisoners.[50] Only under the circumstances of capitalism (enabling time to be calculable), the length of the period of incarceration can be calculated depending on the seriousness of the criminal behaviors. Depriving criminals of their time is a punishment that prevents them from creating their own benefits, especially in the case of imprisonment that can be commuted to a fine.

48. Elden, "More Marxist Foucault," 153, 161.

49. Elden, "More Marxist Foucault," 153–54.

50. Elden, "More Marxist Foucault," 154.

Based on this example, Foucault's analysis is still based on the Marxist analysis of the political economy, but it shifts to emphasize what he calls "the genealogy of capitalism," revealing the deep association of capitalism with the modern world and our daily life.[51] On the one hand, Foucault rejects Marxism—which merely focuses on commodity, labor, and market. On the other hand, he is still committed to the whole Marxist tradition, holding onto some features of Marxism but broadening the scope of understanding the *technique* in capitalism. As Balibar points out,

> Foucault does so in *Discipline and Punishment*, "taking up Marx's analysis in *Capital* regarding the division of labor in production, in order to show how disciplinary procedures increase the utility of the body of workers by neutralizing their resistance, and more generally how this permits the unification of the two processes of the accumulation of labor and the accumulation of capital.[52]

Clearly, for Foucault, capitalism still matters but broader considerations and more delicate analysis of its techniques are demanded.

If capitalism still has a decisive influence in Foucault's analysis, the further question which should be raised is: Does Foucault believe in "economic determinism," as most Marxists do? Does he believe in any form of determinism? Foucault's answers to both these questions will be a "no" and he certainly rejects all kinds of determinism, including Marxist economic determinism.

For Foucault, the strategy used in the fight against class struggle is not exclusively to contest, or to seize back, the means of production from the bourgeoisie. This is because we cannot attribute all exploitation in the system of capitalism to the *sole* fact that proletarians do not own the means of production. Marxists have failed to recognize physical labor *and* time as exploited properties, and they misleadingly reduce capitalist exploitation to the division between owners and non-owners of the means of production. This narrow definition of economic exploitation in Marxism is rejected by Foucault.[53]

Moreover, Foucault is even not bothered by such typical Marxist curiosity as: "Why are proletarians oppressed and exploited?" I argue that Foucault generally is not interested in asking or answering *why*-questions. Similarly, he does not explain why sexuality was repressed, or why time started to be calculated. Rather, Foucault is much more interested in

51. Gordon et al., "Considerations on Marxism," 100.

52. Balibar, "Foucault and Marx," 51.

53. Elden, "More Marxist Foucault," 151.

questions about "what and how modern society dominated by capitalism is."[54] As we have seen in the last section, Foucault attempts to describe and critically analyze how different modes of power relationships work and function in different contexts, instead of explaining these situations as most liberation seekers do.

The difference between Foucault and Marxists is also revealed in their separate purposes in researching history. For Marxism, a universal history of all human beings and their destiny is assumed. Their historical agenda serves to explain how the bourgeoisie takes an advantageous position and why all proletarians should revolt to change their oppressed situation. This historical view implies the existence of a society that has not yet been manipulated by capitalism. Capitalism is regarded as a specific kind of market-based system, which emerged in modern Europe and spread all over the world. The fact that it becomes the dominant system of economic system is by historical contingency.[55] Marxism believes, taking a positive side, that capitalism is not an inevitable consequence of human history. Therefore, exploitation in capitalism is not inevitable either.

The capitalist economic system—which distributes materials unfairly and unequally, and which causes an exploitative society—does not have the last word. As Marx and Engel's famous quote calling for revolution says, "the history of all hitherto existing history is the history of class struggles."[56] If oppressed people are willing to stand up for revolution, history can be pointed in the direction of economic equality. Marx's economic determinism offers a metaphysical answer to the condition of class struggle and labor exploitation. To make a change, Marxism must build up a solid foundation on evaluation of the impact of capitalism because the shape of modern society is determined by it.

This kind of "strict" economic determinism is criticized by neo-Marxism and it becomes the basis for Foucault to continue and discontinue his conversation with Marxism. Neo-Marxists, such as Raymond Williams, have noticed that the division of the material/economic Base and Superstructure (including religion, culture, art) does not help. In Williams's view,

54. Foucault has shown his critique of capitalism and neoliberalism in his final work: Foucault, "Security, Territory, and Population."; Foucault, "Birth of Biopolitics." This issue is concerned by some Foucault's queer critiques. See: Winnubst, "Queer Thing," 79–97; Sawicki, "Queer Feminism," 74–87.

55. See, Polanyi, *Great Transformation*. Economic anthropologists, in particular the Marxist anthropologists, following and continuing the discussion of Polanyi, attempted to answer questions such as whether capitalism, or market-based society, is the only destination in the evolutionary process of human history.

56. Marx, *Communist Manifesto*.

Superstructure and the Base are interdependent and interactive, inasmuch as Superstructure includes various cultural practices, rather than merely a reproduction of the economic base. The Base, then, is not just a notion of fixed economic abstraction but exists in the mutable process of having relationships with social and cultural activities.[57] Considering a more mutable process within the broader context of power relationships merely fully echoes Foucault's more dynamic and holistic viewpoint of power.

Also, the Base does not refer to the single economic structure "exclusively" because neither the Base nor Superstructure should be examined *primarily*. For Foucault, these various dimensions of social formation, including economic and non-economic ones, need to be examined together. There is no *simple* dimension of determination. His viewpoint might be shared with Althusser. As Mark Olssen argues, "the non-economic practices" for Althusser, "have a *specific effectivity*, which means that they are determining as well as determined, just as economic practices are determining as well as determined."[58] Non-economic practices and things outside the Base should not be ignored. Through Althusser's criticisms of the economic base, Foucault gets away from the naïve consideration of economic determinism—built on the division of the Base and Superstructure—although he is concerned with the impact of capitalism.

On the other hand, the comparison helps us to start to recognize a fundamental disagreement between Foucault and Althusser when it comes to debating over issues of the *totality* in terms of history and a determination of social structure. Making a fair comparison between Foucault and Althusser, Mark Poster points out that:

> As a Marxist, Althusser theorizes the totality through the category of the mode of production. Foucault, rejecting the category of totality in general and the Marxist version of it in particular, refuses to limit himself to an analysis of the working class.[59]

Poster's comparison reveals the key issue—that Althusser is inclined to a relaxing form of economic determinism, although his analysis attempts to include more factors including economic and non-economic practices. In some measure to economic determination (instead of the economic base), Althusser is concerned with totalizing the practices, but Foucault is not.

In *The Archaeology of Knowledge* Foucault rejects the idea of "total history" or a "total description":

57. Williams, *Problems in Materialism*, 34.

58. Olssen, "Foucault and Marxism," 456–57.

59. Poster, *Foucault, Marxism, and History*, 39.

> A total description draws all phenomena around a single cen-
> ter—a principle, a meaning, a spirit, a world-view, an overall
> shape. . . it is supposed that between all the events of a well-
> defined spatio-temporal area, between all the phenomena of
> which traces have been found, it must be possible to establish
> a system of homogeneous relations: a network of causality that
> makes it possible to derive each of them, relations of analogy
> that show they symbolize one another or how they all express
> one and the same central core; it is also supposed that one and
> the same form of historicity operates upon economic structures,
> social institutions and customs (. . .) .[60]

I argue that Foucault escapes from the dominance of economic determinism, by refusing to totalize different phenomena and experiences. He as-
sures that all oppressions can ultimately be attributed to the economic
factor, no matter whether it is economic or non-economic practices. Although Foucault takes a holistic approach to analyze power relationships
in society, he does not assume the existence of a center of oppression—
which may be an institutional center of many apparatuses or a metaphysical cause of all oppressions.

Foucault refuses to reduce any phenomenon to any single factor or
to assume the existence of a homogenous system. His perspective explains
how economic exploitation and other forms of domination are formulated,
rather than why capital accumulation and state power function.[61] This is
about *how* rather than *why*. It is about capitalism or economic factors rather
than economic determinism or any form of determinism. Foucault challenges us to see how power deployments have gone beyond the economic
base to manipulate us into serving capitalism. Hence, Foucault focuses his
attention on desire, sexuality, and the body.

Sexuality, Desire, and the Body
within Power Relationships

Foucault's attention to sexuality, desire, and the body is motivated by his
attempt to find the trajectory and track of power relationships. Although the
existence of a "given" subject of seeking liberation is not assumed (as Taylor
has noticed), Foucault recognizes the locus in which sexuality, desire, and
the body are objectified by the involvement of power. There is a general misunderstanding that Foucault's writings on sexuality assume sexual subjects

---

60. Foucault, *Archaeology of Knowledge*, 9 (emphasis added).
61. Jessop, "From Micro-Powers to Governmentality," 40.

and propose sexual liberation. In fact, what Foucault wants to reveal is how subjects are *sexualized* by power deployments and how sexuality, desire, and the body are captured and shaped.

As Lynne Huffer suggests, we should read the history of *sexuality* together with the history of *madness*.[62] This is because they both demonstrate how people's sexuality and madness are defined by the new power of knowledge and how people are constructed as sexualized people and mad people. Foucault's writings on sexuality and madness are not his liberating agenda. Huffer sharply argues that:

> *Madness* will show us that Foucault's story is not about an absolute historical shift from sexuality as acts to sexual identities; rather, it is about the internalization of bourgeois morality which produces, eventually, the "fable" of an inner psyche, soul, or consciousness.[63]

The history of sexuality and madness should be read as a reflection on how these individual people become subjects, defined by knowledge and by the practice of bodily discipline within power relationships. The attention to sexuality, desire and the body allows Foucault to analyze power relationships and the deployments of power without fully disregarding State apparatuses (which he inherited from Marxism).

The Construction of Sexuality and Desire

Foucault defines two forms of deployment of power: the one is the deployment of alliance; the other is the deployment of sexuality.[64] Similar to Althusser's understanding of State apparatuses, the former is based on some given relationships and social organizations, including families. This deployment concerns social influence. Its control is mainly exercised through "a system of rules defining the permitted and forbidden, the licit and the illicit."[65] The latter form of deployment, then, is based on the "technologies of power." It focuses on "the sensations of body, the quality of pleasure, and the nature of impressions, however tenuous or imperceptible these may be."[66] The body, pleasure, and feeling (which have been off the radar of Marxism) are now considered as loci on which power exercises.

62. Huffer, *Mad for Foucault*.
63. Huffer, *Mad for Foucault*, 76 (emphasis in original).
64. Foucault, *History of Sexuality*, 1:108.
65. Foucault, *History of Sexuality*, 1:106.
66. Foucault, *History of Sexuality*, 1:106.

Foucault argues that all power strategies, which operate on every individual body, should be viewed as "a major factor of sexualization," rather than "a powerful agency of prohibition."[67] Sexuality—under this circumstance of implementing these power strategies—eventually becomes recognized and means "something." This provocative observation contradicts what sexual liberationists have claimed, which is that power strategies repress sexuality. For Foucault, sexuality used to mean nothing, but it is now defined and produced by these power strategies (which serve "bourgeois hegemony") to mean something.[68]

If the existence of sexuality and desire is created by and in the deployments of power, sexuality and desire are unlikely to be biological entities, purely driven by our physical lust and passion. Indeed, Foucault does not reject its biological connection, but it is not like the distinction between "gender" and "sexuality," which has been misunderstood in English-speaking academia. While introducing Foucault into queer theories, Gayle Rubin narrowly translated *le sexe* as *sex*, which by definition is connected with biological sexual desire and anatomy.[69] In contrast to *gender*, *sex* becomes a term to define male and female, the difference being defined by their sexual/reproductive organs.

However, as Huffer points out, *le sexe* in French or at least in Foucault's context is a word with ambiguous meanings. It includes all meanings of sexuality, sex, and gender that we generally use in English. It means "sex-as-organs, sex-as-biological-reproduction, sex-as-individual-gender-roles, sex-as-gendered group-affiliation, sex-as-erotic-acts, and sex-as-lust."[70] We should not comprehend *le sexe* as a contrasting concept of gender when gender is defined as something more fluid, unfixed, and identity-orientated. Nor should we fall into any category of biological sex and identity gender in our understanding of Foucault's concept of *le sexe*. His notion of sexuality and desire cannot be understood simply as a biological urge at an individual and biological level.

On the contrary, Foucault argues that human sexuality and bodies must be considered in their interaction with power relationships. As he insists,

> We must not make the mistake of thinking that sex is an autonomous agency which secondarily produces manifold effects of sexuality over the entire length of its surface of contact with

67. Foucault, *History of Sexuality*, 1:114.
68. Foucault, *History of Sexuality*, 1:114.
69. Rubin, "Thinking Sex," 100–133.
70. Huffer, *Mad for Foucault*, 47.

power. On the contrary, sex is the most speculative, most ideal,
and the most internal element in a deployment of sexuality
organized by power in its grip on bodies and their materiality,
their forces, energies, sensations, and pleasures.[71]

As we have recognized the teleology of power relationships in Foucault's
thought, we can recognize that the shape and definition of sexuality and desire have been incorporated into power deployments to satisfy the demand
of capitalism. More importantly, the body with sexuality and desire must be
a *docile* one, as capitalism and its power dominance cannot be satisfied or
pleased by any random body-forms. These docile bodies must be "productive bodies"—which are constructed by disciplinary techniques both for the
accumulation of capital and the sufficiency of reproduction.[72]

Hence, sexual behaviors do matter because their role is vital when it
comes to sustaining procreation as a part of reproduction—they serve to
supply the laborers of the future. Stuart Elden proposes that this is what
Foucault means by the concept of "political economy of bodies" in *Discipline and Punish*.[73] Rendering the bodies of prisoners docile is a typical
example—which demonstrates that, for the optimal rate of reproduction in
capitalism, these disordered and subversive bodies of criminals should go
through the disciplinary process.[74] As Foucault states,

> [The body in prison] must be trained and retrained; its time
> must be measured out and fully used; its forces must be continu-
> ously applied to labor. The prison form of penalty corresponds
> to the wage form of labor.[75]

Utilizing discipline, the prisoners regain their sufficiency and stability of
production, instead of de-radicalization, torture, or punishment. To maxi-
mize the benefit of capitalism, the process of forming and disciplining the
body must be "invested" by sustaining economic production and consolidating the relationship of maintaining economic exploitation.[76]

The control of a population is given as another example in *The Will to
Knowledge*. Foucault, unlike most Marxists, points out that, "the people" is
no longer an object which should be fully controlled—but the "population."[77]

---

71. Foucault, *History of Sexuality*, 1:155.
72. Elden, "More Marxist Foucault," 161.
73. Elden, "More Marxist Foucault," 161.
74. Jessop, "From Micro-Powers to Governmentality," 39.
75. Foucault, "Punitive Society," 35.
76. Foucault, *Discipline and Punish*, 25.
77. Foucault, *History of Sexuality*, 1:25.

This is because the size of the population is an important factor in economic growth and industrial production capabilities. The freedom of the people in physical body and expression is not the main task anymore. What capitalism attempts to involve is sexuality, desire, and the body which are "produced by a whole series of mechanisms operating in different institutions."[78] Although they are constructed within the multiplicity of power relationships, these intertwined deployments of power work cooperatively in fulfillment of capitalism's needs. In terms of sexuality and the body, a big population and healthy bodies are important to maintain the procreation of future laborers. In terms of desire, restless and unsatisfied souls are great for maintaining the consumption of commodities.

The strategy of power deployments of capitalism is not to repress sexuality, but to orientate, refine, and utilize bodies and pleasures. As Foucault explains, "a policing of sex is not the rigor of a taboo, but the necessity of regulating sex through useful and public discourses."[79] The "hypothesis" of sexual repression is proposed to enlarge the capacity of sexual control by means of encouraging (rather than discouraging) articulation of sexuality. On the other hand, the deployments of power have deeply intruded on individuals so that people not only actively "confess to acts contravening the law" but also enthusiastically "seek to transform their every desire."[80] Individuals simply trust that their articulation of sexuality is an expression of their freedom and a sign of liberation, and in no way is it being manipulated by a force of dominance. Sexuality is supposed to be private and personal. It then turns out to be something that is exposed *to* the public and *for* the public.

The Birth of Perversions within Power Relationships

Perversions and abnormalities *must* exist in Foucault's analysis. This is not because Foucault likes these topics (although he probably does!). Considering Foucault's holistic perspective of power relationships, power and counter-power co-exist and rely on the existence of each other. But the birth of perversions is attributed to the work of power deployments, encouraging people to confess their private sexuality and put it under the gaze of the public and medical knowledge. Perversions do not emerge from new moral orders. As Foucault argues,

78. Foucault, *History of Sexuality*, 1:33.
79. Foucault, *History of Sexuality*, 1:25.
80. Foucault, *History of Sexuality*, 1:21.

> The growth of perversions is not a moralizing theme that ob-
> sessed the scrupulous minds of the Victorians. It is the real
> product of the encroachment of a type of power on bodies and
> their pleasures.[81]

Through recognizing and defining perversion as "an analytical, visible and permanent reality" and "a natural order of disorder," the mechanism of power relationships starts to monitor and regulate perversion. Then power can eventually impose itself onto the bodies of the perverted.[82]

For Foucault, this display of power on perverse behaviors and subjects occurs "through the isolation, intensification, and the consolidation of peripheral sexualities."[83] The more we talk about sexuality and desire and expose our bodies to the public and medical knowledge, the more it becomes possible for them to be medicalized and identified as perversions. Sexual liberation turns to sexualize these talking subjects and ends up allowing the subjects to be monitored and measured within power relationships.

Recognizing that perverted subjects are oppressed, monitored, and controlled by power does not encourage them to seek liberation. Conversely, power becomes a force for creating pleasure and excitement. Foucault observes that the interaction between power and pleasure forms a spiral curriculum.[84] This process has three stages, (1) pleasure is enlarged and intensified by power, (2) this enlarged pleasure creates greater desire, and (3) sexuality is more encouraged to expose to power. The more disclosure of sexualities there is, the more power is enlarged. The next spiral then keeps stirring up and intensifying pleasure. In this spiral, sexual perversions are invented through being discovered and revealed. Once they are revealed, power can be observed in action, getting involved and implanting itself onto perversions to regulate them. Ironically, the process is driven in the name of sexual liberation.

Unlike Marxist theorists and activists who only pay attention to singular dominance structure, the multiplicity of power relationship proposed by Foucault is much more complicated. But the attention to sexuality, desire, and the body helps Foucault gradually to identify these exertions. If the subject of power and dominance is the concern of Marxism, then the object contracted by power is Foucault's main concern. As Maurizio Lazzarato notices, Foucault's definition of political economy is no longer just about the relationship between capital and labor exclusively.

---

81. Foucault, *History of Sexuality*, 1:48.

82. Foucault, *History of Sexuality*, 1:44.

83. Foucault, *History of Sexuality*, 1:48.

84. Foucault, *History of Sexuality*, 1:48.

It "encompasses power *dispositifs* that amplify the whole range of relations between the forces that extend throughout the *social body*."[85] This new concern with the pollical economy is called *biopolitics*.

In order not to miss Foucault's point, it is helpful to make a distinction between Foucault's original account of biopolitics and other contemporary interpretations (such as Agamben and Deleuze).[86] Foucault's account of biopolitics should be regarded as his "thick description" of the multiplicity of power relationships, which cooperatively works on the subject. As we have discussed, these power relationships include *both* the deployments of alliance (like State Apparatuses) *and* the deployments of sexuality (like disciplines). Biopolitics is not a new term that refers to "bodily discipline," as Deleuze claims.[87] Here I agree more with Claire Blencowe that the techniques of disciplines are not replaced by the mechanisms of biopolitics because they are on different levels. The techniques that work at the level of the body itself are disciplines rather than biopolitics.[88] Biopolitics is more like a term that describes the system which is built and woven by a series of power relationships.

In Foucault's typical example of the history of sexuality and punishment/discipline, he has shown a picture of how human subjects are *sexualized* and prisoners are *shaped* within power relationships to serve capitalism. All these historical examples of perversions and abnormality nourish Foucault's account of biopolitics in his *Society Must Be Defended* lectures—they are about normalizing and regulating society and excluding and exterminating impurity and danger.[89] Biopolitics always has a dimension of *formation* in history, rather than a history of biosciences or "ahistorical" truth of modern government, in contrast to Agamben's theory of biopolitics as a universal claim of totalization of government power.[90] If we comprehend Foucault's intention clearly, the biopolitical account will draw us to recognize the *dispositifs* (arrangement and management) of power relationships and the loci of their exertions, rather than another biopolitical theory of the state. The birth of perversion, in this sense, is very key to Foucault's analysis of power relationships.

Foucault repeatedly reminds us that these power relationships *within* society must be recognized as living and practical forces, which are

---

85. Lazzarato, "From Biopower to Biopolitics," 102–3.

86. Blencowe, *Biopolitical Experience*.

87. Deleuze, *Negotiations*, 177–82.

88. Blencowe, *Biopolitical Experience*, 59–62.

89. Foucault, *Society Must Be Defended*.

90. Agamben, *Homo Sacer*.

orientated towards capitalism. Power is not a singular force from a rigid center, so when we seek liberation, we cannot merely propose a strategy for escape from "one" power regime. But it does not mean there is no resistance. Foucault explains that:

> If we assume things [like]. . . an omnipotent sovereign whose orders, injunctions, commands would effectively be followed to the letter, this would exclude from the social body through which he exercises this sovereignty the existence of these thousands of relations of power that establish themselves between people that rebel, that contest, etc.[91]

Although resistance may not be something we commonly expect in the Marxist eye, it is not unachievable. As we have discussed, resistance always happens before the re-management of new power relationships (because the emergence of resistance requires power relationships to be re-arranged).

Here I argue that we should read Foucault's analysis *more provocatively* than he intended. For Foucault, resistance stimulates and fuels the whole dynamic series of power relationships. If there is no resistance, it is pointless talking about the dynamic creation of new power relationships. In this light, the existence of power relationships also *supports* and *sustains*, rather than undermines, the emergence of resistance. Resistance occurs when power relationships are recognized. Although new deployments of power may come out and be re-arranged as quickly as possible to stamp resistance out, resistance has to emerge in the first instance.

Based on this *absurd* principle of resistance and power relationships, we should read *The Will to Knowledge* again to see the problem of "liberation." In the first instance, sexual liberation emerged to subvert Victorian sex-phobia. This liberation might temporarily achieve great success in messing up decent morality. But we cannot remain there in over-enjoyment of the fruit and forget the coming rearrangement of new power relationships. Sexual liberation activists have made this mistake so that the perverse subversion has complied and practices of sexual liberation are incorporated into new deployments of power. Perversion is no longer subversive but abnormalized under the normalization of society and decent sexual morality.

Foucault does not lead us to a pessimistic viewpoint of subversion. Sexual liberation is still possible, but it would not be achieved in a simple and straightforward way, or before we know how power dominance works actively and creatively. The practice of indecent sexual perversions and the emergence of perversion cannot be regarded as a settled solution. To resist must not be to seek a concrete or stable situation, which is a place

---

91. Gordon et al., "Considerations on Marxism," 107.

where all power relationships have been eluded. There is no option to find a power-free zone. Hence, recognition of the *precariousness* of any liberations—through constantly discerning how these power relationships are re-arranged—is a more sustainable strategy of resistance.

Here we can see that the position of the perverted within dynamic power relationships is intricate. On the one hand, perversion is resistive; on the other hand, perversion is part of dominance. This draws us to a further question: How do the perverted exist? What is their "identity"? Or do they have any identity? These questions are all related to how Foucault understands the "subject" and its relation to resistance and freedom.

The Subject of the Self in Seeking Freedom

When Foucault discusses sexuality, desire, and the body, when he presents the emergence of perversions, we probably sense that his attitude toward the "subject" is ambiguous. Taylor criticizes Foucault for not believing in the existence of the subject. When we talk about how sexuality, desire, and the body are disciplined and constructed, it seems that we imply that the subject does not have too much autonomy and is merely socially constructed. Conversely, when we read about Foucault's concept of resistance, he appears to imply that there is the subject that has already existed before power relationships, and which activates resistance. This paradoxical understanding of the subject is indeed why Foucault thinks the subject is being constructed as well as constructing within power relationships.

Becoming the Subject within Power Relationships

Foucault rejects the kind of understanding of the subject that regards a phenomenological or existentialist theory of the subject as the foundation of the given knowledge.[92] As we have seen in Foucault's account of the sexualized subject in sexual liberation, the subject may have existed. But without the involvement of knowledge of sexuality, that sexual self cannot be recognized or known. This gap between the subject and self-knowledge is what Foucault wants to examine. As Foucault explains, "[the subject] is not a substance. It is a form, and this form is not primary or always identical to itself. You do not have the same type of relation to yourself (. . .) ."[93] In

92. Foucault, "Ethics of the Concern for Self," 290.
93. Foucault, "Ethics of the Concern for Self," 290.

Foucault's view, it is questionable whether the subject knows about himself or herself, and how they have knowledge of who they are.

On the other hand, because there is a gap between the subject and the self who is recognized by self-knowledge, the subject is always on the journey of *becoming* that subject of the self. Bearing in mind that all relationships are involved with power, this journey of becoming cannot avoid having the involvement of power relationships either. Here we can see how the relationships between the subject and power are not limited to an "external" environment and political-economic structure. These relationships are always involved in the process of becoming the self—more accurately, in the *orientation* of becoming *what kind* of the self.

This may explain the rationale of Foucault's further development of *The Use of Pleasure, The Care of the Self,* and *The Confessions of Flesh* (*The History of Sexuality, Volumes 2, 3, 4*)—which analyzes the practice of the body, desire, pleasure, and sexuality (*flesh* in Christian term) in relation to the self. As he states in *The Use of Pleasure,*

> With this genealogy [of sexual subjects], the idea was to investigate how individuals were led to practice, on themselves and on others, a hermeneutics of desire, a hermeneutics of which their sexual behavior was doubtless occasion.[94]

Foucault himself has noticed that his History of Sexuality project does not follow his original plan and it seems that there is a "gap" between *The Will to Knowledge* and *The History of Sexuality Volumes 2, 3, 4.* But, because of this gap, Foucault goes deeper into the issue of the subject-within-relationships, in which we may find the paradox of dominance and resistance.

Remembering this paradoxical image of the subject, we can understand Foucault's word-play "subjectification" (*assujettissement* in French, or translated as "subjectivation," or "subjectivity"). In describing this process of becoming, there are two senses of subjectification—which means "the constitution of the subject, and at the same time the way which we impose on a subject in relations of dominance."[95] If subjectification means both "becoming a subject" and "being subject to dominance," it also means that we cannot be the subject of the self without being subjugated to power. This contradicts our conventional understanding of subjectivity, which assumes that we will be free subjects without restrictions. Becoming a subject is identical to a free subject.

---

94. Foucault, *History of Sexuality*, 2:5.

95. Gordon et al., "Considerations on Marxism," 107.

For Foucault, our concern with freedom and restriction is dominated by the binary idea of repression and liberation. For liberation believers, freedom is based on an escape from power-over and the achievement of this freedom is then proved by self-determination. As Thomas Lemke points out, this kind of self-determination has fitted into the techniques of neo-liberalism (which shifts the responsibility for social risk "into the domain for which the individual is responsible, transforming it into a problem of "self-care").[96]

In this sense, Foucault's concept of freedom radically challenges the consideration of liberation as self-determination. Seeking the freedom of power-to in subjectification becomes the first step of his strategy. But the subject should recognize this as the first step considering resistance has to keep going. It should also take the ineradicable relations of dominance as a given. The binary of freedom and unfreedom then is subverted. This is because freedom will not be achieved automatically when the systems of unfreedom are removed, as the structures of dominance will constantly build up in different forms and with different techniques. Freedom is not a tangible object to achieve. Hence, Foucault cannot be more realistic than to suggest: "Let's seek freedom within power relationships of dominance."

Foucault may ask: Why do the deployments of power want to control, seize, manipulate and form the subject? This is because, in his sense, the subject resists! The deployments of power relationships—working on sexuality, desire, and the body of the subject—reveal the fact that the subject did successfully resist. If so, the possibility of resistance will be there in subjectification too. What power wants is to form and orientate the subject of the self. This certainly means that resistance acts in disobedience to being formed and orientated by power.

This strategy sounds simple, but Foucault's suggestion implies a *restless* wrestle with power in the process of subjectification, in terms of the formation of sexuality, desire, and the body. This is what Foucault means by the practices of "self-regulation" or "technologies of the self." These subjects are suggested to constitute and control themselves "to determine their identity, maintain it, or transform it in terms of a certain number of ends, through relations of self-mastery or self-knowledge."[97] Foucault has a positive image that the subject of the self would find their freedom under the circumstance of unfreedom—when they reject becoming what they should become and deny complying with power. More interestingly, Foucault suggests that the subject should *master* and *know* the self, rather than determine it.

96. Lemke, "Foucault, Governmentality, and Critique," 59.
97. Foucault, "Subjectivity and Truth," 87.

Subjectification as the Practice of the "Self"

Foucault argues that knowing and analyzing who we are is a "practice of the self." As Edward McGushin points out, Foucault's subjectification is what he calls the "care for the self"—which is defined as "what we make of ourselves when we do devote ourselves to taking care of ourselves."[98] The self in Foucault's sense is something that can be examined, discerned, and reflected on. The self and the subject are in relationships (in plural)—which are kinds of power relationships too—as power gets involved in every relationship. McGushin gives a simple example to explain the ways these relationships are formed: "When I express myself, I am both the self who is *doing* the expressing and the self who is *being* expressed."[99] This example shows the mutual relationships between the self and the subject.

The relationship between doing the expressing and being expressed can be understood in the grammatical relationship between the subject and the self. For example, the subject, which acts from the first person, holds a sovereign and active position in comparison to the self which is positioned as a reflective pronoun. As Sergey Horujy points out, this subject with the reflectivity of the self is "the subject actualizing the return of every action toward the self."[100] By means of knowing the reflection of the self, the subject can know more about oneself. In this sense, we can understand that the process of subjectification—the subject becoming the subject of the self—is also about techniques of self-knowledge, self-examination, and then the interpretation of the self.[101]

While exploring various forms of technologies of the self in ancient Greco-Roman culture (in *The Care of the Self*) and in early Christianity (in *The Confessions of Flesh*), Foucault notices that Christianity requires a form of truth obligation—confession (*exemolgesis*):[102]

---

98. McGushin, "Foucault's Theory," 128.

99. McGushin, "Foucault's Theory," 128 (emphasis in original).

100. Horujy, *Practices of the Self and Spiritual Practices*, 21.

101. Foucault, "Hermeneutic of the Subject," 93.

102. Foucault thinks that "the penitent's exomologesis is a double manifestation (of the renunciation of what one is and of the being of defilement and death that one renounces) as a purifying test of oneself conducted by oneself." See: Foucault, *History of Sexuality*, 4:292. I do not fully agree with Foucault's evaluation of Christian practice of confession, as I am uncertain as to whether the renunciation of the self in confession means the "eradication" of the self. At this point, James Bernauer has a more positive interpretation of Foucault's critique of the renunciation of the self. See: Bernauer, "Michel Foucault's Ecstatic Thinking," 92–93.

> Each person has the duty to know who he is, that is, to try to know what is happening inside him, to acknowledge faults, to recognize temptations, to locate desire; and everyone is obligated to disclose these things either to God or to others in the community and, hence, to bear public or private witness against oneself.[103]

These individual subjects find their subject of the self through knowing who we are and reflecting on what we have done. They also find it through punishing the self and denying themselves in penitence for sin. As Foucault adds, "self-punishment and the voluntary expression of the self are bound together."[104]

This process of subjectification shows that the practice of the self is not just a mental activity of the self (like talking to oneself). This is because the interpretation of the self has already included recognizing how power deployments orientate the direction of the self. For example, temptation does not come from the self—it comes from the external environment and others. Recognition of temptation must mean recognition of how our desire has been influenced and orientated towards something tempting us. This is an example of how the interpretation of the self is involved with broader contexts of other power relationships.

Foucault also finds a similar practice of the self in ancient Greco-Roman culture. This case may help us understand why Foucault uses the term "self-mastery" to describe the practice of the self. This is because being a *master* had a significant meaning at that time.[105] Mature or adult men were so afraid of being enslaved that they made efforts to school themselves to be masters. Being a master means having no desire for boys or girls while looking at them. People are worried about being slaves of their desires, so they try to master themselves completely.[106]

The principal of the practice of the self in Greco-Roman culture then is to orientate one's desire to be under control. Of course, Foucault consciously recognizes that the practices of the self may be varied rather than universal.[107] But the Greco-Roman practice of the self is contrasted to the practice in sexual liberation particularly when the former attempts to avoid indulging

103. Foucault, "Technologies of the Self," 242.

104. Foucault, "Technologies of the Self," 244.

105. See: Foucault, *History of Sexuality*, 3:94-95.

106. Foucault, "On the Genealogy of Ethics," 260. Foucault also points out how the love of boys (considered as a "perfect virtue" though) should be overcome in conformity to marriage in Foucault, *History of Sexuality*, 3:226–27.

107. Foucault, *History of Sexuality*, 2:14–15, 25.

themselves in sexuality and desire. Re-considering the use of pleasure in the Greco-Roman time, Foucault *problematizes* the knowledge of sexuality, pleasure and the body, which has been normalized by sexual liberation.[108] When we survey different practices of the self, we might be puzzled by how sexuality and sexual behaviors became something so important.

The Practice of the Self and Governmentality

It is important to remember that the practice of self-knowledge in subjectification is not an independent mind activity, nor is it an autonomous practice of self-affirmation within a power-free context. No matter whether someone is insane, a prisoner, a sexual pervert, a Greek-Roman free man, or a Christian confessor, all these examples by Foucault reveal the materiality of the self in the subjectification—particularly the body and desiring pleasure. The body is always there and part of the practice of the self.

Foucault's example of psychiatry is another great example of the triangle of the subject, the self, and the power of knowledge—which shows how the body involves the subjectification of becoming the self of insaneness within power relationships of medical knowledge and the hospital. The subjectivity of the insane is constituted by physicians through observing and defining the expression of their madness. What the patients bodily and mentally *express* will be presented as evidence (which helps further build up medical knowledge) for the hospital to diagnose their madness. The patients will be required to accept their identity (who they are) based on what is expressed by themselves. If due to their expression, they are diagnosed as insane, the subject of the patient will be formed as the self of the insane. As Foucault says, "the physician's power enables him to produce the reality of mental illness characterized by the ability to reproduce phenomena completely accessible to knowledge."[109]

Although the subjectification of becoming the insane self is about self-examination, this self-knowledge is not purely based on the self-understanding of the subject (claiming who we are) but is produced within power relationships (how medical knowledge tells us who we are, and what we think we are told to be). Because of the materiality of our body and desiring pleasure, the self vulnerably becomes an object—which can be examined and interpreted within the broader biopolitics. Hence, the self is not fully subjugated to the subject but to all power relationships.

---

108. Foucault, *History of Sexuality*, 2:14–24.
109. Foucault, "Psychiatric Power," 44.

The recognition of the self, as distinct from the subject, helps Foucault to analyze how the subject of the self is constituted by power relationships and how significant the role of the self is played in connecting the subject with the external world, the thought with the body. Foucault's analysis of subjectification is not exclusive to the analysis of the construction of the abnormal, the perverted, and the insane. Every subject has this experience of encountering the self, knowing the self, interpreting the self, and then being constituted by the self in order to become the subject of the self. We are all capable of the practice of the self.

Because of this practice of the self, I argue that resistance can be arranged persistently like power relationships can be re-arranged constantly to control us. In the analysis of the subject, techniques of dominance and techniques of the self are considered together. Foucault coins the term "governmentality" to identify "the relationship of the self to itself." This concept "covers the whole range of practices that constitute, define, organize, and instrumentalize the strategies that individuals in their freedom can use in dealing with each other."[110] As we have known that Foucault's analysis of power relationships is far beyond government-as-apparatus, the concept of governmentality is designed to identify broader relationships of power outside the state apparatuses.

Governmentality has its techniques. It focuses especially on participating in the process of subjectification when the self is modified. Foucault adds,

> Governing people is not a way to force people to do what the governor wants; it is always a versatile equilibrium, with complementarity and conflicts between techniques which assure coercion and processes through which the self is constructed or modified by himself.[111]

We may be able to understand Foucault's words in another simpler way (and hopefully not misinterpret his message): if we want to recognize how governmentality works on the self, we should reverse our understanding of the subject-self relationship. In the light of Foucault, the subject is the reflectivity of the self because the figure of the subject, which we can observe, is the production of the reflectivity of the self—which is constructed through governmentality.

Foucault still states that the subject constitutes the self. But he also implies that the self plays the role of constituting the subject. As he states,

110. Foucault, "Ethics of the Concern for Self," 300.
111. Foucault, "About the Beginning," 204.

"in governing people, there is always a structure inside those who are governed that makes them governable by others."[112] Through the practice of
the self—which has been constructed by power and is constituting the subject—the subject interiorizes social formation and accepts the insertion of
power. Hence, power and structure are no longer external anymore. They
have been embodied in the practice of the self.

The Practice of Freedom as Resistance

According to Foucault's logic, if the triangle of the subject, the self, and
knowledge allow power to involve, becoming resistance is also allowed
to happen. It means, therefore, that freedom will come from there too.
We have discussed how Foucault struggles with accepting the utopian
idea that freedom (or so-called liberation) is found in power-free zones.
Foucault suggests pursuing "a practice of freedom"—which will always be
situated within power relationships.

For Foucault, freedom is not a condition that can be secured and
maintained for good—but a practice that always emerges in our activity,
behavior, and action. In terms of Foucault's understanding of freedom, John
Rajchman concludes that "our freedom is found not in our transcendental nature but in our capacities to contest and change those autonomous
practices that constitute our nature."[113] Freedom is a capacity to change.
Freedom is so dynamic that it can only appear when we use it.

In the case of sexual liberation, Foucault suggests pursuing "freedom
of sexual *choice*" rather than "freedom of sexual *acts*" "because there are
sexual acts like rape which should not be permitted." Even "some sort of
absolute freedom or total liberty of sexual action" should not be something we are looking for.[114] Foucault implies that freedom that includes
full liberty does not offer any real freedom as it allows oppression to happen more violently. Freedom of action without restraints is just created by
new power deployments, which consolidate sexual abuse in the name of
freedom of sexual acts.

On the contrary, freedom of choice gives freedom to choose to do and/
or not to do for everyone, instead of forcing everyone to accept a certain
kind of freedom (e.g. sexual liberation). Considering "freely" articulating
sexuality (which has been normalized), this freedom becomes a new force of

112. Foucault, *L'Origine de L'Herméneutique de Soi*, 118. Cited from Gordon,
"Christian Art," 258.

113. Rajchman, *Michel Foucault*, 105.

114. Foucault, "Sexual Choice, Sexual Act," 143 (emphasis in original).

power—that enables people to lose their ability to choose. Due to the mani-festo of sexual liberation, people gradually lose their capacity *not* to express their sexuality. This offers Foucault a *queer* foundation when he talks about homosexuality and freedom. He does not suggest that homosexuality should be re-introduced into society or seek normalization.[115]

Foucault appeals, "Let's escape as much as possible from the type of relations that society proposes for us and try to create in the empty space where we are new relational possibilities."[116] He then adds, "by propos-ing a new relational right, we will see that non-homosexual people can enrich their lives by changing their own schema of relations."[117] Here Foucault uses homosexuality-as-choice to explain freedom of choice. Fou-cault knows that freedom for homosexuals will not come just because gay culture is a choice *of* homosexuals *for* homosexuals. Freedom of choice will be presented when these relations in gay culture are transferable to non-homosexuals.[118]

What Foucault suggests about freedom of choice should be under-stood as a practice of the self because that is based on Foucault's under-standing of the subject, the self, and knowledge. How can homosexuality become both the practice of freedom and action of resistance? When ho-mophobic sexual morality dominates society, and even medical knowl-edge pathologizes homosexuality, the self is expected to be normalized through denying its desiring pleasure of homosexuality. Under this cir-cumstance, resistance emerges when the subject chooses to self-express as a homosexual and at the same time, allows the homosexual self (which is expressed) to constitute the subject.

The case here shows how subjectification works to resist the social norm. But the subject is still within power relationships, which keep re-arranging themselves in exerting power. Foucault emphasizes practices of freedom over processes of liberation because the former maintains its agility and flexibility to deal with the dynamic relationships of power. He critically points out that several liberations are definitely "necessary from an oppres-sive morality." Oppression loves the creation and emergence of liberations as they are supportive of their dominance. Foucault further adds:

> This liberation does not give rise to the happy human being imbued with a sexuality to which the subject could achieve a complete and satisfying relationship. Liberation paves the

115. Foucault, "Friendship," 138.
116. Foucault, "Social Triumph," 160.
117. Foucault, "Social Triumph," 160.
118. Foucault, "Social Triumph," 160.

way for new power relationships, which must be controlled by
practices of freedom.[119]

This echoes what Jon Simons argues, which is that the practice of freedom
is consciously to create new power relationships and then to know how to
maintain their freedom within them. Freedom can be practiced in various
forms such as resistance, insubordination, counter-conduct, and ethical
subjectification.[120] When the forms of power relationships are created
variedly, what we need is to have another form of resistance to deal with
them. If subjectification manifests two meanings (being a subject and being subjected to), governmentality of the self can be part of dominance,
but of resistance too.

Foucault's positive message about freedom is that we are not "trapped"
within power relationships as "we always have possibilities of changing the
situation," even though "we cannot jump outside the situation."[121] Recognition of our reality will refresh our vision of reframing our strategies of
resistance. As Simons argues, staying within a power relationship does not
mean that we are always dominated by others.[122] Accepting the given situation and choosing not to detach ourselves from all power relationships does
not mean choosing to be dominated. (In fact, choosing *not* to leave power
relationships is resistance in Foucault's view if liberation is doomed to be
under the dominance of power.) Here we can see that the practice of freedom points towards the action of political resistance, as the subject discerns
the strategy of choosing not to comply with social norms.

This political resistance is seen as new *ethics* by Foucault. As Rajchman
says,

> Foucault advances a new ethic: not the ethic of transgression,
> but the ethic of constant disengagement from constituted
> forms of experience, of freeing oneself for the invention of new
> forms of life.[123]

The ethic displays the subjects that are constructed but fully engaged with
new power relationships. This ethic has nothing to do with "whether a decision is moral," but is about "how we can be moral," and "what it means
for us being an ethical subject." In *The Use of Pleasure*, Foucault develops
being an "ethical subject" with "self-awareness," "modes of subjectification,"

---

119. Foucault, "Ethics of the Concern for Self," 283–84.

120. Simons, "Power, Resistance, and Freedom," 314.

121. Foucault, "Sex, Power and the Politics," 167.

122. Simons, "Power, Resistance, and Freedom," 314.

123. Rajchman, *Michel Foucault*, 37.

"ascetics" and "practices of the self." Foucault goes deeper into the issue of freedom and "being" or "becoming" in order to respond to his old interests in dominance, oppression, and resistance. As he contends, "freedom is the ontological condition of ethics. But ethics are the considered form that freedom takes when it is informed by reflection."[124] (There will be more discussion about ethics and freedom in chapter 5.)

124. Foucault, "Ethics of the Concern for Self," 284.

4

The Critiques of Political Theologies
of Sexuality and Desire

CHAPTER 3 POINTS OUT how Foucault may help liberation theologians en-large our understanding of power and dominance through his delicate dia-logue with Marxism. Foucault's insight into power relationships points us in the direction of us paying attention to sexuality, desire, and the body to recognize how the practice of the self (subjectification) is constituted within power relationships. Foucault also asserts that because power is there, re-sistance is there too. The consideration of sexuality, desire, and the body in liberation theologies is of course not new, as it has been done by Marcella Althaus-Reid, Jung Mo Sung, and Daniel Bell. In this chapter, I will scru-tinize their theologies through the eyes of Foucault. I will propose that our further task of political theology should be based on what they have success-fully done and revised in the light of what they have failed to recognize.

I will firstly introduce their theological viewpoints and contributions in each section and I will then show my criticisms and point out their limi-tations and problems. There are two main sections:

1. Althaus-Reid's concern with sexuality and desire and its relation to the resistive practice of perversion.

2. The dialogue between the ethical with desire in Sung's theology and the ontological concern with desire in Bell's theology.

Marcella Althaus-Reid on Sexuality and the Body

Althaus-Reid seeks to bring Latin American liberation theologians and feminist theologians to recognize the entanglement of colonialism, sexual oppression, economic exploitation, and genocide of indigenous peoples in

Latin America. In her view, Latin American Liberation Theology has failed to extend its criticism of imperialism and capitalism to encompass the suffering of women and the excluded—due to its narrow definition of the poor. Drawing on her Argentinian roots, Althaus-Reid maintains her application of the liberating hermeneutical circle—which insists on reading the text in community and connecting the Bible with real human experiences.[1] But when Latin American Liberation Theology develops its own orthodoxy, it stops exploring the diversity of theologies.[2]

For Althaus-Reid, the resource from womanist theology (which has been introduced in chapter 2) is very important. Sharing the insights of the experience of other women from the Third World, Althaus-Reid identifies women in Latin America as sufferers from multi-oppression from both political-economic and sexual oppressive structures. For example, women who are economically deprived not only suffer the disadvantages of a lack of social mobility but are also subject to domestic and sexual abuse.[3] If poverty and sexual abuse are inseparable, subversion of sexual oppression should come together with political-economic liberation.

Althaus-Reid then proposes her postcolonial critique because colonialism is another oppressive experience shared by many women from the Third World. As Kwok Pui-Lan echoes, from a Hong Kongese postcolonial feminist perspective, although postcolonial critique has been more sensitive to how colonial governance manipulates people in colonies psychologically and physically, it is not always recognized how sexual decency norms impose on the oppressed, particularly on women, in support of imperialism.[4] The silence of sexual oppression, utilizing the sustenance of heterosexual norms, turns out to privilege (male) Latin American Liberation Theology and (white) feminist theology.

In Althaus-Reid's view, decency indeed secures the oppressive structure left behind by Western imperialism. Until theologies in Latin American cease to critically concern themselves with sexuality, their criticisms will never recognize the most fundamental structure of oppression and deal with the reality of hierarchy. This is why Althaus-Reid proposes Indecent Theology to continue the work of Latin American Liberation Theology but radically discontinue colonial theology. As she clarifies:

> My purpose is not to demolish Liberation Theology *a la Europea* (in a European academic fashion), but to explore the contextual

1. Quero, "Risky Affairs," 207–18.
2. Althaus-Reid, "Introduction," 1.
3. Althaus-Reid, "From Liberation Theology," 20–38.
4. Kwok, "Theology as a Sexual Act?," 153.

hermeneutical circle of suspicion in depth by questioning the
traditional liberationist context of doing theology.[5]

Imperialism, Decent Mary and Economic Exploitation

Althaus-Reid explains how imperialism, working with sexual oppression, is deeply rooted in Christianity in Latin America. Mariology in
Latin America is a typical example. The image of the Virgin Mary, which
is widely accepted by Latin American women, is far from being a liberator
of women—it is an oppressor of poor women while it defends the morality of decency. Althaus-Reid is of the view that the veneration and worship of Mary as a Goddess may orientate and construct women's solidarity
because Mary-as-a-woman can be more sympathetic to the suffering of
women than any male deity. But she is critical of the fact that this naïve
belief has ignored the colonial context that shapes the image of the Virgin
Mary in Latin America.[6] Althaus-Reid sharply points out that this image
of the Virgin Mary is, in reality, the representation of a historical figure of
Mariana—who was Latina but a notorious traitor. Not only was she the
lover of and collaborator with a Spanish conqueror, but she was also unable
to be in solidarity with her people, due to the abandonment of her Latina
identity. Mariana served the interest of colonizers instead.[7]

This Virgin Mary, shaped by the image of Mariana, is definitively not
someone who stands with oppressed women. Her role as a traitor means
that she knows how to act as a mediator to figure out what the oppressors
want and help them to exploit the colonized. The way that the Virgin Mary
"comforts" women who pray to her is to require and convince the oppressed
women to accept their suffering tamely and humbly. In this sense, the Virgin
Mary is far from being a liberator of poor women. Instead, she is "a woman
who oppresses women."[8] This is particularly the case when the Virgin Mary
is put forward as a "perfect" role model for mothers, and as a perfect example of an obedient woman—one who suffers but who tamely accepts her
suffering.[9] These women's bodies are disciplined by a system of decency and
sexual norms, which is offered and supported by Christianity. In accordance

---

5. Althaus-Reid, *From Feminist Theology*, 5.

6. Althaus-Reid, *Indecent Theology*, 50.

7. Althaus-Reid, *From Feminist Theology*, 40.

8. Althaus-Reid, *From Feminist Theology*, 41.

9. Althaus-Reid, *From Feminist Theology*, 41.

with normativity, the system of decency and norms is established through colonialism and political-economic oppressions.

Althaus-Reid draws our attention to recognize that the governance strategies of European colonizers included not only guns and weapons but also the notion of "civilization." This is particularly in the context that colonizers convinced themselves that Latin American local culture was "savage," so their mission was to "help" the indigenous people to be civilized by "governing" them. When evangelization ministries, which were part of colonialist strategies, introduced the Christian God to the local people, they also imposed North American and European moral culture on native Latin American people. This mission utilized the standardization of Christian moral values, complying with the moral culture of North American and European people, the loves of whom are considered civilized and normal.[10] Western civilization and moral norms, with the spread of imperialism and Christianity, establish the hierarchy which devalues the culture of indigenous people and their "indecent" lifestyle. Unfortunately, this system of oppression will be constantly sustained by the church and Latin American Liberation Theology untill what "decency" means is fully scrutinized.

In Althaus-Reid's critique, the word "decency" is used to refer to all forms of colonial civilization, moral norms, normalities, and so on. As she argues, all political-economic structures in Latin America are "based on the naturalization of sexuality following a western Christian notion of 'decency.'"[11] Decency secures everything "under the governance of norms." It excludes all subversive dangers, which create uncertainty, marginalization, and perversion. The Virgin Mary of Decency is expected to wear beautiful and "proper" clothes to cover her body and breasts. She should then never be seen as an *ordinary* woman who breastfeeds the Son of God. Althaus-Reid suggests that Mary should be represented by the Deceased Correa (*La Difunta Correa*).[12]

> The Deceased Correa is an unstable and generous virgin who redistributes wealth and health amongst the poor but also redistributes the grace of the poor women, the prostitutes, the *mujeres con pasado* (women with a sexual past), and sees the

10. Althaus-Reid, "'Let Them Talk,'" 5–17.

11. Althaus-Reid, *From Feminist Theology*, 87.

12. Deceased Correa was a legendary woman. Her husband, Clemente Bustos, was forcibly recruited to the army around 1840, during the civil wars. While they were separated, she was so eager to be reunited with her husband that she took her infant son on a journey through the San Juan Desert. Sadly, she died of thirst, hunger, and exhaustion in the desert. But when people found her body, her son was still alive, sucking her breasts from which milk was still flowing.

divine in the indecent acts of the everyday struggles of life for
bread and for love.[13]

For Althaus-Reid, Virgin Marys (in plural) in Argentina are not decent
at all. If their lived experiences are shared by other Latin American women,
how can these Marys be as decent as a white Western lady, dressing in a clean
and shiny manner like the Virgin of Guadalupe? The Virgin Mary should be
indecent like Latin American women whose breasts show in public even in
death. Similarly, due to the concern with decency, Jesus is never imagined as
a naked man on the Cross, redeeming human sin. The church, then, should
never be thought of as a place that is full of smelly, filthy, and unclean people
(particularly women). Decent theology has disfigured the nature of the gos-
pel—which should be scandalous.[14] It excludes those who are identified as
not as decent and civilized as those who own power.

Althaus-Reid rejects any "Vanilla"[15] or "Disneyland"[16] theology that
is detached from real human lives. Indecent Theology must be founded on
the experiences of the lives of poor women and those who are too poor to
wear underwear and too indecent and smelly to be in the church.[17] She
cries out that the theological reconstruction has to be radical enough to
doubt the whole theological language—which makes us feel secure and
comfortable—to subvert the present structure of theological norms. Otherwise, what we try to do in liberation theology will be in vain. We will not
even be free from the "old patriarchal/parental metaphor of god-fathers."[18]
Therefore, through articulating and disclosing what is considered to be
indecent, marginalized, and perverse—"indecenting" (as a verb) Christianity is itself a subversive strategy. She adds:

> I deliberately use the term *indecenting* here in relation to the un-
> masking of ideologies. *Indecenting* is a term that reminds us that
> Liberation Theology's first act was that of troubling the status

13. Althaus-Reid, *Indecent Theology*, 85–86.

14. Althaus-Reid, *Queer God*, 33–36.

15. "Vanilla theology" has a sexual implication in Althaus-Reid. It means the theology which does not want to take any risk. For example, in leather fetish culture, "vanilla
sex" means something unadventurous and without the intention of trying different
sexual practices and expressions. See: Althaus-Reid, *Indecent Theology*, 51–57.

16. "Disneyland theology" is a theme park theology—which means a theological
work at the level of expressive symbols but being no different from European theologies. Althaus-Reid uses this term to criticize Latin American Liberation Theology for
functioning like a theme park "at the level of popular attractions." It has "done a lot for
the book market of the western world." See: Althaus-Reid, *From Feminist Theology*, 129.

17. Althaus-Reid, *Indecent Theology*, 17–19.

18. Althaus-Reid, *From Feminist Theology*, 77.

quo and that it was part of provocative and heavily contested transgressive discourse.[19]

As Thia Cooper concludes, the theological method of indecenting "requires us to examine what we have been taught, subjecting it all to suspicion, and be honest about our own experiences."[20] What Althaus-Reid demands us to do is to just be honest about our experiences, however dirty or "shameful" we are. We do not need to look at or desire others or ourselves who are in a "decent" image because we all share the image of God.

Theologians are forced to review why our attention is caught by these decent and chaste women and why it ignores those who may discomfort and shock us sexually. Althaus-Reid encourages theologians to speak out on topics that people are normally unwilling to mention, due to the fact that they are perceived as indecent, or even taboo.[21] She also makes the particular demand that liberation theologians should recognize "the unrecognized" who are of no value to the state, allowing them to "occupy the legal space of the construction of the social system." There is a group of the excluded that has "an invisible existence" and "for whom to be exploited would be a dubious but real privilege."[22] For Althaus-Reid, the liberation of "the poor" is much more difficult than Latin American Liberation Theology claims if the experiences of the excluded are considered. As Claudio Carvalhaes notes, Indecent Theology is determined to include black women, LGBT people, drag queens, and all perverse characters, those who are unable to fit in with the "typical" image of the poor.[23] Indecent theology in this sense is not about creating a new category of the excluded to build up its theology. It is about giving voices to those who are excluded from the social norms—which are established under colonialism, decent morality, and political-economic oppressions. Indecenting itself is resistance.

Indecent Resistance in the Body and Sexuality

I argue that Indecent Theology has proposed two theological strategies and that these strategies are connected with resistive action. The first of these strategies is enacted on the body. The second works at the level of language in terms of indecent sexuality.

19. Althaus-Reid, "From Liberation Theology," 25.

20. Cooper, *Queer and Indecent*, 102.

21. Althaus-Reid and Isherwood, *Controversies*, 36.

22. Althaus-Reid, "Hermeneutics of Transgression," 252–53.

23. Carvalhaes, "Oppressed Bodies," 167.

The body is determined by Indecent Theology as the locus where power relationships can be observed and tracked. The bodies of women and men are "inscribed" with gender roles and "the bodies of women have carried a very heavy burden under patriarchy."[24] The body is no longer an abstract concept, but an *object*—on which social norms inscribe and impose themselves. It is also an objectified agent—which actualizes social norms and reproduces the practice of normalities intentionally or unintentionally. Because of the body, normalities can be "alive."

Interpreting Foucault,[25] Althaus-Reid argues that "our bodies have become victims to the normalizing power of an external discourse." The subject cannot be seen as a mind-based being, perceived by Western Enlightenment philosophers, but should be "found within the material practices of everyday life."[26] Of course, Althaus-Reid would criticize previous feminist/womanist theologies for *idealizing* women's bodies in opposition to male mind-centric theology. This makes feminist/womanist theologies no different from other male-dominant theologies. The body is not just an exponent symbolizing and pointing to the location of experiences that deserve to be heard. Althaus-Reid wants to take the real, smelly, and filthy bodies back, and consider this "physical body" with a vagina. Thanks to Foucault's insights, Althaus-Reid recognizes that the bodies themselves are loci of resistance and have strategic possibilities "through acts of deviance and perversion."[27] We do not need to translate our bodies's experiences into rational theological arguments like other feminist/womanist theologians have done. The enactment is on the bodies, and she adds:

> For Foucault [a multiplicity of resistance] was embodied and he advocates seeking new pleasures which liberate our desires from the male genital discourse, for him fist-fucking, S&M and fetishism could be viewed as ways to dislocate this discourse as they all place desire and satisfaction in other and unexpected parts of the body. There is then a genuine body relocation and with it the chance of a new discourse.[28]

Foucault's idea of sexual "liberation" strengthens her task of Indecent Theology because it shows the relationship between body and sexuality, and

24. Althaus-Reid and Isherwood, *Controversies*, 22.

25. Althaus-Reid clearly refers to Foucault, but she does not indicate where the reference or other resources of interpretation come from. In her *Queer God*, she mentions more about Foucault's thoughts of sexuality, the body and dominance.

26. Althaus-Reid and Isherwood, *Controversies*, 22.

27. Althaus-Reid and Isherwood, *Controversies*, 23.

28. Althaus-Reid and Isherwood, *Controversies*, 23.

power domination. It is possible for the body that has been sexualized to en-act resistance, proposed by Indecent Theology, to sexual norms established by Christianity and imperialism.

The second strategy of Indecent Theology in Althaus-Reid's sense of Foucault is at the level of language or discourse. She encourages theologians to talk more about sexuality and erotic desire, which have been taboo topics in society. Talking more about sexuality and desire is not simply about in-corporating them into their theology but *articulating* them in subverting the decent theological norm. Articulation of indecent sexuality and the vagina casts doubt on "rationality"—the bastion of the power of decent theology and its support of patriarchy—since it authorizes the voice and viewpoint of men and identifies them as being more scientifically objective, and having more rational knowledge.[29] Decent theology, which disguises itself as ratio-nal and civilized Enlightenment theology, avoids talking about erotic desire and sexuality because they are dangerous and uncontrollable. It commands other theologies to conform to social norms of decency and attempts to put every potentially subversive element under control. Decent theology scares those indecent explosives which may destroy the theological hierarchy and undermine their order of ruling power.

Indecent Theology recognizes that the hidden truth, which has been covered up by decent theology's phobia, is that erotic desire and sexuality are transformative and resistive. As we have pointed out, the bodies and sexuality themselves are loci of resistance. Hence, articulation of sexual-ity, erotic desire, and the body in theology is the *disclosure* of the truth. The phobic reaction of decent theology—in demonizing queer theol-ogy—proves the powerful threat of Indecent Theology and Queer God (in Althaus-Reid's later use). Althaus-Reid argues that the traditional theol-ogy of redemption requires "conversion" because it considers redemption to be 'retention' of and reproduction of decent or proper order—which is given and imposed on the converters. This redemption does not welcome or include anything outside heterosexual ideologies. It excludes Queer God and fails to recognize loving relationships outside conversion.[30] Althaus-Reid is indecenting and queering redemption, by presenting the experience of *masturbation* as a form of rebellion. For her, redemption is not a piece of doctrine—it is real practice.

> Masturbation gives us an angle of ambiguity in our sexual re-flections on theology, from which sexual ambiguity manifests it-self by affirming the community basis of the act of theologizing,

29. Althaus-Reid and Isherwood, *Controversies*, 26.

30. Althaus-Reid, *Queer God*, 134.

while enjoying at the same time maintaining a fierce self-sustaining independence.[31]

Some people might be furious and upset when Althaus-Reid compares God's redemption with masturbation, but she intends to disclose how indecency has been demonized and how theological decency is deeply rooted. Althaus-Reid argues that the heterosexual redemption misrecognizes Godself as a discrete sexual Other and forgets how redemptive practices of God include "the same flowing desire and a memory (much richer than simply a retention) of desire to be actualized."[32] Althaus-Reid appeals for an alternative language to be used, which we can use to understand God better than the language offered by heterosexual decent theology. Articulation of sexuality and desire, especially non-heterosexual erotic desires, is a strategy of resistance.

Indecent Theology successfully pinpoints how political-economic power systems (including imperialism and capitalism) can be maintained by the sexual norm of decency to consolidate the structure of multi-oppressions in sexuality and erotic desire and exclude women and the perverted. For Althaus-Reid, indecenting theology and exploring Queer God itself is resistance to conformity to the heterosexual norm, which is defined as decency and rationality. The task of Indecent Theology is to draw our attention back to real human lives and to shake the stability of theological imagination employing articulation of sexuality and non-heterosexual erotic desires. What Althaus-Reid has done undoubtedly turns decent theology upside down, but I argue that, from the perspective of Foucault, her proposal of Indecent Theology is incomplete and even puts her theology at risk of becoming powerless to subvert.

Indecency as Counter-Decency?

Althaus-Reid embraces the idea and practices of indecency to resist the theological and socio-political structure of decency. Thus, she believes that indecency helps us to explore God outside the heterosexual framework, and the way to liberate ourselves is to fundamentally "queer" social order and normality. Her theological language is powerful, but I doubt whether she still falls into that dualism—which has been consolidated by decency. For example, the way she defines indecency is based on the definition of decency and heterosexuality, so homosexuality is indecent, and the Queer

31. Althaus-Reid, *Queer God*, 138.
32. Althaus-Reid, *Queer God*, 138.

God is homosexual. If we want to encounter God, Althaus-Reid would suggest challenging decent sexual knowledge and finding God in homosexual love and desire.

I agree with regarding Indecent Theology as a *hermeneutical* method—that is if we want to find God, we need to find God beyond the limitation of our current knowledge. Althaus-Reid contends that "the Queer God is the God who went into exile with God's people and remained there in exile with them."[33] God is not always presented on a glamorous altar but on the way to escaping from that kind of suffocating decency. From a Trinitarian perspective, God sent the Son to the muddy world and Jesus was born in a dirty manger. Althaus-Reid challenges our expectation to find God who is restrained, cleansed, and purified in a decent place. On our walking (*caminata* in her word) journey of seeking God, Althaus-Reid adds, the desire is "not to make of God an occasional and compassionate visitor to the margins of the margins but to *rediscover* that God is a truly marginal God."[34] Seemingly what Althaus-Reid means here is that God should be seen as being in movement "from a God at the margins (still partaking of central definitions) to a more radical 'marginal God.'" As Cooper clarifies, this does not mean that God's movement is just from the center to the margins, because this assumes that the God-at-the-margins is only the same God from the same center—but in different locations.[35] This is the reason why Indecenting theology encourages us to rediscover God at the margin through *caminata* to the margins.

However, I am dubious about what *the* marginal God means in terms of the essence of this marginal God, particularly when Althaus-Reid gradually expands her understanding of the Queer God—which essentializes the God at the margins. She repeatedly defines the Queer God as something opposite to heterosexuality, dissents from heteronormativity, and is distant from the current state of affairs.[36] Hence, the division of indecency and decency, in fact, is still based on the division of homosexuality and heterosexuality—when heterosexuality refers to totally corrupted decency and homosexuality refers to the hope of liberating indecency. It turns out that the existence of decency must continue to *rely on* rather than banish the structure of heterosexuality.

The fact is that "transgression" for Althaus-Reid just means turning away from heterosexuality to homosexuality (which is sometimes called

33. Althaus-Reid, *From Feminist Theology*, 146.
34. Althaus-Reid, *From Feminist Theology*, 146 (emphasis added).
35. Cooper, *Queer and Indecent*, 138.
36. See: Althaus-Reid, *Queer God*, 4; Althaus-Reid, *Indecent Theology*, 88.

bisexuality.)[37] Her strategy of subverting heterosexuality is through shifting her focus on homosexuality and at the same time giving up any resistive possibility *within* a heterosexual structure. Although she claims not
to replace heterosexuality with homosexuality, her ignorance of heterosexuality leads in the opposite direction to what she claims. Carvalhaes's
critiques share the same observation that:

> By emphasizing and centering perverted sexual habits of poor
> people over and against normative sex, she runs the risk of
> switching the binary normative/perverted sexualities upside
> down. The binary is not undone, just replaced.[38]

When homosexuality is defined as everything which is excluded from heterosexuality, the consequence is that it becomes completely meaningless
because it merely means counter-heterosexuality. Similarly, indecency also
becomes meaningless as it, too, simply means counter-decency.

As we have discussed in chapter 3, Foucault may be cautious about
whether Althaus-Reid's counter-decency can subvert heterosexuality, since
he has pointed out how so-called liberation action takes an important role
in consolidating power dominance. In terms of power relationships, the
emergence of counter-decency (indecency) is welcomed and is soon incorporated by the structure of decency and heterosexuality, rather than fully
subverts the current structure. I suggest that, if Althaus-Reid's proposal is
not an "inversion" of heterosexuality, her criticism also needs to *include*
heterosexuality.[39] Some ambiguous and unwanted individual subjects and
those who are forced to *become* decent within heterosexuality should be
concerned because they are crossing the binary boundary and confuse the
dominant system of heterosexuality.

---

37. Althaus-Reid's understanding of "bisexuality" is awkward because it is based
on the stereotype of bisexuality—which only implies polygamy, promiscuity, perversion and infidelity. Her idea of bisexuality is far from the real lives of bisexual people,
especially bisexual women. The limitation of Althaus-Reid's bisexuality is briefly noted
by Robinson, "Reading Althaus-Reid," 108–20.

38. Carvalhaes, "Oppressed Bodies," 195.

39. Judith Butler has argued that the idea of Monique Wittig (a radical lesbian feminist) is impossible to work out. Wittig and Althaus-Reid are similar because they both
criticize a heterosexual system for creating a hierarchical relationship between men
and women, so the sexual oppression can be solved when this heterosexual system is
destroyed. Responding to Wittig's proposal of inversion, Butler argues that "my own
conviction is that the radical disjunction posited by Wittig between heterosexuality and
homosexuality is simply not true, that there are structures of psychic homosexuality
within heterosexual relations, and structures of psychic heterosexuality within gay and
lesbian sexuality and relationships." Butler, *Gender Trouble*, 165.

As an example of including heterosexuality, I suggest Althaus-Reid should more closely consider "hegemonic masculinity" as it may help her recognize different kinds of masculinity and articulate a specific way of sexual oppression instead of a rough and vague idea of heterosexuality. Some sociological analyses have pointed out that internal oppression within hetero-sexuality exists and that men suffer from pressure on the expression of mascu-linity. They also recognize how oppression and incorporation may both come together in contemporary urban gay masculinities—whose experiences are described as "ranging from homophobic violence and cultural denigration to toleration and even cultural celebration and political representation."[40] We should recognize that gender hierarchy is not a single pattern of dominance of men over women, heterosexuals over homosexuals. Masculinity is socially defined, and it is relational to different forms of femininity—it is something to *become* rather than to own. Women and homosexual people are not im-mune from this hierarchy pf masculinity.

Considering that Althaus-Reid's concept of indecency is not as fluid and anti-structural as she claims it is, I argue here that Indecent Theology does not extricate itself from a reliance on structural analysis (which is in-herited from her background of Latin American Liberation Theology and feminist/womanist theology). Althaus-Reid still defines the perverted, queers, and indecent by means of structural analysis of heterosexuality. For her, because of heterosexuality, queers are the most oppressed group. It is no different from the feminist claim that because of patriarchy, wom-en are the most oppressed group. And this kind of formula is reproduced by liberation theologians in constructing different liberation theologies. These re-formulations of defining the most oppressed group turn into a competition for the "crown" of the poorest people, who can know God most, and who are most worthy of being listened to and cared for. (See the discussion in chapter 2.)

In this light, Indecent Theology results in the essentialisation of the Queer God with the most oppressed people. Although this consequence might be unintentional, it certainly contradicts Althaus-Reid's herme-neutical method of indecenting. This Queer God keeps walking—but just leisurely *strolling* along streets in the slum and going *nowhere*. As Cooper interprets Althaus-Reid's image of the marginal God, she comments that:

---

40. Carrigan et al., "Toward a New Sociology," 551–604. Further discussion about masculinity can be seen in: Connell and Messerschmidt, "Hegemonic Masculinity," 829–59.

> People at the margins have their own maps, unrelated to the
> center. There, God is present, living and struggling with them.
> God becomes Godself at the margins, unrelated to the center.[41]

Indeed, *God the Margin* is an empowering message for those who
are excluded as God comes to be with them. But does this marginal God
keep transgressing the theology from the center and the whole structure
of decent theology? Althaus-Reid falls into this binary division again no
matter how indecent and aggressive her theological language may be. As
Foucault has inspired us, the power dominance of decency loves and wel-
comes these counter-decency challenges because their harmless uproar
strengthens their authority while the new power relationships are created
and deployed again.[42] If Althaus-Reid wants to overcome the binary, she
must take an approach that transgresses the boundary rather than one that
establishes another utopian picture of the marginal God who stays at the
margins and enjoys walking in them. The Queer God needs to walk freely
back to indecent people in the center.

The Construction of Perversion

Following the first criticism of Althaus-Reid's binary of decency and indecency, I argue that the fundamental problem of repeating the binary
system is that she cannot see the process of subjectification—that is, how
subjects become perverted selves. Althaus-Reid still relies on the identification of oppressive structures in the first instance. Therefore, while focusing on the oppressed group which is defined by the structure analysis, she
loses the flexibility required to maintain her indecenting power to trace
the active works of oppression in newly developing deployments of power.
Althaus-Reid's method of indecenting is dead when it sticks to achievements that satisfy the queering critiques and make them docile. This situation reminds us of Foucault's critique of sexual liberation—when sexual
liberationists celebrate their freedom to talk freely about their sexuality,
they sacrifice the vigilance needed to maintain a recognition of how new

---

41. Cooper, *Queer and Indecent*, 138.

42. Lesbianism—which is seen as the counter-heterosexuality—is very close to what
Althaus-Reid means about indecent and queer. But Judith Butler sharply points out
that lesbianism does not really subvert heterosexuality. "Lesbianism would then *require*
heterosexuality. Lesbianism that defines itself in radical exclusion from heterosexuality
deprives itself of the capacity of resignify the very heterosexual constructs by which it is
partially and inevitably constituted. As a result, that lesbian strategy would consolidate
compulsory heterosexuality in its oppressive forms." Butler, *Gender Trouble*, 174.

power deployments recapture them in a new form of power relationships. Perversion is one such example.

Althaus-Reid's application of perversion in Indecent Theology begins with an underlying problem—that the "perverted" in her definition do not *choose* to be perverted. No doubt, they are excluded by the structure of decency because they cannot fit into the heterosexual structure. But they do not choose to be perverse or to act perversely. The "perverted" are exploited instead of choosing to be in poverty. They are sexually abused instead of enjoying taking a submissive role in sadomasochism. They are innocent under persecution instead of fighting against authority without fear of death. If we have considered these questions and realistically sense the lack of freedom of the perverted, how can we discern the message of liberation and freedom in Indecent Theology? When we praise the Queer God for being naked, for not wearing a clean suit, and for self-exiling in slums with the poor, perhaps the question should be asked: Does this indecent God really have anything to do with places that exile God and exclude people?

Foucault's concern with perversion and resistance indicates freedom of choice, instead of freedom of acts.[43] Perversion can be seen as *strategies* of resistance only under the circumstance that perversion is not steadily categorized. This idea of strategic perversion as transgression is shared by Judith Butler when she proposes "cross-gendered drag" as sexual performativity that subverts heterosexuality. She argues that this subversion is not through opposing heterosexuality or proliferating genders—but that it is "with the exposure or the failure of heterosexual regimes ever fully to legislate or contain their own ideals."[44] Although drag is enabled by the freedom of choice, this choice is not based on random acts of subversion and perversion. This freedom should be practiced within the norms which "precede, constrain, and exceed" the perverse action so that it is enabled to interrupt a reiteration of the norms (by which heterosexual norms are constructed).[45] And the possibility of resistance is open when the subject is related to its practice of the self (in Foucault's sense), so Butler adds:

> The agency denoted by the performativity of "sex" will be directly counter to any notion of a voluntarist subject who exists quite apart from the regulatory norms which she/he opposes. The paradox of subjectification (*assujetissement*) is precisely

---

43. Foucault, "Sexual Choice, Sexual Act," 143.

44. Butler, *Bodies That Matter*, 181.

45. Butler, *Bodies That Matter*, 178.

that the subject who would resist such norms is itself enabled, if not produced, by such norms.[46]

I argue that if we read Foucault and Butler together, it will show that "resistive perversion" requires three elements, which unfortunately Indecent Theology lacks. Firstly, resistive perversion requires freedom of choice—which means that transgressors are free to cross boundaries that have been established by heterosexual norms. The subjectivity of homosexuality has been so firmly constituted by heterosexuality that their existences fully rely on each other. Hence, the emergence of homosexual subjects does not cross the boundary at all but consolidates it. Lesbians and gays are products of heterosexuality. In this sense, Althaus-Reid's perverted subjects do not have freedom to transgress heterosexuality either. The existence of poor women, homosexuals, and queers depends on the existence of heterosexuality to such an extent that no matter what they do, and however indecent they claim to be, this heterosexual structure is merely consolidated.

Secondly, if perversion is to be resistive, it requires constant acts of resistance happening within the oppressive structure. It is impossible to find a utopian space in which the oppressed can escape from oppression. This kind of liberation does not work. As Butler says, "gender is always a negotiation with power" so "there is no gender without this reproduction of norms."[47] What we *can* do to subvert gender norms established by the heterosexual structure is to *undo* and *redo* the norms in unexpected ways. In this sense, Indecent Theology misses the point of the Queer God—who should move between the center and the margins and who should cross the boundary that is set by decent norms. The Queer God should not be opposed to its reiteration of becoming (heterosexual) God—which regulates God to stay in the center of decency. The Queer God should sneak out to the slum and invite other queers to come back to the center in unexpected ways. God and queers should have their freedom to stay at indecent margins and go to the decent center.

Finally, resistive perversion requires concern with the process of *becoming* the self (subjectification). As we have discussed in chapter 3, Foucault points out that resistance comes from the practice of the self when the subject and the self are constituted by each other. Butler also mentions that because of this process of becoming, the subject has opportunities of undoing and redoing the norms. However, Althaus-Reid completely ignores the process of becoming perverted subjects when she uncritically identifies the perverted with those who are excluded from the heterosexual structure.

46. Butler, *Bodies That Matter*, xxiii.

47. Butler, *Notes toward*, 32.

This drives Althaus-Reid into relying on structural analysis as other liberation theologians do. But her turn to structural analysis limits her ability to recognize the dynamic deployments of power, thereby gradually essentializing the nature of the Queer God and losing the ground of her critical, hermeneutical method of indecenting.

Althaus-Reid and Foucault both pay attention to sexuality, desire, and the body, and are concerned with social norms and power dominance. Even Althaus-Reid, in her discovery of the complexity of multi-oppressions, has already recognized imperialist domination, indigenous genocide, and sexual oppression when she finds the complexity of multi-oppressions, which is how sexual norms and the heterosexual structure cooperate with social, political, and economic oppression. However, from Foucault's perspective (with the help of Butler), a close reading of Indecent Theology shows that Althaus-Reid merely puts new wine into old wineskins.

Jung Mo Sung and Daniel Bell on Desire

Sexuality, desire, and the body have been explored by Althaus-Reid in terms of their relations to sexual norms and heterosexuality. Due to her attention to multi-oppressions, the oppressed can be recognized beyond political-economic structures. But at the same time, Althaus-Reid's idea of desire seems to be disconnected from her critiques of poverty and capitalism, and it becomes strongly connected with sexual pleasure—which resists heterosexuality in collusion with capitalism. Althaus-Reid runs the risk of romanticizing desire as our "natural" drive, which we can trust in exploring God. We should not be surprised by her confidence in identifying desire with "liberation" and "transgression."[48] This danger of romanticization of desire does not fully slip under the radar of political theologians. Jung Mo Sung from Latin American Liberation Theology[49] and Daniel Bell from Radical Orthodoxy take different approaches to assess desire, but they both seriously consider how capitalism manipulates human desire. This direct link between desire and economic exploitation has been missed in Althaus-Reid's Indecent Theology if the desire is insufficiently resistive.

48. See: Althaus-Reid, *Queer God*, 23.

49. Jung Mo Sung (in Hanja 成定模) is a Roman Catholic lay theologian in Brazil. He was born in Seoul, South Korea and grew up in Brazil. He is a professor at the Methodist University of São Paulo, where he also received his PhD in religious studies.

Limitless Desire and Limited Need

Sung's critique begins with the recognition of capitalism as an *inventor* and *manipulator* of limitless desire. Latin American Liberation Theology misses the point of "limitless desire" because the idea of human needs, instead of desire, appears in Marx's writings. When Marxism talks about the object of commodity, it means everything that is produced by human laborers to be sold, or exchanged, in the market. The production of the commodity itself is not fully evil. Based on the interpretation of *Capitalism*, Sung argues that a commodity is necessary because it may satisfy human want, regardless of whether human beings are motivated by basic need or by a desire for luxury.[50] Here, it seems, Marx assumes that both what human beings want and what they need result from basic human nature. Commodities that exchange in the market meet the needs of daily living. Human lives still get some benefits from the market exchange and the production of commodities.

Sung urges the making of a distinction between "desire" and "need." Unintentionally, Marx has recognized that a certain degree of necessity matters. Not all commodities that satisfy people's needs are motivated from the stomach or from the need to survive. Some are from fancy, or imagination, or *Phantasie* (Marx's word).[51] Sung characterizes desire as the drive of "limitlessness" in comparison to basic need—which is necessary and able to be satisfied. As he says, "we human beings need more than material goods to survive and we need to feel that it is worthy to live."[52] Human beings are driven not only to meet their basic and minimal need of survival but to feel and recognize the value and the worth of being alive. Although need and desire should be considered separately, they are inseparable and undeniable as they are part of human nature.

However, need and desire are usually confused for the sake of capitalism—which reduces all desires to the needs of our survival. As Philip Kotler points out, there are two ways to solve the unsatisfied "need" of people. One way, particularly in industrial societies, is to develop more commodities satisfying their desire. The other way, usually in poor societies, is to reduce their need.[53] In the view of liberal and neoliberal economic theories, desires are considered to be the continuation of human needs, so that when we try

---

50. Sung, "Commodity Fetishism," 89.
51. Sung, "Commodity Fetishism," 89.
52. Sung, "Commodity Fetishism," 70.
53. Sung, *Desire, Market and Religion*, 32.

to satisfy basic human needs, their desire needs to be satisfied. The satisfaction of needs turns out to be the satisfaction of desire too.

If Sung is correct to characterize desire as limitless, how can our economic system satisfy a human need—including desire? The short answer may be that it is *impossible* as he adds:

> When one thinks from the standpoint of desires there are no limits. One pursues the limitless. And when one desires the limitless there is never anything left to share. There is never enough. Therefore, one does not accept a dialogue on income and wealth redistribution.[54]

This strategic confusion of basic need and limitless desire conceals the indispensable distinction between what we truly *need* and what we *desire*. People always feel that their needs cannot be satisfied. But what Sung highlights is the fact that "desire" is something they cannot satisfy, instead of basic need. People need food to fulfill their needs, but they do not "need" to have a meal in a Michelin three-star restaurant. What a nice meal offers is temporary satisfaction of their desire.

When people have been misled by capitalism, they start to believe that what they desire is identical to what they need. This is the "magic" of capitalism. By confusing need with desire, capitalism transforms desires into needs. As Friedrich Hayek says, "the luxuries of today are the necessities of tomorrow."[55] This kind of limitless desire created by capitalism is called "mimetic desire." It is vital for capitalism to constantly create motivation and stably sustain its circulation throughout the whole system.

> The basic structure of mimetic desire consists in the fact that I desire an object, not for the object itself but because another person desires it. Thus, desired by both, the object is always scarce in relation to the subjects of the desire. It is because it is scarce that it is the object of desire.[56]

Mimetic desire, in Sung's view, cannot be represented as what people really need—if our basic need can be estimated by physical fulfillment. For example, we stop eating when we no longer feel hungry and do not want/ need to eat anymore. But mimetic desire shifts our focus onto what we *believe* we feel rather than what we *really* feel. We start to *believe* that we need something when we see others have already needed it or have wanted it beforehand.

54. Sung, *Desire, Market and Religion*, 33.
55. Sung, *Desire, Market and Religion*, 36.
56. Sung, *Desire, Market and Religion*, 37.

The Legend of Development and Religion of Capitalism

The need/want of others triggers our mimetic desire to have something that might not come from our own needs. We are convinced by our mimetic desire to believe that we want something that is not needed. The role of this mimetic desire is significant in capitalism because it keeps enlarging the need to consume—which sustains the demand for production and accumulation. When commodities are produced in excessive amounts, we are trapped in a situation in which we can always see and feel something that we do not have. It does not matter whether we really need these commodities. What matters instead is that the mimetic desire is gradually enlarged and becomes too great to satisfy. The more we pursue, the more the commodities are produced. This vicious circle of pursuing the unattainable takes us onto an endless road on which our desire can never be truly satisfied.

On the other hand, when pursuing the desirable becomes an endless journey, capitalism crafts another legend of the ceaseless progress of modernity—one which promises that limitless need and desire can be satisfied. Capitalism brands itself as the best system of distribution to provide people with what they desire—although the desirable goods are always too scarce to be distributed to everyone. (In fact, due to the principle of mimetic desire, what people desire is never something they have owned. When they are owned, they become no longer desirable.) It is an illusion, created by capitalism, that production will be increased and will then become so efficient that our needs will be satisfied. So if people believe that desire will be satisfied in the end, they need to have faith in the progress of modernity which will keep increasing its supply to meet the demand of everyone.

However, capitalism avoids tackling the real issue, which is that scarcity is the basis for the creation of mimetic desire.[57] Capitalism fails to prove that satisfaction of desire can be promised by means of constantly increasing the supply—when demand is created in scarcity. The progress of development will never catch up with desire when mimetic desire is triggered by seeing what people have that I do not have. The economy of desire does not follow the conventional principle of supply-demand. The increase of the supply of production does not reduce the degree of desire—it creates more mimetic desire. Development is never a satisfactory remedy for limitless desire.

In this light, capitalism and its legend of development cannot overcome poverty if poverty is caused by the lack of supply. Instead, through maximizing production and profits, scarce resources are redistributed

---

57. Sung, "Greed, Desire and Theology," 257.

unjustly.[58] While proclaiming itself as the "best" system of just distribution, nation-states and individuals are persuaded to hand over their power to "economic rationality." They are traded off to maintain the freedom of the market to provide the best operational environment without any restrictions.[59] They are even requested to trust this system wholeheartedly though it might "sometimes" go wrong or unsteadily. The market never fails. The failures always come from our "little faith" and the environment that is criticized for not being free enough. People are required to believe that they are witnessing the progress of development—which will perfectly balance supply and demand through economically rational distribution—if we allow the market to perform at its best.

Sung issues a warning about the danger of having faith in the "illusive" legend of development. He argues that a change in our relationship with possession will also change the understanding of the self, thereby changing our direction toward finding our happiness. In this light, who we are is defined by what we own because it is related to how we achieve happiness.

> The opposition commonly placed between "having" and "being" makes no sense. For the "having" has become the only way to achieve being. Whoever has, is; whoever does not have, is not. The being that a person looks for to feel more human is not in the people or the direct human relation but in the commodities of luxury that we desire to buy.[60]

What we have makes us *happy*, instead of who we are. Happiness is the foundation of human fulfillment. Sung points out that in capitalism, people are driven to seek temporary happiness while pursuing their acquisitions and possessions. But this process of pursuing value does not itself lead to any real happiness in the end.[61] If value means something which is most important to human beings, then obtaining possessions turns out to be the thing of prime importance for human value. The value of an individual is therefore defined by what they have. It is ironic that, because human beings are pursuers of value, they *are* their possessions. This gives capitalism an opportunity to alter what it means to be a human being.

Sung criticizes capitalism for creating mimetic desire and shaping humanity in its relationship with commodity objects. This is a new *religion*—one which turns people away from God. God is meant to be the most

58. Sung, "Save Us from Cynicism," 43–59.
59. Sung, "Greed, Desire and Theology," 256.
60. Sung, "Commodity Fetishism," 95.
61. Sung, "Greed, Desire and Theology," 257.

desirable thing for people to pursue. But God becomes less desirable in the face of glamorous but unattainable commodities. Sung then remarks that:

> Nowadays, the place to be in contact with the sacred forces, which give back "being," are no longer churches but the shopping malls, "real" or "virtual." That is why many shopping malls have architecture reminiscent of temples, cathedrals, or other sacred places.[62]

This means that people may have lost the meaning of their life and the value of being human if they start to profess the "creed" of capitalism. People are indoctrinated by capitalism to go shopping to find what they desire most. They then persuade themselves to believe that "healing" can be found in buying and owning commodity items. While *consuming* the commodities, people are *consumed by* their new relationships with them.

Capitalism becomes a religion and replaces God—who gives meaning through being desired and worshipped by human beings. In this sense, the reason why capitalism is idolatrous is not merely because a deity whose name is Mammon is worshipped. It is also because the possessions desired by people become the most desirable thing, over and above any relationship with God. Having recognized that capitalism has become a god—which controls the world and manipulates human desire—we should seriously consider resistance to capitalism to be an economic issue as well as a theological issue. And desire certainly cannot be seen as a natural driver of resistance.

Sung's Ethical Concern with Desire

Sung insists on making a distinction between limitless desire and the basic need to survive, but he does not cast doubt on the existence of desire. Thus, he argues that this desire to *be*—as opposed to the desire to *have*—can only be satisfied in loving God, who freed the oppressed from slavery, and in love for our neighbor.[63] Human beings and their value should be defined by their relationship with God rather than by possession of a commodity item.

Considering capitalism as an economic system as well as an ideology of understanding of the self, the strategy for the subversion of capitalism should be the discernment of how capitalism shapes and distorts humanity. Sung's theological premise is to restore humanity to its default setting in God's creation because humanity has been driven by mimetic desire toward

---

62. Sung, "Commodity Fetishism," 91.
63. Sung, "Greed, Desire and Theology," 261.

a restless journey to the unattainable and has been defined by the commodities they possess. The most effective strategy for the subversion of capitalism
is to restore humanity to "factory settings."

> To become godlike is to become truly human—to become rec-
> onciled to the constraints inherent in the human condition. It is
> the recognition of the insuperable limit that leads Christianity
> to state that salvation (the complete fulfillment of the deepest
> human desires) can happen only by a free act of God's grace.[64]

In Sung's view, "to be human" means "to follow and imitate God." It
does not mean that human beings either need to be or will be identical
with God. In the creed of capitalism, people profess to become like a god
who controls and transcends everything. They have full freedom to pursue
what they want and desire. But it is contrary to the Christian faith. In the
confession of sin, in which people are required to examine themselves and
learn their limits, the arrogance and egomania of humanity are challenged.
The practice of confession indicates the imperfection and powerlessness
of human beings. It also means that human beings are subjugated to their
limited capacity and restriction. Human beings are not as powerful as capitalism promises. What capitalism offers, in this sense, is merely an illusion
of human beings as free agents to fulfill their limitless desire, whereas the
reality is that there are limits to our ability to access everything we want
and to own everything we desire.

It sounds frustrating that human beings are at their wits' end with
limitless desire. But it is not what Sung means, because the recognition of
our helplessness draws our attention to the reality that we should look for
"something else" to satisfy our desire. That "something else" is God and
leads us to approach God's salvation. If capitalism is unable to offer a road to
happiness with meaning and true value, the only way of fulfilling our desire
is to have a relationship with God. As Sung points out:

> We human beings cannot attain the infinite (to see God) but we
> are able to experience the presence of God among us, to find
> fulfillment of our infinite desire, as far as is possible, in relation-
> ships of love and solidarity.[65]

Similarly, the mission of the church is "to give visibility to the lives of those
living on the periphery or outside the system, and then to make it possible
for their voices to be heard by the privileged."[66] The myth of capitalism and

---

64. Sung, "Greed, Desire and Theology," 258–59.
65. Sung, "Greed, Desire and Theology," 261.
66. Sung, "Greed, Desire and Theology," 261.

the faith in development—which both attempt to progress human happiness and regress human suffering—should be disclosed. The lie that the doctrine of capitalism remains true and sufficient in seeking the common good should then be exposed too.

Sung contends that liberation theology has some words to say when the evidence that people are still in poverty and hunger has proved the failure of justice and equality under the yoke of capitalism. He urges liberation theology to take the cry of sufferers seriously and seriously reflect on the relationship between "their desire to improve their standard of living, their pattern of consumption and the suffering of the poor."[67] This allows liberation theologians to express their anger when they face injustice. This also encourages people to seek a humane way of living together to subvert the dehumanization of capitalist modes of consumption.

Furthermore, Sung highlights some theological concepts supportive of capitalism that should be avoided. One example is the theological application of sacrifice. It is very common to hear the capitalist notion of sacrifices—it is used to justify the suffering of the poor when "all social problems are seen as 'necessary sacrifices' demanded by the market."[68] The second example is the relationship between evil and freedom. According to the creed of capitalism, evil "is wanting to do good, thus wanting to direct, or intervene in, the market."[69] As we have discussed, trust in capitalism is to give the market full freedom without any intervention. In this sense, a thought of "wanting to do something" (whether good or bad) is an evil and sinful act. Pursuing the common good can be vicious if it disobeys the law of capitalism, or if it starts to cause people to lack faith in the magical power of the free market.

Hence, Sung's strategy of resistance is the recognition of human suffering and giving it visibility. It can be enacted in two ways: The first way is to feel angry while recognizing that the suffering is there in the first place. The second way is to be outraged by the condition of those suffering, especially the poor. Here we can see the methodology of Latin American Liberation Theology shared by Althaus-Reid and Sung. As Sung insists, acts of resistance reveal the truth that the suffering is still there, and it has not yet been brought to an end.

> Opening the Church to the poor, being a Church of the Poor,
> is to give public witness that God is no respecter of persons,
> to affirm the dignity of the poor, and to live a non-idolatrous

67. Sung, "Greed, Desire and Theology," 261–62.

68. Sung, *Desire, Market and Religion*, 90.

69. Sung, *Desire, Market and Religion*, 16.

faith. And the public affirmation of this dignity is a necessary condition for more people to become angry at the situation of the poor and for their sufferings to become a priority for society, with more political will and energy to bring about the necessary transformations.[70]

This transformation for Sung means the abandonment of the current system of economic distribution, which has failed to share equally and justly.[71] Here I argue that Sung's criticism of capitalism is specific to its form of religion—which works with creating mimetic desire and distorting humanity and offers the false illusion of promise in development and just distribution. The problem is not the dysfunction of capitalism-as-exchange itself but the damage of human creation. Therefore, Sung urges Christian theology—which should bear social responsibility and raise ethical awareness—to establish a new order that reduces and restricts the unlimited accumulation of wealth.[72]

Fighting against capitalism is an ethical action, as human desire and basic needs are appropriated and manipulated for serving the interest of capitalism. Thus the responsibility of liberation theology is to examine the *right-or-wrong* that capitalism brings. Sung's theology not only aims to establish an ethical principle, which helps people to live more morally in this capitalist society. Although this is part of the solution, it also charts an ethical course to challenge, or even fix, humanity in the capitalist society. Sung's proposal is clear and sharp. On the one hand, he proposes to reveal the reality of the life of the poor through continuing the tradition of Latin American Liberation Theology, while on the other hand, he proposes to do so by enlarging our understanding of how capitalism *functions* and *works* in manipulating humanity. His recognition of mimetic desire and development myth helps articulate the manipulation of capitalism. This is missing in Althaus-Reid.

However, my concern is that Sung's theological proposal runs the risk of bringing political resistance to an end. This is because he cannot show any realistic alternative solution to capitalism if capitalism cannot be truly abandoned. Even though his premise seems to be practical and ethical, he fails to set up a credible agenda that puts his criticism and premise into practice. Apart from feeling angry for the poor, what can people do after recognizing how distorted their desire has become and how it has been manipulated by capitalism? The primary issue of the ethical solution is to show *how* people

70. Sung, "Poor," 73.
71. Sung, "Save Us from Cynicism," 43–59.
72. Sung, "Save Us from Cynicism."

may have different desires from those shaped by capitalism. How can we—whose desires have been shaped and manipulated by capitalism—have the capacity to desire "something else" if the mimetic desire has been deeply rooted? Can this "other" desire be an option for us? More precisely, when the construction of desire is to fit capitalism, what we might need to do in priority is to de-construct this constructed desire, thereby setting this desire free. The ethical proposal of what desire *should be* is important, but it faces limitations in terms of showing how our desire *can become*. I argue that Sung's concern with desire needs to move beyond the ethical level of right-and-wrong decisions and to reconsider the *process* of shaping the desire. Daniel Bell may contribute to this idea.

Bell's Ontological Concern with Desire

Like Jung Mo Sung, Daniel Bell also argues that resistance to capitalism is not a rejection of this economic system of exchange but recognition of the work of forming human desire in capitalism. He thinks that capitalism attempts to control the order of the world through managing the order of *beings*, which is the most basic arrangement of the power of reality. This consideration defines the issue of capitalism as an issue of ontology.[73] Lacking this ontological dimension of resistance to capitalism, we will fail to recognize how capitalism entails manipulating human desire and constructing the created order in accordance with its interest.[74]

But Sung and Bell put very different focuses on their proposals and responses to the manipulation of desire in capitalism. Bell does not propose an alternative social policy or any ethical principle. Instead, he rephrases Christian theology and regards it as the healing of desire and liberation. In his view, because Christian faith itself is a *therapy* for healing in the social-political-economic sphere, it does not need another process of translation or application to make theology useful. Christian faith is the source of healing power. Therefore, in contrast to Sung's ethical concern, the role of the Christian faith is not to suggest a moral standard for examining the economic system. Instead, it is a medicine for curing desire, which has been distorted by capitalism.

Christian faith should not be simplified as a moral system to evaluate people's behavior and capitalist distribution. Nor should it function as one. It is because it seems to imply that this kind of faith can consult on what to do from a perspective that comes from somewhere outside the current

73. Bell, *Economy of Desire*.
74. Bell, *Economy of Desire*, 87.

social, political, and economic realms. Bell criticizes this kind of Christian faith—the sort that suggests what society can do—for making itself *apolitical* and for merely collecting knowledge that is "non-political."[75] Bell argues that theology does not need to think about how to offer an ethical voice in politics because it *is* politically and socially engaged. Theology does not need any help from Marxism or social theory in the way that Sung does in the tradition of Latin American Liberation Theology.

Bell doubts the value of Marxism. He has no faith in the ability of a social theory to transform society because social theory separates religion and Christian faith from the state and forces theology to forfeit its value in the public realm. If social theory and Marxism have undermined ecclesiology, it follows that building theology on social theory and the unsolid foundation of ecclesiology is doomed to fail ever since it took its first step.[76] His criticism of Latin American Liberation Theology is applicable to his critique of Sung's ethical proposal:

> The serving of any direct relationship between the theological and the political realms of life does not leave the realms unrelated, thereby repeating the errors of idealist or spiritualist theologies. The wall between the realms is bridged by means of what Gutierrez calls a "social appropriation of the gospel," which amounts to a correlation of faith and history, a translation of faith into political activity.[77]

In Bell's view, the Church cannot save or transform society if it is excluded from society. When theology cannot embed as a real political activity, due to the division between the theological and the political, it becomes voiceless and a *spiritual* ideology.[78] This reveals a fundamental predication of doing liberation theologies—which is how to retrieve its political nature and cross

75. The idea of "non-political" here must be understood in the root of Radical Orthodoxy. Daniel Bell shares a similar perspective on "the political" with other theologians in the Radical Orthodoxy Movement, particularly with William Cavanaugh. Mary Doak argues that Bell and Cavanaugh can be categorized into "the anarchic oppositionalism" because they refute the privatization of Christianity and sectarianism. They both regard the state as a hopelessly evil institution so "this thoroughgoing rejection of the state allows for a boldness and consistency in their vision of the church as an alternative to the status quo in its witness against the injustice of the world" (378). In this sense, for Bell, "the political" is not only a matter of society but of the church. And the political can be everywhere rather than any specific issue about society. See: Doak, "Politics of Radical Orthodoxy," 368–93.

76. Bell, *Liberation Theology*, 3.

77. Bell, *Liberation Theology*, 61.

78. Bell, *Liberation Theology*, 60.

the dividing boundary between the theological and the political when they are based on secularized social theories.

Bell argues that the social-political-economic realm should be taken back by theology. To bring about peace and justice, theology must take more "radical" action to subvert the separation of the theological and the political, and should recognize that we should not have any expectation that the free market will bring about justice.[79] In other words, Bell does not think there is any chance of repairing the current system—which is the cause of injustice. If theology cooperates with social theories, accepts the separation of faith and the state, or keeps any hope in the corrupted system, it is impossible to subvert capitalism. Here, Bell is careful *not* to be a secular revolutionary who might even be willing to take violent action to establish an alternative system. He is cynical about being a liberation theologian who is unwilling to question the fundamental issue of any secular political system. Bell urges resistance against capitalism—unlike Sung, without fundamentally challenging the whole idea of the current capitalist system. He requires an ontological imagination which overcomes capitalism and its power deployments.

Bell argues that—through retrieving human desire—theology becomes the tool for resistance against capitalism. Political resistance is an ontological issue—considering that exclusion of theology-as-healing is one of the deployments of capitalism in distortion of human desire. As Bell argues:

> Where capitalism constitutes a veritable way of life that exercises dominion by capturing and distorting desire, resistance must take the form of an alternative way of life that counters capitalism by liberating and healing desire.[80]

For Bell, capitalism is the cause of the distortion of human desire, so the radical examination of capitalism has to be taken; otherwise, we may not be able to see any opportunity to change.

Applying Deleuze's theory of desire, Bell argues that the foundation of capitalism, sustaining the operation of the economic system of production and exchange, is the *production* of desire. Desire creates production. Desire is *productive* in sustaining the mode of production in operation. Although desire itself is not a mode of production, it is always produced in response to the specific needs of production.[81] In this sense, desire never waits passively for satisfaction but is in fact rather positive and active in

79. Bell, *Liberation Theology*, 119.
80. Bell, *Liberation Theology*, 72.
81. Bell, *Liberation Theology*, 33.

stimulation, motivation, and even production. Desire in capitalism is constantly territorialized to fulfill the purpose of capitalist production and comply with the principle of the market. Desire is not something to achieve or a desire for something. "Desire is not a matter of acquiring or grasping an object. It is not about possession."[82]

Desire is about a flow, a current to go, and a process of becoming. As Bell points out, the real predicament we face is that, due to the production of desire, we have already lost our capacity to envision a different form of desire within the confines of the capitalist system.[83] The distortion of desire has corrupted our mechanism of producing a desire to subvert the current reality—which "is constituted by desire, by dynamic flows of desire by an infinite multiplicity of becomings."[84] In this light, we can understand why, following Deleuze, Bell does not believe that human beings continue to have the capacity to desire justice and transformation if desire is wholly corrupted and distorted. When we realize how human beings have been formed as subjects who are incapable of creating political resistance, we may understand that "the political" is not about what we have. It is not an ethical decision. It has been involved in our being. As Deleuze says, "politics precedes being."[85]

By introducing Deleuze's theory of desire into the conversation, we may understand the difference between Sung and Bell. For Sung, mimetic desire is an invention of capitalism in contrast to basic needs as human nature. However, Bell insists that human desire is related to God's work and God's presence. From the medieval monastic tradition, such as Bernard of Clairvaux (1090-1153) and the Cistercians, Bell learns that human desire will not come to an end in heaven. This is because "we find a desire to penetrate deeper which is never quenched, yet which has no sense of unrest about it" in heaven.[86] It is different from the desire formed by capitalism, that desire in God is a kind of love and self-giving force—which comes both from God and from the perfect nature of humanity.

Bell recognizes the original nature of desire, unlike Sung, who arbitrarily defines desire as an illusive product of capitalism. In fact, human desire is not the result of a lack of need, nor has it come about because of human deficiency or the Fall. Instead, it results from "an excess," from abundance. It also comes from the fact that human beings are made in the

82. Bell, *Liberation Theology*, 14.

83. Bell, *Economy of Desire*, 42.

84. Bell, *Economy of Desire*, 42.

85. Bell, *Economy of Desire*, 40.

86. Bell, *Liberation Theology*, 90.

image of God. Hence, desire is not a sinful power. The nature of desire itself can be perfect and beautiful, even though the problem is that it usually lacks direction. Indeed, desire needs some ethical principle when its direction is misguided; for example, when desire is directed to seek joy and pleasure.[87] Desire needs to be redeemed and saved rather than abandoned. When human desire is redeemed, it means that the *chains* of capitalist production are interrupted. This interruption may then lead to political resistance, especially when human desire can be free from the restriction of the political that has been formed by the desire of capitalism.

Justice-Building and the Healing of Desire

Bell argues that the redemption of desire is the basis for the restoration of justice and righteousness. "Recognition of the bondage of desire is a prerequisite of 'sowing righteousness,' repentance, prayer, and works of mercy."[88] Only right and just desire can produce righteousness and justice because, as we have noted, desire is not merely about waiting but about shaping and creating. It also means that the potential for righteous action has to be based on motivation. Unless they are redeemed, these desires in captivity will not be able to produce goodness. Bell criticizes liberation theologians for getting the wrong end of the stick when they pay all their attention to "doing righteousness"—thereby missing the point of how righteousness can be produced. Like Sung's ethical concerns, they regard the exercise of justice as the routine application of a value or rule such as "respect human rights."[89] In Bell's view, seeking justice and righteousness turns out to be a series of "window-dressing" practices—which make their doings look righteous and good. But these practices will not be sustained because they do not have a proper root *in* motivation and desire. This kind of desire for justice and righteousness becomes the desire which tries to make things right, but this desire itself does not produce justice and righteousness.

So Bell's strongest criticism of Sung and other liberation theologians is that none of them can explain *how* people can be fully transformed to do justice and righteousness. Bell adds that they "lack sustained attention to the host of technologies of desire necessary for the formation of just persons."[90] This is the reason why Bell calls for a more radical action to build up the solid foundation of political resistance: If justice is produced by desire that has been

87. Bell, *Liberation Theology*, 91.
88. Bell, *Liberation Theology*, 95.
89. Bell, *Liberation Theology*, 124.
90. Bell, *Liberation Theology*, 124.

formed by unjust capitalism, how can this desire produce any justice that can challenge capitalism? If desire cannot be shaped in a just way, there can be no justice. The justice-building must begin with the formation of a more just form of desire. The radical practice of building justice has to go back to the basic practice of disciplining and directing desire. As Bell argues:

> The formation of just persons is not primarily a matter of getting their value right; it is a matter of redirecting desire, with all that involves, so that it flows the way just persons' desire flow.[91]

Bell points out the irony and the misleading concept of justice in liberation theology because what they propose has fitted perfectly into the ideology of capitalism—which introduces "justice" to protect the property and wealth of the rich and the middle class. This justice was designed to exclude the poor and their "rights." This concept of rights was also designed to assert rights over property to maintain the wealth of the owner of the property. Bell concludes that "rights were first and foremost about removing obstacles not to human fulfillment but to trade and commerce."[92] Hence, once we recognize that they have incorporated the agenda for the rich, the concepts of rights and justice are useless for supporting the poor and subverting capitalism.

God's justice must therefore be different from the justice formed by capitalism. Nor should the economy of God's work fit into any economic theory justifying capitalism. From the perspective of political and capital-ist economics, God's salvation is "unjust" because it is not based on any equal and free exchange between God and human beings in which human beings cannot do anything to achieve this salvation.[93] God's incarnation and salvation give grace to those who never deserve to receive. This giving, including God's self-giving, does not follow any logic of capitalism. Com-pared to the economics of capitalism and its concepts of justice and rights, God's economy of salvation contradicts market economics. This economy of God's salvation, in Bell's view, is *the politics of forgiveness*—which itself is the therapy of desire.[94]

What the economy of forgiveness can offer is different from the "jus-tice" that liberation theologians, revolutionaries, and social activists claim to offer. But as Milbank criticizes, they can only bring violence.[95] Because liberation theologians merely reverse the oppressive structure and turn

91. Bell, *Liberation Theology*, 124.
92. Bell, *Liberation Theology*, 126.
93. Bell, *Liberation Theology*, 131.
94. Bell, *Liberation Theology*, 144.
95. Milbank, *Theology and Social Theory*.

the oppressed into oppressors, the discontinued cycle of oppression creates more violence, instability, and internal conflict. Therefore, the solution is not reversion of oppressive structures but rather discontinuation of oppressive relationships. In Bell's view, this is the power of the politics of forgiveness. "Forgiveness renounces the power of violence to bring it into being. Recall that justice is transformed into terror when it is linked to the violence to enforce it."[96]

Forgiveness refuses to transfer suffering to others. It also means stopping the transfer of an oppressed state. It is aimed at creating a new relationship between the oppressors and the oppressed—which has nothing to do with *revenge*. Bell urges a forgiving relationship between the oppressed and the oppressor to become mutual and reciprocal: The oppressed no longer stay in the oppressed situation when they give the oppressors the gift of forgiveness; at the same time, the oppressors renounce "the option for the wealthy that characterized their previous lives" through an act of repentance.[97]

It is noteworthy that Bell does not mean that forgiveness no longer looks for justice. Based on the idea of capitalist economics, the politics of forgiveness might be accused of promoting a "cheap" action of forgiveness. This accusation is based on the distrust of forgiveness which does not require an exchange in revenge. It is also based on the assumption that justice can only be achieved when we can recognize "who has rights" and "how the rights can be distributed justly and equally." But these evaluations are not from the viewpoint of God but from human beings who want to be a judge, who can identify injustice and oppression, who can calculate "revenge" and "redemption" in an equal exchange. These concepts are all based on capitalism rather than the Christian faith.

Bell reminds us that justice and forgiveness are "two names of the single love of God that desires to draw humanity into communion." They both "share a single end—the return of all love, the sociality of all desire, in God."[98] In other words, justice and forgiveness can meet only when they both come to our desire in God—instead of our desire for doing justice. This again shows the danger of our action when we rush to find an ethical solution in bringing justice and peace for the sake of our judging viewpoint. As Bell points out, the wisdom of Anselm of Canterbury reveals an important message—which is that God's justice can be seen and fulfilled

96. Bell, *Liberation Theology*, 149.

97. Bell, *Liberation Theology*, 178.

98. Bell, *Liberation Theology*, 187–88.

in God's forgiveness.[99] This is because forgiveness produces justice and justice also includes forgiveness. Seeking justice has to be based on God's forgiveness—which human desire seeks.

This distinctive understanding of redeemed justice, provided by Bell, is about a relationship between God and human beings, rather than what people do or what righteous people do. The practice of redeemed justice is based on a group of people who have a relationship with God, rather than on an individual who fights for their rights but reproduces the injustice. Bell still believes that seeking justice is important for God's people. But the method is to live in God's forgiveness and generosity. As Bell argues:

> It [justice] seeks to maintain communion by fostering coop-
> eration in the pursuit of holiness, by nurturing solidarity in a
> common good much more substantial than anything modern
> rights language. (. . .) Redeemed justice is not a matter of
> protecting the rights of strangers but of nurturing the com-
> munion of saints.[100]

In Bell's view, God's people need to be liberated from the desire which transfers suffering to other oppressed groups, and which puts less trust in God's foreignness without any just and equal exchange. They need to be so faithful to God that they can discontinue their desire formed by capitalism and renew with desire for God's forgiveness. A desire for empowerment—which is achieved in terror and violence—must cease. A desire to receive God's forgiveness prevents God's people from replicating the secular notion of justice to protect their own advantages and rights. On the contrary, Bell urges God's people to be "crucified people."[101]

Those who accept the politics of forgiveness—which also means "the therapy of healing desire"—are crucified people whose desires are healed. Some people may be suspicious of whether acceptance of crucifixion might rationalize a ceaseless acceptance of suffering. According to Bell's clarification, though the therapy of forgiveness requires patience (due to the length of its process), it does not follow that forgiveness condones the suffering of crucified people.[102] This therapy of desire not only calls for social action but also restores and heals the nature of (human) beings at the ontological level. It is a strategy of breaking away and discontinuing the current structure of

---

99. Bell, *Liberation Theology*, 187–88.

100. Bell, *Liberation Theology*, 188.

101. Bell, *Liberation Theology*, 190.

102. Bell, *Liberation Theology*, 191.

desire in capitalism, which has formed us in such a way that we are not able to produce justice and righteousness.

In this sense, if having sin means turning away from goodness, this therapy of desire helps us to resist sin—through countering the desire that has established itself in us. It does so in the practice of generosity, hospitality, and embracing enemies.[103] Such practices do not adhere to the principle of the capitalist mode of desire, so the practice of disobedience has to fully rely on God's economy of salvation. This disobedience in our desire then creates powerful resistance to capitalism. As Bell states:

> Redemption entails our participation in the divine economy of ceaseless generosity and superabundance. The economy of salvation is about the healing of desire—the creative, filiative power of love—as it is taken up into the communion of charity that is the divine life.[104]

Accepting the therapy of desire (which restores our being at the onto-logical level) helps us to reflect on the nature of human beings and humanity. Bell points out that humans in our nature are "worshipping beings" (*Homo Adorans*) rather than "economic beings" (*Homo Economicus*). The deepest, most desirable thing to do is to worship the Christian God, who is generous, forgiving, and self-giving, rather than to worship money and power. Worshiping God cannot be real and honest until our desires are healed in forgiveness—which sets us free from being *Homo Economicus* and reshapes us as *Homo Adorans*. When this happens, our desire can lead us to worship God naturally rather than power and money. It will also be formed so as to forgive using God's mercy rather than to seek justice for the benefit of men's rights. Due to this ontological restoration of our desire and nature, the orientation of being will be redefined so as "to worship and enjoy the divine love that provides all that we need."[105]

Bell's solution shifts our focus from one of promoting social action on justice and rights to one of healing the nature of our ontological being and restoring our relationship with God. This is the most desirable end-state for all human beings to aspire to. (Unfortunately, the nature of being—perhaps the most fundamental issue of all—has not yet been properly explored by Sung and other liberation theologians and social theorists.) However, although Bell draws our attention to this primary issue, he raises a question about his ontological strategy: Is it too abstract and philosophical to

103. Bell, *Liberation Theology*, 191.

104. Bell, *Economy of Desire*, 153.

105. Bell, *Economy of Desire*, 168.

organize any real political resistance?[106] How can this ontological shift be related to any ethical and practical action? At the end of his book, *Liberation Theology after the End of History* (2001), Bell himself states:

> The therapy of desire that is forgiveness may fund resistance to capitalism. It may embody a crucified power that amounts to suffering against suffering. But how do we know if this is true?[107]

Bell's own answer to the question is, "No theory can verify it."[108] The answer seems to be humble, but it disappoints. Here I argue that it is not possible to separate an ontological argument from an ethical application because ethical practices have to be rooted in the foundation of an ontological concern. Thus, ontology eventually helps with ethical practices. In this sense, the dialogue between Jung Mo Sung and Daniel Bell, liberation theologies, and Radical Orthodoxy is necessary—because it may help Sung to find his ontological roots and help Bell to explore how ethical and political action can be taken.

An Ontological Concern and Its Ethical Applications

Sung and Bell are similar in that they both recognize the construction of human desire, as shaped by capitalism. But they focus on different levels. Briefly speaking, Sung takes an ethical approach whereas Bell takes an ontological approach. On the face of it, it seems that there is little common ground between them, particularly when one considers Bell's criticism of the whole methodology of liberation theologies upon which Sung's theology is based. However, I argue that the apparent separation of ontology and ethics is an illusion, because "what we do" corresponds to "who we are" and desire is the linkage between them.

I agree with Bell's refutation of the idea that the church and the state are separate, but I do not think it is necessary to refute all social theories in order to prioritize the significance of theology. The knowledge of the political, including social theory, and the knowledge of theology are not mutually exclusive of each other.[109] This is because they both provide different and complementary dimensions for the understanding of God's creation and order. That is, social theory and theology may use different languages and ways to describe what we see in God's creation, even though they both describe

---

106. Bell, *Liberation Theology*, 124.
107. Bell, *Liberation Theology*, 194.
108. Bell, *Liberation Theology*, 194.
109. See: Gill, *Theology in a Social Context*.

the same thing.[110] It is helpful when theology includes, or "cooperates" with social theories because this helps us to know *more* about God's creation, rather than diminishing the theological understanding of God. For example, theology points out the nature of human desire and what human desire "ought to" be in God's salvation and creation. Social theories then show what it means to be human in the contemporary context and how human desire is shaped and distorted by capitalism and oppressive structures. They both show different dimensions of God's work and creation and neither of them can lay claim to sole truth about God's work and creation.

There is another division, which needs to be overcome. When the only way to liberation is through proposing ethical transformation, as in Sung's theology, human desire cannot bring about any justice or righteousness if human desires have all been distorted. When the way to liberation is merely a means of understanding human beings at the ontological level, as in Bell's theology, it is also impossible to propose any social action of political resistance. Sung and Bell have both fallen into the divide between ontology and ethics, with the result that they cannot see the connection between ontological beings and ethical practices.

I argue that desire is the bridge between two levels of the human being. What desire produces depends on the nature of being, because our ontological being is not disconnected from our ethical practices. In this light, we can see how knowing about ourselves, called "subjectification" or "the practice of the self" by Foucault, can bring about political resistance. In my micro-political theology, I urge that a real transformation starts with the transformation of our "being" at the ontological level (which is the root of our human desire) and ends with a complete transformation of society and all ethical practices. This is because the ethical practice of liberation, which is motivated by redeemed desire, can only be assessed when the nature of human desire has been healed (in the sense of Bell's theology).

For example, this new co-relationship of ontology and ethics drives us to ask a deeper question: How can any individual who has been shaped by capitalism desire God? Human beings who are shaped by capitalism cannot sense or discern that they "should" worship God. They cannot even recognize that there is another god who is the most desirable and worthiest of worship. This is not an ethical question about what human beings "should" do.

110. Practical theologians and theologians concerned with ecclesiology and ethnography pay attention to the reality and context of the church. Their observations lead them to recognize the value of working with social theories as they believe that social theory and theology refer to the same reality but probably use different languages to describe it. See: Healy, *Church, World and the Christian Life*; Swinton and Mowat, *Practical Theology*.

It is an ontological question about what human beings can do when acting in accordance with their natural desire. This example shows how ontological transformation produces ethical change and how this ethical change must be based on the fundamental transformation in the ontological self.

Based on this, we can also draw Althaus-Reid into this conversation, as Indecent Theology also ignores the process of how perverted people are constructed by the heterosexual structure, thereby misrecognizing the relationship between the practices of perversion and the "becoming" of the perverted. Althaus-Reid cannot recognize the reality that all perversions simply consolidate the heterosexual structure eventually because these perverted have been constructed as excluded subjects who are incapable of subverting the heterosexual structure.

Perversions cannot subvert oppressive structures until perverted subjects can *discontinue* being constructed as the perverted by heterosexual structures. Here we can see why ontological transformation should be considered in Indecent theology. In this sense, Althaus-Reid's theology of sexuality is no different from Sung's theology of desire, because they both offer an ethical proposal about what the perverted and the poor *should* do as their way of resistance. In my view, by means of proposing the ethics of perversion, Althaus-Reid narrowly regards sexual desire and pleasure as something on which the perverted can play in indecenting social norms. She also fails to recognize that sexual desire and pleasure are driven not only by human nature but also by other power dominance (in Bell's sense).

In this chapter, I have shown the failure of political theologies of sexuality and desire in Marcella Althaus-Reid, Jung Mo Sung, and Daniel Bell. Each of them falls into the division of an ethical application and an ontological transformation, with the result that they cannot cope with a resistance of the oppressed to oppression. Based on this review of sexuality and desire in these political theologies, we have noticed that, although sexuality, desire, and subject are considered by these theologians as Foucault suggests, they do not follow Foucault's insights of sexuality and desire. Hence, in chapter 5, I will bring Foucault back into the discussion, to see how my proposal of a micro-political theology—which seriously considers the production and construction of sexuality and desire—may connect subjectification (ontological transformation) with political resistance (ethical practices).

5

Prayer, Asceticism, and Subjectification as Resistance

FOUCAULT'S THEORY OF POWER relationships draws our attention to desire, sexuality, and the body in relation to power and subjectification. (This was discussed in chapter 3). Then, in chapter 4, we examined what political theologies have so far done in terms of considering liberation in respect of sexuality, desire, and the body. But I argue that although Marcella Althaus-Reid, Jung Mo Sung, and Daniel Bell have incorporated sexuality or desire into theological consideration, they have all failed to consistently recognize the relationship between subjectification, resistance, and sexuality and desire. The result is theological divisions between them—one may proceed with an ethical approach to propose liberation movements while the other may develop their ontological arguments but without a clear political agenda.

In this chapter, I will reintroduce Foucault into constructing political theology as his insights will help us to find the "missing link"—which should connect the "knowledge of our sexuality and desire" with "our action of political resistance," as well as "ontological transformation" with "ethical practices." This missing link is *the practice of the self* (subjectification), which has been neglected by political theologians of sexuality and desire. And this practice of the self resonates with Christian spirituality, especially in the idea of *kenosis* (self-denial) and Ignatian practice of indifference. Based on Foucault's viewpoint, I argue that these Christian practices of spirituality themselves should be regarded as political resistance.

This chapter will explore—through Foucault's insight into subjectification—how the practice of spirituality itself can be political and subversive. The main sections focus on:

1. Foucault's concept of "political spirituality" (in comparison to "spiritual corporality"). This development will be explored to clarify his early

proposal in response to the Iranian Revolution and his later proposal on the idea of governmentality.

2. The confession of sin and the practice of asceticism in Foucault's political spirituality. They will be considered as two techniques of the self in the practice of subjectification.

3. Asceticism as political resistance (in contrast to sexual liberation). Based on this, Foucault's idea of asceticism can help us recognize the political of the spiritual practice in the Christian tradition.

4. The practice of indifference as an example of resistance. This will show how resistance to temptation is political.

Foucault's Political Spirituality

Before developing my argument about political spirituality, it is important to clarify some areas of confusion and dispute. This is because, when we come to connect political resistance with religious spirituality in Foucault's sense, we may suddenly come to his controversial comments on the Iranian Revolution of 1978/79 in relation to Shi'ite religious identity. Various groups across Marxist-Leninism, student movements, trade unions, and Islamic organizations attempted to overthrow Mohammad Reza Shah (the Pahlavi Dynasty). Surprisingly—in Foucault's eye—Iranians did not seek a secularized republican government, in the way the French Revolution did. Most people supported Ayatollah Khomeini (a Shi'ite leader) to create an Islamic state, with Islamic laws. From the Western viewpoint of secularization and liberalism, the Revolution was a "backward" revolution to a theocratic government.

In the middle of the Revolution, Foucault visited Tehran and wrote some journalistic articles for French audiences. His writings were later criticized for what critics perceived as his naïve and slanted observations. Edward Said criticized Foucault's Eurocentric application of his Western theoretical interests to explain a phenomenon taking place in a non-western society.[1] Behrooz Ghamari-Tabrizi fairly pointed out that Foucault's understanding of Shi'ite culture was not suited to articulating the Iranian context in the 1970s. Observations by Louis Massignon and Henry Corbin (two philosophical orientalists) were not reliable or "authentic" either.[2]

---

1. Said, "Michel Foucault," 9.

2. Ghamari-Tabrizi, *Foucault in Iran*, 73. Henry Corbin's interpretation of Islamic texts, which stresses the distinction between the "superficial exoteric meaning" and "the true, inner meaning" is problematic. It has been appropriated by Foucault in his analysis. See: Leezenberg, "Power and Political Spirituality," 107.

Another critic, Georg Stauth, maintained that Foucault simply used the role that Khomeini played in the Iranian Revolution to frame his "romantic" image that religion/spirituality can bring about social action and revolution. He could then "lecture" Marxists who regarded religion as "the opium of the people" that they are too materialist.[3] From these criticisms, we might understand why Foucault said "[religion] was the spirit of a world without a spirit."[4] Indeed, it proves that Foucault became, over time, more interested in and sympathetic to religion.

I agree with these criticisms of Foucault's evaluation of the Iranian Revolution. Foucault seemed obsessed with this new social-political phenomenon. His Eurocentric observations were almost unavoidable considering his writing context—which required him to present something to his French readership from the perspective of a French philosopher. The nature of his journalistic writing is primarily Eurocentric. On the other hand, as Michiel Leezenberg argues:

> He was clearly fascinated, and troubled, by this unprecedented assertion of a unified popular will. He may have underestimated Khomeini's political role, but none of his published writings express anything remotely like a blind admiration for Khomeini or an uncritical enthusiasm for the prospect of Islamic government.[5]

Foucault's voice to his French readers and to those who strictly insist on incorporating religious secularization into their political agenda of liberation was clear. The Iranian Revolution demonstrates the potential of religious involvement in the revolution, irrespective of whether or not it would be appropriated by a newly-created oppressive system. (As he constantly argues, nothing can permanently guarantee liberation or oppression because power is always dynamic and productive.)

In my view, Foucault's writings posed the challenge to the French left that, when they uncritically defined religion as an oppressive source, they were too blind to see how Shi'ite faith could be constructive in revolution to subvert the authority of the Shah of Iran. As Leezenberg highlights, the purpose of Foucault's writing was not to ignore the role of the state but to warn that "over-attention to sovereign power located in the state prevents us from looking for non-sovereign forms of powers exercised elsewhere."[6] As with all strategies of resistance, religion can be resistive, although such

3. Stauth, "Revolution in Spiritless Times," 259–80.

4. Foucault et al., "Iran," 218.

5. Leezenberg, "Power and Political Spirituality," 105.

6. Leezenberg, "Foucault and Iran," xxvii.

resistance might not be permanently sustained. For Foucault, maintaining and sustaining the political message of the Iranian people was achieved through demonstration. This "must be taken literally: a people was tirelessly *demonstrating* its will."[7] And this demonstration should not be divided by political groups but should *unite* the people beyond the division of political interests and their social classes.[8] Foucault goes on to say:

> There was in these demonstrations a link between collective action, religious ritual, and an expression of public right. (. . .) In the streets of Tehran there was an act, a political and juridical act, carried out collectively within religious rituals—an act of deposing the sovereign.[9]

I argue that, for Foucault, religion is no more resistive or less resistive than any other strategies deployed by revolutionary movements. It would be unwise to exclude the contribution of religion to political resistance in the first instance, due to the ideology of secularization. And it is also unwise to believe that the doctrine of Shia belief can be capable on its own of bringing about liberation in this one-off Revolution.[10] (Otherwise, if Shia Islam is "the" strategy of political resistance, Foucault would have promoted an Islamic political revolution in France.) Unlike other leftists who obsessively incorporate secularization into their agenda of liberation, Foucault certainly wants to re-evaluate religion in his agenda of political resistance, even though his attention inevitably comes back to his Western Christian roots.[11]

---

7. Foucault et al., "Iran," 216.

8. Foucault et al., "Iran," 219.

9. Foucault et al., "Iran," 216.

10. Foucault has clearly recognized that religion is not a solution either. See: Foucault, "Is It Useless," 133.

11. I appreciate Alain Beaulieu's insight on locating Foucault's writings on the Iranian Revolution (in 1978) in the middle of his 1977/1979 lectures—published as *Security, Territory, Population* and as *The Birth of Biopolitics*—and his essay on Kant and the Enlightenment (published as "What Is Critique?"). See: Beaulieu, "Towards a Liberal Utopia," 801–18. As Beaulieu argues, "Foucault's Iranian experience finally convinced him to look to the western tradition to find forgotten views of the improvement of the self as a first step leading to the transformation of others by the means of spiritual exercises" (815).

However, I disagree with Beaulieu's argument that Foucault is convinced by the consequence of the Iranian Revolution to believe that revolutions have nothing to do with spirituality or religion (811). If this was what Foucault thought, it would not make sense for him to develop his lecture on the Christian experience of sexuality and its technology of the self (in the 1980s), write volumes 2 and 3 of *The History of Sexuality*, and even explore more about Christian spirituality in volume 4.

Foucault's Political Spirituality in Development

Foucault revisits some potentials of political spirituality in the Western roots of Greco-Roman antiquity and Christianity. In his examination of other writings by Foucault on religion, Jeremy Carrette identifies two strands, which he terms *spiritual corporality* and *political spirituality*.[12] I find the notion of spiritual corporality very useful to distinguish Foucault's enthusiasm for the Iranian Revolution from his later development of the practice of the self.[13] They are not in a split relationship as Foucault explicitly appreciates the Shi'ite involvement in the revolution. However, he also recognizes that spiritual corporality *alone* is not enough in political resistance, based on the lesson he learned from the result of the Iranian Revolution.

I insist that Foucault attempts to expand his notion of political spirituality whilst continuing to include spiritual corporality. He may see both of them in a mutual critical relationship to avoid sliding into each of the extremes: One may simply believe in spiritual corporality bringing about political liberation, thereby forgetting that religion can be deployed by newly-created power (as we have seen in post-revolutionary Iran). The other may simply regard political spirituality as the practice of the self to construct their "apolitical" subjectivity and then misjudge religion as an "opium," which smooths over the revolution. I believe that if we want to keep spirituality politically resistive, Foucault would suggest not only maintaining this creative tension between spiritual corporality and political spirituality but also being vigilant to consider that neither side of religion can offer a "final" solution.

In this sense, political spirituality has something to offer when liberation theologians identify with the way in which Shi'ite believers participate in the revolution—because this is literally what liberation theologies have been doing (as we have discussed in chapter 2). Liberation theologies are expressive of spiritual corporality, which means that religion embodies itself

---

12. Carrette, *Foucault and Religion*, 139. Carrette argues that Foucault's "spirituality corporality" is distinctive from "spirituality corporeity" in Corbin's study of Islam, which assumes the dualism of body-spirit.

13. Carrette loosely defines that Foucault's notion of a spiritual corporality was more prevalent in his writings prior to 1976. But after 1976 Foucault paid more attention to Christianity, his religious emphasis changed. This resonated with another significant observation—that Foucault began exploring some materials about Christianity and probably in 1977 got a chance to read John Cassian. Based on this "discovery," the Christian pastorate is re-considered and introduced to his discussion with governmentality. And this consideration of Christianity is different from his former viewpoint on religion and from the time when he wrote *The History of Sexuality, Vol. 1*. See: Carrette, *Foucault and Religion*, 20, 135.

into politics and becomes a force of resistance. They are organized in solidarity to mobilize a change, listen to the suffering of oppressed people, and liberate them. This resonates with what Foucault said in 1979:

> It is through revolt that subjectivity (not that of great men but that of whomever) introduces itself into history and gives it the breath of life. A delinquent puts his life into the balance against absurd punishments; a madman can no longer accept confinement and the forfeiture of his rights; a people refuses the regime which oppresses it.[14]

Foucault no longer sees revolution a turning-upside-down of the structure. Instead, he sees an affirmation of the existence of oppressive systems and oppressed groups. This spiritual corporality is expressed well by Indecent Theology—which allows the excluded to be recognized, to speak, and to exist (as we have discussed in chapter 4). For Foucault, a *demonstration* by the people itself is important for every oppressed subject because it re-assures their existence when they assert their will and break their enforced silence.[15]

It is clear that Foucault emphasizes the perspective of spiritual corporality in his developing project of political spirituality. As Bernauer and Mahon suggest, one question that has become knotty for Foucault is, how should one have the capacity to develop a form of subjectivity which founds the basis for effective resistance to power?[16] Foucault's response to this question is expressed in his concern with the triangular relation of power-knowledge-subjectivity. The way to subvert power and construct subjectivity is to bespeak the oppressed subjects. Through the revolution, individuals achieve their liberty, which implies autonomy and the capacity of practicing liberty.[17] Liberation theologies and the participation of the Shia in the Iranian Revolution both embody the spiritual in political resistance, as expressions of spiritual corporality. Both have fulfilled their goal in political action of liberation. Both also perfectly *witness* the spirit of religion in the secularized world without a spirit.

However, it would be problematic or at least partial to focus only on spiritual corporality while trying to understand Foucault's political

14. Foucault, "Is It Useless," 133.

15. Foucault, "Is It Useless," 133–34. More interestingly, Judith Butler comes back to this idea of "demonstration as demonstrating the will of the people" she proposes her "performative theory of assembly." For example, Butler states "that enactment [exercising the freedom of assembly in which "we the people" is spoken] is performative inasmuch as it brings into being the people whom it names, or it calls upon them to gather under the utterance." Butler, *Notes toward*, 169.

16. Bernauer and Mahon, "Michel Foucault's Ecstatic Thinking," 147.

17. Bernauer and Mahon, "Michel Foucault's Ecstatic Thinking," 153.

spirituality. Firstly, neither the Iranian Revolution nor the efforts of liberation theologies have proved the limitation of spirituality corporality (in
chapter 3). In fact, Foucault constantly warns us not to rely on a moral
system of judging good/bad or defining oppression/liberty. We should not
over-trust any political engagement which attempts to promise to sort out
oppression. As William Connolly says, "a *politics of engagement and insur-
gency* often generalizes conflicts so that one set of concerns becomes over-
whelmed by others; it opens up the probability of more totalistic definitions
of one side by its opponents."[18] On the contrary, we are called to cultivate
an ethical sensibility (in Connolly's words)—which "applies tactics patiently
and experimentally to the self" and "affirms ambiguity and uncertainty in
the categories through which ethical judgment is made."[19]

Secondly, according to Carrette's insight, the focus on spiritual corporality alone ignores Foucault's discussion of *governmentality* (which has
become his primary concern after reflecting on his comments on political
spirituality in the Iranian Revolution) and his dual meanings of the word
"subject" (which constantly appears in Foucault writings).[20] Carrette argues that, based on Foucault's 1982 lecture series, the spiritual "involves a
transformation of the subject." Hence, it also means "the construction of
the subject through a series of power relations which shape life, the body,
and the self."[21] If everything has to be constituted within power relationships (as we have discussed in chapter 3), political spirituality should call
for an "active" response to power relationships, by allowing the subject to
create the self within power relationships instead of passively escaping and
liberating oneself from power.

From Confession to Asceticism in Political Resistance

If the practice of the self has already created a space for becoming the
self, then the practice of freedom should come from that space. The self-
constitution or self-determination in Foucault's sense is far from any autonomous idea of who we claim we are, or of will-power. The constitution
of the self means, in the process of subjectification, that the self can be
constructed not by knowledge power, but by the subject. This is the reason
why Foucault insists that governmentality must get involved in power-
knowledge-subjectivity relations. Governmentality is a strategy of taking

18. Connolly, "Beyond Good and Evil," 383 (emphasis in original).
19. Connolly, "Beyond Good and Evil," 383.
20. Carrette, *Foucault and Religion*, 138.
21. Carrette, *Foucault and Religion*, 136.

back the control of the self, through firstly allowing the self to be governed by the subject *in advance of* a re-arrangement of the relationships between the subject of the self and other powers.

In his broader project of *The History of Sexuality* and *On the Government of the Living* we can observe the motivation underlying Foucault's exploration of some examples of techniques of the self from Greco-Roman antiquity and Christianity. Foucault clearly notices the connection between the structure of political authority and the spiritual direction of the pastoral. For Foucault, the "combination of the development of an administrative political power and a whole series of institutions of spiritual direction, of the direction of souls and individuals, again both Protestant and Catholic" is evident, though their "forms" might be heterogeneous.[22] As Colin Gordon recognizes, there is always a connection between techniques of direction and soteriology in the Western political domain.[23]

These techniques of the self (or the practice of the self) should be considered as Foucault's extension of "political spirituality" while re-evaluating his comments on the Iranian Revolution and his critique of spiritual corporality. Considering a mutual critical relationship between spiritual corporality and political spirituality in his post-Iranian Revolution context, the technology of the self—involving all kinds of spiritual and sexual practices—should definitely be regarded as his political spirituality, which is fully political and fully spiritual.

The Confession of the Self as Subjectification

We should not forget that Foucault's practice of freedom is part of his response to the theory of the state and power dominance (see the discussion in chapter 3). Foucault's exploration of the Christian pastorate demonstrates the potential of the practice of freedom. Although Foucault may not be interested in the Christian faith, he is interested in Christian pastoral *techniques* themselves, and what they may offer in political resistance. (But of course, the other side of the coin is that these pastoral techniques can be part of oppression and dominance.) In this sense, these pastoral techniques show two sides of subjectification: the subjugation of others and the subject's constitution of the self.

Foucault's first stage of exploring Christian pastorates is *confession*, which is about telling the truth (*parrhesia*) about faith and self. Foucault states that "Christianity is, at the fundamental level, a religion of confession,

22. Foucault, *On the Government*, 232.
23. Gordon, "Christian Art," 262.

to the extent that confession (*confession*) is the hinge of the regime of faith and the regime of confession of self (*aveu*)."[24] Foucault argues that Christianity used to be recognized "merely" as the confession of faith (dogma and non-reflective truth acts), and as ideology. For him, this misrecognition fails to see the other meaning of "confession," which is about the self. Foucault then argues that the act of Christianity itself is the confession of self—which, for Christians, is about a "continuous relationship to themselves of knowledge," about their obligation to discover secrets that elude them, and about their obligation to manifest these secret and individual truths.[25]

In this sense, telling the truth in Christianity is not just telling the "Truth" of God in the confession of faith—but also telling the truth of the self in the confession of sin. The self to be confessed is not even based on behaviors and practices. As an Anglican penitential prayer says:

> We confess that we have sinned against you in thought, word, and deed, by what we have done, and by what we have left undone. We have not loved you with our whole heart; we have not loved our neighbors as ourselves. (. . .)[26]

Repentance for Christians is confessing what they have done and how they have erred against God's commandments. It is confessing these things which are not yet even done, or which will not be done. Repentance scrutinizes the self on behaviors as well as what is in minds, orientations, and motivations (including what the penitent love, how much they love and what they have not yet loved). The confession of the self even involves that identity of the self which is not yet disclosed.

Hence, Foucault argues that the whole regime of truth in Christianity is not around the act of faith (the proclamation of faith)—but the act of confession (the manifestation of sinful self).[27] Foucault further points out that: "The penitent is expected not so much to "tell the truth" ["*dire le vrai*"] concerning what he did as to "do the truth" ["*faire vrai*"] by manifesting what he is."[28] From the perspective of power relationships, government of Christianity is not about controlling what people confess in what they say. It is about constructing and practicing the subject who is obligated to disclose what they have done and left undone—the secret truth of the self. By means of the techniques of confession, the subject (who verbalizes the truth of oneself)

24. Foucault, *On the Government*, 84.
25. Foucault, *On the Government*, 83.
26. The Episcopal Church, *Book of Common Prayer*.
27. Foucault, *On the Government*, 83-84.
28. Foucault, *History of Sexuality*, 4:97.

is becoming the self (who is a sinner). This self is manifested, expressed, and recognized in subjectification. Or in Foucault's words, the act of confession is "the practice of the self" because the self is manifested in the process of subjectification.[29] We should clarify the relationship between the self and act in accordance with Foucault's practice of the self. As Carrette points out, Foucault is seemingly inclined to propose an "expressionist" theology when he puts emphasis on the obligation ("you have to") and on the demand to "show yourself." This kind of "expressionist theology" founds the basis for truth-subjectivity in the Western context. But in Foucault's thinking, it does not mean that an "interiority" of the self is assumed to be "waiting to be discovered and brought out."[30] His understanding of expression is not in the Augustinian sense of outward signs and inner grace, or of external manifestations and internal states.[31] For Foucault, the self and truth are *produced* rather than retrieved in practice.[32] Expression is about *politics* rather than self-performance. (This resonates with Foucault's analysis of power relationships—which relies heavily on recognition and expression—as he emphasizes that power is created in display only when it is resisted.)

Furthermore, we can see that, due to the "power" of the techniques of penitence, the self is constituted as a sinful subject who is required to repent. This subject of the self is manifested in their disclosure of sin, in their examination of the self, and in their expression of repentance. This repentant self is contradictive to a "positive" image of the self which is shaped by contemporary culture. It is not the self—which can be expressed in doing something great for the sake of liberality, autonomy, and empowerment. On the contrary, it may surprise many people that, for Foucault, the self is manifested in confession of sin and in the subjugation of self to others—from which the subject becomes the self.

Foucault's Move-on from the Confession of Sin

The confession of sin demonstrates how subjugation to others manifests the self—instead of demonstrating how the subject constitutes the self. This is

29. Disappointingly, Philippe Büttgen argues that the confession of faith is replaced by the confession of self but what Foucault means in the confession of self is *not* the confession of sin. See: Büttgen, "Foucault's Concept of Confession." But I do not agree with Büttgen's interpretation. In my view, Foucault might not be interested in Christian faith, but he certainly was interested in analyzing Christian confession of the self as his example of the techniques of the self.

30. Carrette, "'Spiritual Gymnastics,'" 282.

31. Carrette, "'Spiritual Gymnastics,'" 283–84.

32. Foucault, *On the Government*, 308–9.

because the practice of penitence merely shows the relationship between subjectivity and knowledge. For example, the subject of a "confessant" is constructed by the knowledge of the self (in committing one's sin) and by the knowledge given by another (in forgiving one's sin). For Foucault, this confessant is like a mad person, a prisoner, and a sexualized person. They all find their subjectivity—by means of subjugation to such fields of knowledge as psychiatry, law, and the science of sexuality—when they confess their thoughts of madness, undisciplined behavior, and the secret truth of their sexual life. Foucault discovers that this technique of government of the self—which is from external knowledge but works on the physical and spiritual self—can be traced back to the Christian pastorate. The same pattern of the technique of governing the self in various forms of confession can be observed throughout Western history.

However, Foucault does not stop at the confession of sin, which is at the level of subjugating oneself to others and to knowledge. Otherwise, he would have been satisfied with sexual liberation in which subjectification is found in sexualizing the self. Confessing sin is just the *first* step towards knowing the truth of the self. More fundamentally, the second step is to prevent the self from sinning again. This then leads Foucault to explore a more basic issue, which is how *not* to sin. If sinning allows power to be involved in controlling the subject by creating knowledge—which not only constructs a sinful self but obligates this self to confess their sin—the radical way of resistance is to put the self under the subject's control by means of *not* committing sin. This resonates with Foucault's critique of sexual liberation. The way for the subject to not be sexualized is to not talk about their sexuality or to not fully obey the instruction of sexual liberation. It is better not to give the science of sexuality any opportunity to sexualize the self.

In other words, when the self is constituted by the subject as a not-to-sin self, the subject is temporarily free from that power relationship. (It is not permanent of course if we consider a power relationship to be always created and dynamic when resistance creates.) As Foucault himself states:

> If there is a subjectification, it implies an indefinite objectification of oneself by oneself—indefinite in the sense that, never acquired once and for all, it has no end in time; and in the sense that one must always push one's examination of thoughts as far as possible.[33]

Foucault realizes that practicing the examination of the self and one's thoughts should be required as often as possible. This is because it is primary to act to

---

33. Foucault, *History of Sexuality*, 4:189.

prevent oneself sinning and it is secondary to respond in a confession of the done sin. If a sin confessant attempts to be free from being constructed, it is better to take the initiative of dealing with the knowledge of the self rather than to wait until construction takes place in the confession of sin.

Foucault continues to explore the techniques of self in Christianity. Foucault notices that the writings of Augustine of Hippo (354–430) have suggested taking radical action to draw the confession of the sinful self to a deeper level of controlling the self in order *not* to sin.[34] For Augustine, it is not just about what confessants have done in their body, but what they have *thought* in their mind and spirit. The corruption of the human mind began with Adam's "original sin." Since Adam wanted to gain his own will and escape from God's will, he lost control of himself as well as control of his body.[35] Foucault argues that the reason why Adam covered his genitals with a fig leaf was not that he was ashamed of recognizing himself as a sexualized being—but because his sexual organ was moving out of his control without his consent.[36] Adam could not control his genitals.

Thanks to Augustine, the knowledge of the self in confession is no longer about knowing the self as a sexualized being. It is more about the sin of the self who cannot control their body and sexuality. For Augustine, sex in *erection* is "the image of man revolted against God."[37] Foucault then concludes that "the arrogance of sex is the punishment and consequence of the arrogance of man. His uncontrolled sex is the same as what he himself has been towards God—a rebel."[38] The issue of confession turns to be the question of whether the self is under control.

After reading Augustine, Foucault turns his concern to *desire* or libido to reflect on how the self can be controlled. Desire is regarded as a key "valve"—which may control the flow of sexuality and orientate the behaviors of sinning or *not*; hence, the control of desire may help the subject to take back control of the self. Again, according to Augustine, desire (libido) is a core issue of free will particularly when human will has gone beyond

34. Foucault has his interpretations of Augustine and other Christian writings, which do not necessarily comply with orthodox understanding in Christian theology. But I do not think this is what Foucault is concerned with. I argue that his reading of Augustine's and other Patristic works is "genealogical" because he reads them to interpret the present and to understand the techniques of governing the self in Christian tradition. For Foucault, the point might not be what Augustine really said but those Augustinian ideas that have been received into Christianity and Western society.

35. Foucault, "Sexuality and Solitude," 185–86.

36. Foucault, "Sexuality and Solitude," 186.

37. Foucault, "Sexuality and Solitude," 186.

38. Foucault, "Sexuality and Solitude," 186.

God's providence.[39] Foucault then argues that a technique of the self to govern desire *cannot* be found in re-claiming what we have known about desire and in an attempt to put desire into an order originally created by God.[40] We reviewed this kind of technique in chapter 4—Althaus-Reid, Sung, and Bell all wanted to show how desire works well in God's original plan so their strategies are just putting our desire into a proper order (indecent or decent). However, in terms of assuming the potential of desire in God's order, Foucault is "ironically" more of a realistic than these Christian theologians, recognizing that desire primarily comes from human rebels. Due to its nature, desire is uncontrolled or uncontrollable.

How desire has been involved in our thoughts and behaviors is, in this sense, something which should be understood, interpreted, examined, and discerned in the technique of the self to govern desire. In Foucault's words, these techniques of governing desire, or "the means of the spiritual struggles against libido" are the exercises which require "turning our eyes continuously downwards or inwards to *decipher*, among the movements of the soul, which ones come from the libido."[41] Revealing the rule to comply with would not automatically lead desire onto the "right" track. What can possibly control desire is constant monitoring of the orientation and flow of desire, rather than showing how it ought to be performed. It is similar to a valve because the function of a valve is not to change the whole pipe system or to lead the water in another direction. What a valve can do is to control the volume of the water-flow and when it is allowed to flow. Through reading Augustine's writings, Foucault figures out that we cannot control ourselves in such a way as to eliminate desire. But the control of desire is fundamental to the government of the self. This is the next step for Foucault in the process of techniques of the self because the confession of sin to others is not sufficient.

Foucault's Turn to Asceticism

Following this journey of exploration, we should not be surprised by the controversial fact that Foucault moved on to think about *asceticism* after reading the writings of John Cassian (360-435). Cassian was a monk who brought the ideas and practices of Christian monasticism to Western Christianity. Here Foucault distinguishes *continence* from *asceticism* because continence merely applies the principle of abstinence to prohibit

39. Foucault, "Sexuality and Solitude," 186.
40. Foucault, "Sexuality and Solitude," 186.
41. Foucault, "Sexuality and Solitude," 186 (emphasis added).

sexual desire.[42] But asceticism is about monastic living in chastity and virginity. It is "the life of perfection, or of working at perfection, it is the way towards a perfect life."[43] As Bernard Harcourt notes, "by contrast to ancient Greek notions of continence and abstinence that are merely repressive, the idea of chastity is a positive force that gives rise to the concepts of the soul and body, and relations to self."[44]

Seeking asceticism means that Foucault is concerned with an action of cultivating the self instead of an action of eliminating desire. The ultimate purpose of controlling desire is to transform the self to be indifferent to sexual desire. Henceforth, the subject does not need to reject temptations because one becomes in no way bothered, distracted, or seduced by sexual desire. Reaching this level of the techniques of the self, the subject does not need to take any action against desire since desire has no *power* over the subject of the self.

As Foucault has been considered as a pioneer of sexual liberation, it is conflicting to see Foucault embracing and encouraging chastity and asceticism. But it should not be unexpected, for three reasons which consistently follow.

Firstly, Foucault does not consider repression to be opposite to liberation. But equally, he does not embrace repression as his way of liberation. Movements with or without repression are related to pleasure. Considering his spiral of power and pleasure (See chapter 3), continence merely creates more sexual desire—because the more sexual desire is repressed in the practice of continence, the more pleasure is created. Continence, which stimulates the spiral of power and pleasure, will make desire more uncontrolled rather than bring it under control. (This is like trying to block the flow of water from a tap with hands—the water finds a way of getting around the hands.) Hence, as Foucault says:

> Compared to these stresses of continence, chastity appears to be an end state in which one would no longer have to combat "the urge of carnal concupiscence"; then, and only then, the soul can become "the dwelling place of the Lord," which is never in "the battles of continence."[45]

In this sense, we can understand why chastity is proposed by Foucault as the strategy for responding to sexual liberation. We should be clear that Foucault

42. Foucault, *History of Sexuality*, 4:116.
43. Foucault, *On the Government*, 260.
44. Harcourt, "Foucault's Keystone," 63.
45. Foucault, *History of Sexuality*, 4:167.

supports sexual liberation for creating the freedom of choices of human sexuality. But he is always reserved about unrestrained freedom of action—which contradicts his idea of *ethical* freedom of practice (which demands the freedom *not* to act). He is also cautious about the expression and confession of sexuality and its relationship with knowledge-power. Therefore, we should not be surprised by his intention to go beyond sexual liberation and his eventual discovery of chastity and asceticism.

Secondly, Foucault wants to find the practice of *philosophy*, which means "a way of life" and "a way of existing in the world, which should be practiced at each instant and which should transform all of life."[46] He has found some possibilities for cultivating the self in Greco-Roman culture. For example, it is "ethical" for a man to lie down with a young and beautiful boy if he can control himself not to touch the boy. This is not because this man does not have any desire which comes out in his mind and thought. Rather, it is because his self-control and choice not to touch the boy have proved that he cultivates and masters himself well. He is an ethical man. Being ethical is not incompatible with the desire to touch the boy—he can *control* himself. In this sense, being ethical does not put desire under control, but the self. Desire continues to seduce and tempt an ethical man. The behavior is under control because it is not mastered by desire, thanks to the cultivation of the self. In other words, the demonstration of ethics is through control of behaviors and rejection of temptation. It is not concerned with mastery over desire.

Continuing to explore the techniques of the self, Foucault finds that Cassian offers something which is even *more* ethical than the practice of Greco-Roman men. In Cassian's writings, Christian techniques of the self go deeper into the level of controlling the *emergence* of desire rather than controlling the self. The Greco-Roman practice of being ethical is not enough or radical at all. Foucault explains that:

> A monk was really chaste when no impure image occurred in his mind, even during the night, even during dreams. The criterion of purity does not consist in keeping control of oneself even in the presence of the most desirable people: it consists in discovering the truth in myself and defeating the illusions in myself, in cutting out the images and thoughts my mind continuously produces. Hence the axis of the spiritual struggle against impurity.[47]

46. Davidson, "Ethics as Ascetics," 123.
47. Foucault, "Sexuality and Solitude," 187.

Cassian urges "real purity," instead of continence or repression, because the way to cultivate the self should not stay at the level of rejecting temptation or desire. The cultivation of the self should include the orientation of desire. The former technique is passive because it merely cultivates the self in *constant rejection* of being driven by sexual desire. But the latter one is more active because it truly masters the self in *dissociation* with sexual desire.[48] Foucault believes that chastity, instead of continence, is a radical method of self-mastery. Hence, because of ascetic practices, "we are now far away from the rationing of pleasure and its strict limitation to permissible actions."[49] Foucault adds:

> But what does concern us is a never-ending struggle over the movements of our thoughts (whether they extend or reflect those of our body, or whether they motivate them), over its simplest manifestations, over the factors that can activate it. The aim is that the subject should never be affected in his effort by the obscurest or the most seemingly "unwilled" presence of will.[50]

Finally, the practice of chastity for Foucault is not a higher moral principle that we should comply with. Foucault's concept of ethics has nothing to do with a right-wrong decision. It is always about living a life of wholeness in practice. Through clarifying the difference between chastity and continence, an ascetic practice should be considered as the freedom of the practice of the self rather than a "code of permitted and forbidden acts."[51] It is noteworthy that the confession of the self is not replaced with ascetic practice. On the contrary, the confession of the self with other techniques of the self is incorporated into the practice of asceticism. According to his explanation:

> [The involvement of asceticism] is a whole technique for monitoring, analyzing, and diagnosing thought, its origin, its qualities, its danger, its power of seduction, and all the dark forces that may hide beneath the appearance it presents.[52]

Foucault regards this ascetic practice as one side of subjectification (in *The Confessions of the Flesh*).[53] I argue that asceticism can also be seen as part of the government of the self (in *1977-78 Lectures at the Collège de France*), a

48. Foucault, "Battle for Chastity," 193.

49. Foucault, "Battle for Chastity," 193.

50. Foucault, "Battle for Chastity," 193.

51. Foucault, *History of Sexuality*, 4:188.

52. Foucault, *History of Sexuality*, 4:188.

53. Foucault, *History of Sexuality*, 4:189.

process of the hermeneutics of the self (in *1980 Lectures at Dartmouth College*), and a form of cultivation of the self (in *The Care of the Self*). Asceticism is not to ensure compliance with sexual ethics. Rather, it is about how the subject can govern the self to create a space—which may be offered by the practice of freedom.[54] In this sense, Foucault connects self-transformation with political resistance. If we use the language of the dialogue between Liberation Theology and Radical Orthodoxy (in chapter 4), it is a connection between ontological formation of the self and ethical practice in resistance.

Sexual Liberation and Asceticism in Political Resistance

Why does ascetic practice matter for political resistance? I argue that according to Foucault's exploration of power analysis, resistance must come from self-mastery, such as ascetic practice rather than sexual liberation. It is not a straightforward answer that we can find in Foucault's writings from the beginning. I consider the development of Foucault's analysis of power to be his journey of chipping away at the dynamic deployments of power relationships, through analyzing different forms of dominance and power relationships. Foucault did not know what he would discover at the beginning of his project of *The History of Sexuality*. He did not know where we may find the basis for political resistance or what the alternative action to liberation might turn out to be. (It is evident that he changed his writing proposal while exploring the issue and considering his reflections on the Iranian Revolution.) However, I argue that in terms of extending his discussion of political spirituality, Foucault has found *subjectification* as his alternative strategy to a Marxist sense of liberation. What asceticism offers Foucault is a *strategy* of resistance—in which the self is constituted by the subject to be an ethical being who can be indifferent to sexual desire. The strategy is definitely not in compliance with sexual ethics to repress desire.

Foucault's conversion to the practice of the self may be criticized as abstract, apolitical, and too "philosophical." However, considering his rationale (discussed in chapter 3), it may make more sense for his strategy to work closely alongside his analysis of power. As we have noted, Foucault is not satisfied with the Marxist understanding of repression and dominance, which over-relies on structural analysis and the theory of the State. He does not think liberation is possible or that it has any future because a power-free zone is not attainable. He insists that every relationship and resistance creates new power relationships, so we should consider power deployments in the forms both of government (from external apparatuses) and governmentality

54. Foucault, "Battle for Chastity," 193.

(of the self). This is the foundation of Foucault's reconsideration of political resistance. And it must be different from liberation, which fails to recognize in subjectification a form of governing the self.

Although Foucault seemingly fails to justify how religious piety can be a power strategy of political resistance in the case of the Iranian Revolution, some anthropologists of Islam provide some complementary examples of "spiritual corporality." Saba Mahmood offers a compelling example of a woman's piety movement in Cairo, Egypt between 1995 and 1997 to counter the "secularization" of Egyptian society.[55] She argues that the subjectivity of these Muslim women can be constructed by means of practicing Islamic virtue—including the "proper" acts of worship and the "decent" expression of piety. Pious Muslim women gain their subjectivity through being subjugated to pious Islamic faith as well as in the bodily practice of liturgy.

Exemplifying the ritual practice of morning prayer, Mahmood shows that the repeated practices, for securing God's pleasure, strengthen the pious women to obey God's will. This results in a pious self being created and constructed through the techniques of cultivating pious desire.[56] Through the lens of Foucault's idea of subjectification and the cultivation of the self, Mahmood highlights—in shaping a docile body—that the subjectivity of pious Muslim women can be constituted in virtuous techniques of the self. This challenges Western liberal assumptions of freedom and agency.[57]

However, I argue that Mahmood's interpretation of Foucault's subjectification, in terms of the Egyptian political context, can be problematic. A piety movement can easily fit into the agenda of secularization when it leads to voluntarily withdrawing religion from politics—due to its "disobedience" to secularization. On the other hand, Mahmood redeems agency and subjectivity of pious Muslim women, but she misrecognizes how pious spirituality dissociates itself from political resistance when their sectarian movement becomes "apolitical" in opposition to secular politics. In my view, Mahmood's conclusion—that Muslim women do not need western feminist liberation because they have found their agency and subjectivity—results from the key linkage between subjectification and resistance.[58]

55. Mahmood, *Politics of Piety*.

56. Mahmood, *Politics of Piety*, 124–26.

57. Mahmood, "Feminist Theory," 202–36; Mahmood, *Politics of Piety*, 15.

58. Rachel Rinaldo thinks that agency and piety may have different ways to balance and express within the Muslim female community. So, she proposes two other modes of agency: "pious critical agency" and "pious activating agency" to enlarge Mahmood's notion of "pious docile agency." See: Rinaldo, *Mobilizing Piety*. The issue of piety and politics is particularly relevant in the context of wearing the veil in Indonesia. Also see: Smith-Hefner, "Javanese Women," 7.

She fails to present how new power relationships can be created by pious women in their techniques of the pious self. If Foucault is right about becoming an ethical subject, the government of the self is inseparable from the government of others. The self does not, then, have to find autonomy in Kant's sense or in the Western sense of liberty. At this point, Mahmood neglects the significant role of governing others in creating new power relationships, thereby failing to recognize the relationship between agency and the practice of freedom, and between subjectification and resistance. In this sense, the politics of piety itself becomes the termination of Muslim women when their docile body is produced for pious disciplines rather than the fruit of the techniques of the self.[59]

Foucault regards freedom as a practice (in the process of subjectification) rather than a status. If the status of freedom is fixed, it will be vulnerable to manipulation by new deployments of power relationships. In other words, keeping freedom as flexible and agile as possible is the best response to all newly created power relationships. Sexual liberation is a typical case, showing how the fruit of liberation is suppressed and hijacked by new deployments of power dominance. Foucault's early research on the excluded also demonstrates how the subject is constructed by knowledge. Mad subjects are defined by psychiatry. Sexualized subjects are constructed by the science of sexuality. These cases are Foucault's example of one-dimensional subjectification—in which the subject is constructed by subjugation in a passive way.

Foucault is excited by the idea of political spirituality that is developed in the light of his reflections on the Iranian Revolution. He is awakened to the subversiveness of religion (considering religion has been seen as a symbol of subjugation for French secularized intellectuals). He believes that the spiritual has something to do with the other side of subjectification—self-mastery—in which the subject actively constitutes an ethical self. This idea is proved by his exploration of Greco-Roman culture and Christianity in his project of the History of Sexuality. There are two techniques of the Christian self—one is confession of faith and self, and the other one is the ascetic practice of controlling desire.

I contend that it is Foucault's turning point in response to sexual liberation. Becoming a sexualized subject is like becoming a Christian in confession because the self is constructed with the obligation to explore and tell the truth about their sexuality. The subject is indeed constructed by the

---

59. I argue that if we cannot distinguish discipline from the techniques of the self, we may not be able to recognize the difference between repression and self-mastery. For Foucault, the experience of prisoners who are disciplined to have docile bodies is *not* identical to the practice of the technique of self.

knowledge of the self but at the same time, the process of articulating their sexuality to others re-introduces them into new deployments of power relationships. This explains why Foucault is not convinced that sexual liberation brings about the practice of freedom—demonstrated in giving freedom to choose to do and/or not to do. Sexual liberation merely offers freedom-as-status, in which sexualized subjects are subjected to others in obligation. In Foucault's exploration, an alternative to sexual liberation can be found in asceticism—which demands a practice of freedom *not* to be driven or controlled by desire—if the self is cultivated to become ethical in control over the self as well as desire. For Foucault, asceticism demonstrates real freedom of choice because the subject is free from obligation.

More importantly, asceticism is a practice of political resistance to the constitution of a sexualized self. On the one hand, by means of asceticism, the subject takes its initiative in constituting the self *not* to be sexualized. Self-mastery becomes a strategy of disallowing the self to be constituted by others. On the other hand, asceticism rejects what sexual liberation serves behind subjectification—which is capitalism. As Foucault has remarked, population in increase is a crucial issue for capitalism, so sexuality has been manipulated to maintain future availability of labor. The political action in asceticism is straightforward in its denial of compliance with the agenda of capitalism, which is served by constructing sexualized subjects.

Following the same logic, seeking chastity is not about repression of sexual acts and desire—it is about political resistance in which freedom of choice is created by means of controlling desire. Chastity creates a political space that is excluded by sexual liberation and capitalism when choosing *not* to be sexualized becomes a practical option. In all probably Foucault was fascinated by the fact that his idea of political resistance was shared by Cassin, a fifth century monk, who "apocalyptically" pointed out how fornication is coupled with greed. Foucault may also agree with Cassin's suggestion—which is "the ascetic of fasting."[60]

Christian Spirituality as Political Resistance

If Foucault's project of exploration in *The History of Sexuality* is to discover an alternative strategy to liberation that turns upside down the repressive structure of sexuality, I argue that he has found it in the practice of asceticism. This is because sexual liberation (in his understanding) remains in the model of subjectification in truth-telling. Foucault has shown that this knowledge-subjectivity has a long history in Western culture. The subject

60. Foucault, "Battle for Chastity," 189.

is constructed as a sinner in their *confession* of sin, as a mad person in their *confession* to psychiatrists, and a sexualized person in their *confession* of sexuality. If being a sinner, mad and sexualized fully rely on knowledge and *confessions* (albeit expressive of various forms), these forms of liberation as a reversion of the oppression fail to really subvert oppression. In other words, even after reversing oppressive structures, this structure is consolidated instead of banished, because hegemony relies on the existence of counter-hegemony.

More significantly, oppressive structure is maintained by the practices of the subjects who have been constructed by this oppression—irrespective of whether what they do is directly against or in support of the structure. Applying Althaus-Reid's theological language, indecent theology in fact consolidates decent theology. Although the practice of perversion, resonated with the practice of sexual liberation, seems to challenge heterosexuality and decency, the existence of the perverted (constructed by heterosexuality) promises the authority and normalization of decent theology. Dominance paradoxically depends on the emergence of liberation, if liberation simply means counter-dominance.

How can we subvert dominance and oppression? This question is Foucault's "anxiety," if I can so describe it. If we can understand the predicament with which Foucault tries to grapple, we may come to know why he must rule out the possibility of finding resistance in any forms of liberation and counter-dominance without considering the process of subjectification. He holds faith in the certainty that resistance exists outside the box, which presumes a binary opposition. If the subject has been constructed by knowledge and in any other power relationship, the way of retrieving their freedom and resistance is to construct the self *by* oneself. If the subject cannot get away from a power relationship, he or she should actively and constantly create new power relationships. In this way, the subject should not passively accept their constitution or negatively respond to social structure in liberation. Foucault calls for an *active engagement* with power relationships. The subject should act in an *initiative* way—in order to respond to existent power and even to create power relationships—as he believes resistance always goes before newly created power relationships.

We may question how seriously Foucault considers Christian faith. However, in my view, Foucault has offered plenty of insights into religious practice and political resistance for political theologians (especially for liberation theologians). He reminds liberation theologians that religion—which calls for action and participates in political revolution—was a powerful factor in the Iranian Revolution, but not the whole story. Religion in politics even runs a risk of immerging into an ideology that is easily manipulated by the newly created power relationships. In other words, what spiritual corporality can offer is limited. What we are looking for in coping with the dynamic creation of power relationships is *political spirituality*, including the governmentality of the self. Foucault has talked a great deal about the "political." While analyzing the different forms of power and subjectification in the Western history of Greco-Roman and Christianity, he has demonstrated some elementary but useful resources. As a theologian, my aim is to continue his exploration in Christian "spirituality" to show how the practice of spirituality *itself* is fully political.

An Example: *Indifference* in Ignatian Spirituality

What Foucault means by "chastity" is certainly not the stigmatization of sexuality and desire. Chastity should be understood as a practice of not being dominated by sexuality—which is driven by a *blind* attitude toward "sexual liberation." Chastity is not a sexual ethic to comply with but a practice of resistance. Based on this, I argue that Foucault's proposal of chastity resonates with some spiritual practices in Christianity. One example is the Ignatian practice of indifference. We might be surprised to discover that Foucault actually collaborates well with Ignatius of Loyola (1491–1556).

Desire as the Motion of the Self in God

In his *Spiritual Exercises*,[61] Ignatius pays a lot of attention to human desire and its relationship with the self. Like Foucault, Ignatius does not regard the self as an autonomous and self-contained being—but a being-in-motion and a being-within-the-environment. The self can be recognized only when one is in action and one discerns its relationship with the environment in which one is situated. The understanding of the self is therefore a question of what we perceive about our movement, instead of a metaphysical question of who we are. The first example suggested by Ignatius is discernment of the surrounding environment in retreat because our physical location and feelings matter in knowing the self. We cannot know the subject independently (who we are) by means of fully focusing on the self.

> If we desire to experience pain, sorrow, and fear for our sins, any thought of happiness or joy will be an impediment. . . . For the same purpose, I will deprive myself of all light, by closing

---

61. Ignatius, *Spiritual Exercises*.

the shutters and doors while I am in my room . . . . (*Spiritual Exercises*, 78, 79)

In this practice, the experience and perception of the environment is part of our motion because the self is interactive to where they are situated. This example of discerning the self and their relationship to the physical environment is small and easily ignored. But it shows Ignatius's idea of being-within-the-environment, which means that the self is never separated from their location and how they are situated.

The second example is about how Ignatius suggests fasting and eating to the exercitant to recognize the self in the world. Resonated with Foucault's self-mastery, Ignatius points out that the subject can master the self when he or she can reject the inclination to eat and control what is consumed.

> One should be on guard against being totally absorbed in what one is eating and letting oneself be completely dominated by the appetite. Rather, one should be **master** of oneself, both in the manner of eating and the amount one takes. (*Spiritual Exercises*, 216; emphasis added)

Of course, Ignatius does not deny the vitality of eating for sustaining life. The practice of fasting for him is the practice of setting the self free from the dominance of our appetite and the uncontrollable desire to eat without moderation. Here the self emerges as "one who is eating" and "one who can resist their desire." This self is in motion!

Considering the self as a being-within-the-environment and a being-in-motion, Ignatian spirituality challenges the secular understanding of spirituality. As Jeremy Carrette and Richard King argue, this secularized knowledge of spirituality works tightly with individualistic psychology—for the purpose of serving the benefit of capitalism.[62] For the sake of individualistic psychology and privatized spirituality, the self is constructed as an independent entity—which is obsessed with self-love, self-pity, and the experience of the self. The self in this sense is disconnected from the reality and the world in which one is situated. And Christian spirituality is restricted to something privatized and has nothing to do with the political.[63] However, Ignatian concern with the self *subverts* this established structure of power-knowledge-subjectivity—considering the triangular relationship between capitalism, individualistic psychology, and the autonomous self. As Dyckman clarifies, Ignatius draws attention to the self and our experience, insisting that the discernment

---

62. Carrette and King, *Selling Spirituality*.

63. Carrette and King, *Selling Spirituality*.

of the self "has to do with the *perception* of reality, with *receptiveness* toward the real in all its dimensions."[64]

For Ignatius, paying attention to our motion and experience is to recognize what we are seeking and where we are going to. This is about desire—our orientation and intention of the self—rather than our desire of craving and needing. We meet God while discerning our motion as God manifests himself in our desire. There is a paradox in that, as David Lonsdale explains, we may sense in our experience of struggles, pain, sorrow, and suffering the goodness and the love in God's movement. We may encounter the unfamiliar side of God, but we meet him while questioning and doubting his love and goodness.[65] In this sense, reading the experience of ourselves is far from self-indulgent because Ignatius never suggests that the exercitant should follow their feeling and emotion, or seek joy and pleasure. Ignatius emphasizes that when we are in spiritual lowliness and disquiet due to agitations and temptations (called "desolation"), it is not suggested that we should make any change in order to escape from that uncomfortable situation. On the contrary, we should "strive to preserve ourselves in patience" in order to "counterattack against the vexations which are being experienced."[66] Here, we can also see that, for Ignatius, the subject of the self is constructed while, in desolation, consciously declining to follow our inclination.

On the other hand, although it seems that we have power and capacity to resist these temptations in "desolation," Ignatius believes that the power to resist self-indulgence (seeking the pleasure of the self) cannot be achieved by our internal mind activities or good intention. Here Ignatius is fundamentally different from Foucault because Foucault does not recognize the involvement of the divine power (as opposed to religious ideology and spiritual corporality). This power of resistance comes always from God's love and grace, and God's motion always goes before us and involves itself in our motion. As Ignatius himself suggests:

> For we can do this with God's help, which always remains available, even if we do not clearly perceive it. Indeed, even though the Lord has withdrawn from us his abundant fervor, augmented love, and intensive grace, he still supplies sufficient grace for our eternal salvation. (*Spiritual Exercises*, 320)

In this light, the spiritual practice in "desolation" is subverting individualistic spirituality when we recognize that our desire is not an independent

64. Dyckman et al., *Spiritual Exercises*, 4.

65. Lonsdale, *Eyes to See*, 77.

66. Ignatius, *Spiritual Exercises*, 321.

event. Knowing our experience and motion is always about recognizing God's motion of love and grace.

As Roger Haight points out, Ignatius draws us from a "self-centered desire" to "imitate Christ" when we practice self-denial.[67] This practice of self-denial does not erase the position of the self—but reassures the self that only exists with the help of God's love and grace. The self *never* exists independently, in the sense that it is assumed to exist in individualistic spirituality. The self always relies on God, no matter whether the providence of God is perceived. When the exercitant examines and discerns their motion (including orientation and desire), what is examined is not the self *alone*, but includes God's motion in the motion of the human being. Lonsdale uses the term *collaboration* to describe how God invites human beings to join his work of salvation.[68]

In the journey of knowing more about our desire, we know more about God's motion in us. Knowing ourselves is deeply connected with knowing God. The first-week focus of Spiritual Exercises aims at recognizing our sin but at the same time recognizing God's infinite love. It can be very intense but, as Dyckman highlights, the focus of the week is "a desire for a deeper spirituality"—which "results from an initial or renewed discovery of God."[69] When we offer our gratitude to God, we can then recognize God's graciousness in all of his motions that participate in our daily life. This is the reason why the exercitant is required to reflect on what God has done for us, particularly the involvement of the Holy Spirit in our inner and outer movement. Only through recognizing God's motion can we find our motion—which is our desire. Moreover, our desire is the locus where the Holy Spirit works directly. As Dyckman points out, "the Holy Spirit reveals the true condition of the heart by allowing one to see desires for what they really are and what they move one toward."[70] But the orientation of this desire is ambiguous, so it usually requires discernment.

The Practice of Indifference

Here we come to a fundamental question for Ignatius: how can we know we are led by the Holy Spirit if our desires are mixed with God's motion? Or, how can we possibly go wrong or do evil if our motion includes God's motion? These questions are primary if we want to see how Ignatius may help discern

---

67. Haight, *Christian*, 32–34.

68. Lonsdale, *Eyes to See*, 84.

69. Dyckman et al., *Spiritual Exercises*, 177.

70. Dyckman, et al., *Spiritual Exercises*, 57–58.

various power relationships which have been constructed and have been involved with constructing the self in Foucault's sense. For Ignatius, there is no "God's will" which we need to comprehend and with which we must comply, so what we need to do is the "discernment of spirits, within a living relationship God."[71] We need to discern our desires (which are interior and exterior) in their relationship to God. As Lonsdale further explains, we might sense a lot of unknown feelings whilst finding it difficult to recognize their origin and source. Knowing these feelings are not the primary task, though it may be helpful. Nor is it the end of the discernment. Discernment is about *interpreting* and *evaluating* desires, particularly about sensing "the direction in which we are moved by feelings." It is about examining how we are driven and how we are constructed and defined by power relationships.

The interpretation must be concerned with "the context in which it occurs."[72] The same feeling is not always good and not all desires are always harmful. For example, the definition of "desolation" does not depend on what we "feel" but where we are led to in this motion and where this desire draws us to go. Concluding Ignatius's rule of discernment, Dyckman offers us a clearer step of discernment: Firstly, we should notice these motions, name them, and then assess their origin and direction, finally encouraging some and discouraging others.[73] Noticing and naming them is just the beginning of the practice. The ultimate goal is to orientate desires and find the balance within all these motions of ourselves and of God. Ignatian spirituality suggests *discouraging* some of them, rather than denying or *repressing* them, because these motions have been part of us and we cannot just get rid of them. They are even stimulated by some of our deep needs and longings. We cannot deny that these desires are still part of our motions. Similarly, we cannot neglect how power relationships have constructed these desires and orientated our motions towards a certain direction and purpose.

The Ignatian way to discourage part of our desires is *indifference*. Commenting on this special term used by Ignatius, George Ganss argues that being "indifferent" means "being undetermined to one thing or option rather than another." "In no way does it mean unconcerned or unimportant."[74] Margaret Hebblethwaite suggests that *detachment* may be a better and less confusing term to understand Ignatius' concept of indifference.[75] This is because when our desires are attached to, and are driven

71. Lonsdale, *Eyes to See*, 92.

72. Lonsdale, *Eyes to See*, 97, 98–99.

73. Dyckman et al., *Spiritual Exercises*, 252–53.

74. Ignatius, *Spiritual Exercises*, 151.

75. Hebblethwaite, *Finding God*, 39.

simultaneously by, various strands of inerasable motions, what we can do is to accept that we have these desires, and then to reduce their influence on our motions. This kind of detachment may help us take an "objective" attitude to these driving desires, so that we do not need to make any choices that are based on them.[76]

The practice of indifference is the practice of discerning our desire and how we are in motion. It is also the practice of discerning our relationships with all power relationships that construct the self. When we can choose our preference to follow one of our desires, we will experience how this desire drives us, and at the same time, comprehend how this desire may be different from other strands of our desire. Discerning these desires is like discerning how the strands of power relationships are bound to the self in leading and directing the motion. But Ignatius does not expect that our discernment is a one-off practice and can always evaluate these relationships accurately. He expects all kinds of mistakes. (Similarly, Foucault also expects the "failures" of discernment as power relationships are created quickly in response to resistance.) The more we fail to discern our desire, the more experienced we are to discern where these desires may lead us, and how we can make decisions in the future based on this failure. As Hebblethwaite argues, in the practice of indifference, we may experience that "the more our love of God grows, the less the other things seem to matter."[77] But before enabling ourselves to detach from various strands of desire, we cannot find the real agency of the self because the self is just driven by these entangled strands of motions in our desire.

In the sense that discerning desires and motions is like discerning power relationships, this practice of indifference gives us *inner freedom*. As Dean Brackley argues, indifference "is the capacity to sense and then embrace what is best, even when that goes against our inclination."[78] This is because indifference means that we are free from our driving motions by means of choosing what we want and what we need. (Here we may build up our capacity to distinguish what we need from what we desire.)[79] The self can then achieve a certain level of freedom when it is not determined by any desires, especially disordered inclinations.[80] This inner freedom is impossible to achieve by eradicating and repressing disordered desires. As Foucault argues, there is no power-free zone which we can achieve. Inner freedom in this sense means

76. Hebblethwaite, *Finding God*, 40.

77. Hebblethwaite, *Finding God*, 41.

78. Brackley, *Call to Discernment*, 12.

79. Brackley, *Call to Discernment*, 13.

80. Brackley, *Call to Discernment*, 12.

that we are free from being driven by all our desires and motions without any examination. What spirituality can offer in this inner freedom is that we are free from being constructed by other power relationships and that we build up our capacity to make a choice.

We need to remember, as I have discussed above, that this indifference as inner freedom is not just an intention in our mind. Indifference is related to our context and situation in which we develop our habits, inclination, and ways of motion. As Mark Rotsaert points out, we need to be more aware of "what makes us *un*free."[81] We should practice indifference so that we can detach from things that make us unfree. The more we can discern and name the forces of unfreedom, the more we can understand how we come to this situation in our motions. This helps us find our way to choose to be free. As Rotsaert concludes, "such experiences make us what we are now, marking how we act or neglect to act, how we think or feel."[82] Our freedom in our motion and desire is rooted in discernment of who we are in our interior mind and in our exterior environment.

Resistance to Temptation

I argue that *resistance to temptation* in the Lord's Prayer—*lead us not into temptation* or *save us from the time of trial*—is the expressive of the practice of indifference as the practice of resistance. The prayer to resist temptation is sometimes considered not clear enough for Christians to "take a practical action," apart from praying to God for deliverance from evil. In this light, although the prayer reminds Christians of full dependence on God's grace, it allows Christians to be irresponsible in respect of resistance to temptation if they have no power of resistance. Here I think Ignatian theology of desire and the practice of indifference can fill the gap between God's protection and human responsibility, particularly for the growth of Christian discipleship.

For many Christians, temptation means driving forces leading them to evil and wrongdoings, and temptation usually appears in the human intention which tempts them to leave God. Therefore, these Christians prefer to make a binary division between the intention of the self and God's predestinated will, between the evil human body and God's holy action. Everything from the self becomes suspicious and devalued because the choices that are based on human intention and related to the body are unreliable. However, the Ignatian way of reconciling body and mind, intention and action, God and human beings, offers a solid foundation for

81. Rotsaert, "Loving Union," 85.
82. Rotsaert, "Loving Union," 85.

recognizing the complex and entangled motions of God and of human beings. This draws our attention to see the orientation of God's motions and
the motions of human beings in our desire, and the direction in which we
are led. Understanding temptation in Ignatian insight helps us be aware
of God's motions—which have already worked in our desire. Resistance to
temptation is not the eradication of the entire self and of desires but the
discernment of God's motions in ours.

Leading us not into temptation, therefore, should be understood in
Ignatian words as "helping us detach from the inclination to temptation."
Indeed, like power relationships, temptation will always be there and cannot be wholly eradicated. Temptation is not an object which is external to
us and attracts us to fall. It is part of the motions that drive and orientate our
direction and inclination to do everything. More importantly, temptation is
usually entangled and confused with the motions of God, so that we might
misrecognize where they come from. However, the practice of indifference
firstly requires Christians to examine the self-in-motion carefully in order to
recognize temptation—which is a strand that drives us away from God to
indulge the self and be addicted to our own need. This addiction to the self
makes us unfree when we illusively feel that we have no choice not to do it.

By means of practicing indifference, we can gradually recognize, distinguish and name the various strands of motions in our desire. We grow the
capacity to detach ourselves from the driving strands that might eventually
lead us to evil and fulfill our interest. This detachment has to rely on having
an even *stronger* attachment to God's lead and motion. What we can do in
resistance to temptation in a passive way is to make our attachment to God
stronger than to evil. We then allow ourselves to be driven by the motion of
God rather than the motion of the self, toward the greatest satisfaction (the
greatest desire). As Philip Sheldrake says:

> The place of deepest desire is one where we know that we are
> touching a deep well of peace and truthfulness that speaks of
> the infinite—even if we have passed through disturbance and
> pain on the way, it is also a place where we engage with what
> we ultimately realize is intimately associated with our identity.[83]

I think what Sheldrake says, "touching a deep well of peace and truthful-
ness," demonstrates the meaning of "deliver us from evil." This is because
merely detaching from the drive to temptation does not lead us to any goodness. Only when we attach the self to God's motion and desire are we led to
the deep peace and the identity of the self.

---

83. Sheldrake, *Befriending Our Desires*, 119.

On the other hand, I argue that Ignatius also offers an *active* method of resistance to temptation in the concluding period of meditation of the Exercises—known as the Contemplation to Attain Love:

> [To] ask for what I desire. Here it will be to ask for interior knowledge of all the great good I have received, in order that, stirred to profound gratitude, I may become able to love and serve the Divine Majesty in all things. (*Spiritual Exercises*, 33)

Ignatius's guidance on resistance to temptation is to pray that the direction of our desire to God is so strong that we will not incline to temptation. Ignatius invites us to pray for wisdom—which may grow our gratitude for all that is great and good from God—because this is the way we can recognize how God has already been in motion within desires. Our gratitude becomes a stepping-stone to discern God's motion in our entangled desires.

Resistance in Discernment and Indifference

Through creatively reading Ignatius's *Spiritual Exercises* with Foucault's theory of political spirituality, I show the example of how Ignatian practice of spirituality itself can be politically resistive in Foucault's sense. In this section, I attempt to summarise what we have achieved in the cross-reading.

Firstly, I argue that the Ignatian practice of discernment offers the basis for resistance through discerning where the self is situated and how power relationships work on the construction of the self. By means of discerning our desires and motions, the spiritual subject gradually senses and recognizes how the self is constructed by power to have its inclination and orientation. These orientations and inclinations are not neutral, natural, or apolitical. Their existence is defined and driven by power. Therefore, when Ignatius suggests discerning our desires and motions, it is not just discerning how the self—which is an autonomous and out-of-context being—thinks and feels. Far from self-love and self-pity, the discernment of our desires and motions is a process of interpreting and recognizing how we are constructed within power relationships.

Secondly, when we can recognize how we are driven in our desires and motions by power relationships, we gradually build up our capacity to *detach* from these drives and *deny* the inclination. This is called "indifference." Resonating with Foucault's idea that there is no power-free zone, Ignatius does not believe that we can live in a situation without desires and motions. Our life is always in the process of becoming and being driven. Hence, the issue is not to get rid of desires, motions, and power relationships—but to know how to orientate them and how *not* to be orientated by them. At this point, the practice of indifference matters because it helps detach the self from one's desires. Henceforth it creates the space of freedom from detachment, no matter how long it may last.

In this sense, the Lord's Prayer is political because resistance to temptation is real political resistance. Temptation is not something purely "spiritual" like something Satan speaks to us, or something leading us to do evil and immoral things. Temptation is a driving desire which orientates us into the condition of unfreedom and dominance. Being driven by temptation means the loss of our freedom to take control of our desire and motion. In temptation, we lose our capacity to resist being oriented towards unfree and unwilling inclinations. Therefore, the passive strategy to resist temptation at this level is to detach the self from these power relationships, which drive our motions and control our desires. The practice of indifference helps resistive subjects to constantly keep detaching from the web of power relationships in which they are situated. Although indifference is a passive strategy to resist, it actively creates the space of freedom.

Finally, in addition to the passive strategy, Ignatius offers an active strategy of resistance in rethinking of Lord's Prayer—our gratitude for God. For Ignatius, the best strategy for detachment is to attach the self onto God, onto one who secures our freedom. Therefore, detachment does not mean that the subject of the self will rely on oneself as an autonomous being. On the contrary, detachment means that the subject should attach oneself to another subject so that this attachment creates a stronger relationship to resist being attached to other powers. Resonating with Foucault's "confusing" argument of subjugation-as-resistance, I argue that Ignatius's idea of attachment to God demonstrates well the paradox of attachment and detachment and how being attached and subjected to God leads to detachment from other powers. In this sense, gratitude for God—which helps us recognize God's motion and desire in us—offers an active strategy of resistance by means of active engagement with the creation of a new power relationship. But paradoxically, this active strategy is passive because it requires the subject to attach and subjugate oneself to God to create that freedom.

Conclusion

By seeking to clarify the difference between spiritual corporality and political spirituality in Foucault's thought, my intention in this chapter has been to show how Foucault recognizes the limitation of spiritual corporality and why, after the Iranian revolution, he begins to expand his idea of political spirituality. I argue that Foucault's idea of spiritual corporality is closer to liberation theologies in terms of their religious/spiritual involvement in politics (such as revolutions and social movements). But Foucault's comments on the revolution, which have been criticized as "naïve" and "optimistic," signpost the direction he then takes towards political spirituality. This means that religious/spiritual practice should be more flexible in response to newly created deployments of power relationships. Like any other strand of power, religion cannot offer the final solution to oppression and dominance, although it can offer a powerful force of liberation. This is the reason why Foucault cannot be satisfied with spiritual corporality.

Following the logic and exploration of Foucault's self-criticism, we can see how he recognizes the practice of the self (subjectification) as the strategy of resistance by means of rejecting being sexualized and being constructed as madness. In particular, in his response to sexual liberation, Foucault does not think that talking more about sexuality is the way to resist. He then turns to analyze the techniques of the self in the confession of sin, in which the construction of the subject still relies on knowledge of the self and subjugation to others. This practice of confessing sin is no different from admitting one's sexuality and seeing a psychiatrist. In his final years, Foucault moves on to the more controversial and paradoxical stage in exploring freedom—in which he realizes that the potential of resistance is connected with the construction of the self in the Christian practice of asceticism. The practice of asceticism creates the space for the subject to construct the self in order not to be constituted by other power relationships. Here we can recognize how subjectification is politically resistive rather than an abstract philosophical idea.

In this light, cross-reading of Ignatius and Foucault can be a useful way to show how the practice of indifference is politically resistive and is not restricted to contemporary spirituality of individualism and privatization. Ignatian spirituality pays attention to the discernment of desires and motions. This discernment is not for self-pity or self-love—but for the recognition of the relationship between the self and other power relationships. By means of discerning desires and motions, the subject gradually recognizes how the self is constructed. Then, in the practice of indifference, the subject can constantly detach the self from power relationships which construct them. On the other hand, the subject should also attach the self to God as their strategy of helping to detach from power relationships. In this sense, resistance to temptation is not to resist something immoral but to resist all powers that are not from God.

Toward a Micro-Political Theology

Exploring my Micro-Political Theology

THE EXPLORATION OF MY micro-political theology began with empirical observations on the contribution of political revolutions and social movements (this was covered in chapter 1). In recent decades, various oppressed groups have tasted the fruit of political and social actions which subverted the oppressive social structures and systems. They also enjoyed the success that came from the ideas of liberty and liberation. Women, LGBT people, non-white people, and the poor—indigenous people, the disabled, immigrants, and others who are marginalized—have achieved a "certain" level of equality and freedom in terms of amending laws and raised public awareness. However, we also know that the journey of fighting against oppression and inequality is not yet finished. These revolutions and social movements should not end, nor should they be satisfied with what has been achieved. Freedom and liberation are incomplete and will never be fully achieved. And it is clear that the needs arising from unfinished actions in both society and politics have been recognized by revolutionaries, social activists, and political theologians.

So it is undoubtedly the case that these revolutions and social movements have not yet liberated us *fully*. And it was a betrayal when revolutionaries and social activists did not articulate the "limitation" of their actions and political proposals. They rarely admitted that full liberation is not something that can be achieved as they claimed. They clung stubbornly to the belief that full liberation and complete freedom would come if they kept fighting against social structures. On the other hand, as empirical observations have shown, the issue is not whether or not the current achievement is complete. Instead, the issue is that the fruits of revolutions and social movements have been taken over by new power relationships. If these achievements are taken and manipulated by new oppressive relationships, how can we continue to build our action upon them? Henceforth, the first step of revisiting and reimagining political theology is to recognize the limitation of revolutions and social movements, thereby reconsidering the idea of liberation.

Through the lens of empirical observations on the incomplete achievements of revolutions and social movements, this book has explored how different liberation theologians have replicated the agendas that were proposed on the back of the ideas of liberation and freedom—agendas that failed to address the areas in which revolutionaries and social activists were not successful. Based on Marxist insights, liberation theologies (exemplified in chapter 2 by Latin American Liberation Theology, feminist theology, and Womanist theology) draw attention to the experiences of the oppressed and structural oppression.

Although we may agree that there are diverse viewpoints of liberation theologies with different origins, we cannot deny the fact that they more or less shared the same ground and ethos as theological construction—particularly when they began by prioritizing a specific oppressed group over other oppressed groups, and were concerned more with one kind of experience than with others. When liberation theologians paid attention to the suffering of oppressed people and then attempted to propose their solution and political action, they gradually increased their reliance on structural analysis to tell them why the oppressed were suffering. Ironically, liberation theologians became more focused on a sociological method that helped to define the oppressed and locate their social position rather than on the empirical experiences of the oppressed. In other words, they gave the impression of caring more about these social structures for analytical purposes than they did about individual sufferers and the oppressed. Liberation theologians insisted that their primary attention was oppressed "people" but their theological method distracted them from being attentive to the actual experiences of the oppressed at the individual level—such as their unique story and agency in subjectivity.

The obsessive attitude toward structural analysis in liberation theologies is rarely reviewed and challenged, though different strands of liberation theologies attempted to revise the failures and weaknesses of each other. Latin American Liberation Theology established some theological foundations for later traditions through prioritizing the poor as the most oppressed group and demanding that theologians listen to their voice and experience. Feminist theology challenged Latin American Liberation Theology by identifying sexism as the most fundamental and primary oppression in human history. Women were even hidden in Christianity and silenced from telling their own stories. Womanist theology from the Third World stood up in a challenge to the "whiteness" of feminist theology, which ignored multi-oppressions from racism, classism, imperialism, colonialism, and Christian orthodoxy. Womanist theology opens up our understanding of how different structures of oppression may be interlocked. Their proposal attempted to "optimize" the problem of liberation theologies—which was revealed in the way they simplified structural analysis (in a form of monochromatism).

However, what they called "multi-oppressions"—in alliance with "intersectional analysis" (or the idea of intersectionality)—was no different from other forms of structural analysis, except that it added *more factors* to complicate the already-simplified analysis. A Black Feminist, Kimberlé Crenshaw, coined the term "intersectionality." This concept was to disclose the prejudice of the legal system in the USA that repeatedly ignored the existence of black women by treating racism and sexism as mutually exclusive ideas.[1] The purpose of Crenshaw's idea of intersectionality was to open up a space for the recognition of "black" "women" so that the legal system can more *accurately* identify systems of discrimination against black women. Her approach was more like a tool that *calibrates* structural analysis than a new analytic tool of oppression. (Here my micro-political theology criticizes intersectionality studies, not because it refuses to recognize multi-oppressions but because neither intersectionality nor multi-oppressions overcome the whole package of structural analysis.)

At this point, Michel Foucault offers more systemic critiques of structural analysis, particularly when his critical conversation with Marxism and the concept of liberation is considered (see chapter 3). One of Foucault's most significant contributions was his criticism of a utopian expectation of the quest for a power-free society. He encouraged us to see how society is maintained and constructed by power relationships and how using the viewpoint of power relationships may help us to recognize that oppressions go beyond social structures. For Foucault, the issue is no longer how many social structures are interlocked or who should be defined as the most oppressed group. Foucault helped us to realize that oppression and power come up all the time and in all relationships. They even come about immediately after any resistance. In Foucault's light, "liberation" becomes a problematic concept, as it promises the goal of "being free from power," but is never achievable. Foucault requires us to regard power relationships as something unavoidable, productive, and dynamic. What we can do to cope with power relationships is to constantly resist them and to anticipate that new deployments of power relationships may seize the freedom we may only just have achieved.

---

1. Crenshaw, "Demarginalizing," 139–67.

On the other hand, Foucault's analysis of power relationships drew our attention to the *constitution* of sexuality and desire concerning the birth of perversion. Although Foucault is often considered to be the Father of queer theory and sexual "liberation," his analysis of sexuality and desire is much more delicate and nuanced than many expect. Foucault was very concerned with sexual liberation because this liberating action has already been seized by the development of sexuality. Following his critique of sexual liberation, we may understand why sexuality and desire, in Foucault's eye, do not serve freedom. This is because both are related to the birth of perversion and the construction of pervert subjects. Employing a revision of perversion and liberation, Foucault helped us to move on so that we can see how the subject is constructed *within* power relationships (subjectification). This analysis of subjectification was regarded negatively as an oppressive process, but it pointed toward an insight that freedom can be practiced in the process of subjectification, which always includes two sides—becoming a subject and being subjected.

Bringing these thoughts of Foucault into the contemporary dialogue of political theology can be inspirational because, as we discussed in chapter 4, it helps avoid taking a *naïve* attitude toward sexuality, desire, and perversion in any further theological construction. Marcella Althaus-Reid was pioneering indecent theology and Queer God when she attempted to subvert the heterosexuality that is sustained by the decency of social and sexual norms. She confidently embraced perversion—which is represented in queer, poor women, prostitutes, and bisexuals—as her theological method for subverting "decent" theology. However, her theological method neglected the fact that the construction of perversion relies on the dominance of oppressive heterosexual structures. The paradox is that the more she embraced perversion and essentialized it, the more she consolidated the power of heterosexuality. If Althaus-Reid considered Foucault's criticism of sexual liberation carefully, she might have realized the naivety of her "romanticization" of perversion and indecency.

Daniel Bell, as an advocate for Radical Orthodoxy, has recognized the *distortion* of desire and how capitalism gets involved in the process of shaping and orientating desire. Bell holds faith in a kind of desire that is created by God and that leads us toward God. Therefore, theology itself is a remedy for our desire that helps us restore distorted desire into the original God-form. In this sense, desire first needs to be healed and then may lead to building up justice and forgiveness. In comparison, a Korean liberation theologian in Brazil, Jung Mo Sung, took a more critical attitude toward the idea of "desire." While both Sung and Bell both criticized capitalism for misusing desire in contemporary culture, Sung assumed—based more on Marxist understanding—that desire is not created by God in human nature but is instead *constructed* by capitalism. What capitalism does is to confuse human need with desire in such as way that people develop the misconception that they are synonymous.

I argued that Bell proposed an ontological approach in contrast to Sung's ethical approach. The former calls for fundamental transformation and restoration of desire in human "nature" because the way to heal desire is to have a "factory reset" of our distorted desire. The latter is more concerned with how, in a practical sense, we should focus on our needs rather than our desire, by discerning the difference between them. Based on this, we may realize that the division between Bell's ontological approach and Sung's ethical approach does not help to formulate a radical and constructive proposal of political theology from Foucault's perspective of subjectification. Nor does Althaus-Reid help in this task, as her failure to recognize the process of constructing the subject of the self leads her to a misrecognition of power relationships that have been involved in the birth of perversion and the definition of indecency.

To fix the failures of these theologies, my micro-political theology aims to introduce Foucault's thoughts of power relationships, subjectification, and political resistance into the conversation. Chapter 5 briefly reviewed Foucault's developing concept of "political spirituality," reviewed his critiques of the Iranian Revolution, and revisited asceticism and religious sources in Christianity. Due to Foucault's recognition of the limitation of "spiritual corporality," we may also recognize the limitation of religious participation in politics and social movements—which have been exemplified in liberation theologies. If political participation by Muslims and Islamic leaders could be incorporated into new power relationships of dominance, how can liberation theologians and other political theologians in social activism be naïve about our immunity from any new power relationships that are created *by* and *in* our resistance? How can we rely on one strategy which we believe can solve the problem for good?

Taking this attitude towards the complexity of power relationships and dominance, we may "make sense" of why Foucault has seemed to contradict the conventional agenda of sexual liberation with his proposed strategy of political resistance as "asceticism." Asceticism-as-resistance can be understood only when we consider the process of constructing the self in subjectification. If we have recognized that power relationships are always engaged with the process of constructing us, the way to resist this engagement is to *disengage* with these power relationships—by actively engaging with the creation of power relationships, both by and for ourselves. Simply speaking, the way to the construction of the self from other dominance is to let

CONCLUDING REFLECTION: TOWARD A MICRO-POLITICAL THEOLOGY   169

the subject of the self master and dominate our "self." From this viewpoint, it becomes easier to notice how the self is sexualized and constructed in sexual liberation and how sexual liberation has turned into a new power relationship that seizes the freedom of subjects.

If we cannot simply persist with a fixed strategy to achieve freedom and liberation (as liberation theologies have suggested), our resistance has to be based on a *preceding* practice of discernment—a practice that helps recognize where we are and how we are constructed by current power relationships. In this light, Ignatian spirituality can be read politically. This is because the *discernment* of our desire orientation and the practice of *indifference* no longer mean withdrawing from social contexts. They are actively constructing a self who can actively and freely detach from the power relationships that orientate them. Using the viewpoint of my micro-political theology to read the Spiritual Exercises shows us a way in which our spirituality connects with our political action. It also shows us how the reorientation of our desire toward God (at an ontological level) can lead to political resistance, as well as how resistance to temptation is not merely at an ethical level of not doing something but is also—at an ontological level—constructing a resistive self.

My micro-political theology is intended to *complement* former liberation theologies when liberation theologies have been too over-reliant on structural analysis to pay attention to how individual subjects are situated within power relationships. (In particular, the work of power relationships is more complicated and dynamic than static structures—no matter how many multi-layers of social structures we consider.) My micro-political theology in this sense demands that theologians give serious consideration to the construction of individual subjects within power relationships—rather than to their social position. And this discernment of suffering subjects from their experience cannot be replaced with the analysis of their stories. Political resistance is based on our discernment on power relationships—more than simplified reliance on structural analysis. The subject of the self cannot be represented by the oppressed group to which they "belong." More importantly, the strategy of resistance should move on from passively *subverting* social structures to actively constructing *subversive subjects* which break down the cycle of reproducing oppressive structures.

The Micro-Political Theology in Action

Rather than fully abandoning liberation theologies and replacing them, this micro-political theology aims to address the limitations of liberation theologies and point out their blind spots. This is because fighting for freedom is the common theological goal and we ought not to be too naïve when judging the context in which we are situated and the complication of power and dominance we face. But how does it work?

As I write this conclusion, many demonstrations and protests are taking place in Asia as people try to secure democracy and freedom. Through the lens of liberation theologies and its Marxist companions, constant participation at different levels of social movements is vital when challenging oppressive power. Liberation theologies also "demonstrate" the power of disobedience to the new system of injustice. We cannot deny the sacrifice of those who have devoted their lives to disobedience and who even risk death. By attempting to stop the transition, their contributions keep *disrupting* the structure. By disclosing the existence of injustice, they keep *grabbing* attention from outside and raising people's awareness.

However, governments have no intention of bringing in reforms, tensions continue to rise and protestors continue to die. So, if these movements struggle to achieve their aims, we are bound to question whether their sacrifice is worth it and whether tension will ever be eased. We may ask, "How can we see the death of people as the way of resistance?" We might also ask, "Can this movement be sustainable if all that seems to happen is that protesters are persecuted, jailed, and killed?" The value of martyrs is always a controversial issue. On the one hand, we believe that they help to pave the way towards liberation and that without their sacrifice, we cannot get there. On the other hand, we doubt whether they need to die to help us achieve that freedom because their death is sometimes of no significance at all to the oppressors. Outsiders gradually become indifferent to their deaths, particularly when persecution becomes "normalized" and an oppressive structure is settled and established.

The oppressors seem to "enjoy" the cruelty of seeing the spread of the spirit of martyrdom rather than fear it or feel embarrassed by it. In the beginning, they may feel irritated by the interruption because martyrdom keeps raising the awareness of the people and does not allow the action of oppressors to remain secretive. But the power of martyrdom is contained, and its resistance is suddenly reduced and incorporated into a new power relationship. In the end, the oppressors appreciate martyrdom when death is no longer subversive. They take advantage of their self-sacrifice so that they can erase the rebellious as much as possible. The more people are encouraged to give their life in the resistance, the more the oppressors can captivate them and control them. Here we can see the need to explore a new strategy of resistance because, following the creation of new power relationships, any political resistance may develop into forces that serve to consolidate structures. Since martyrdom cannot challenge oppression, it begins to *feed* power and work for the benefit of oppression.

Here we reach a fundamental question: Shall we keep following the same strategy, regardless of the risk of losing more lives, to show the resilience and persistence of the oppressed? Or shall we adopt a new strategy, even though it may be seen as withdrawing from the liberation movement or disengaging from challenging the oppressor? Revolutionaries, social activists, and liberation theologians rarely want to be seen as "cowardly" in the face of an oppressor and its structure. But this mindset of persistence easily blinds us to recognize the newly created power relationships that have snatched away what we have achieved and prevent us from seeing the need for a new strategy of resistance. If we want to keep resisting, we must keep changing our strategy of resistance—depending on how new power relationships have been created. According to my micro-political theology, the fundamentally most effective way of resistance is to consciously deny becoming the subject that the oppressors want.

If we do not consciously deny, we will fail to recognize the trick that the oppressors are "glad" to see more martyrs who are willing to sacrifice their lives—they manipulate the spirit of martyrdom. They encourage the rebellious to be martyrs so that they can control them and easily persecute them. Ironically, in this sense, the oppressors want to shape these people into "martyrs" who are subjugated to them. (This is the same as being more open and vocal about sex to control people's sexuality.) The spirit of martyrdom here is honored by the oppressors because, as we expected, it is more submission than subversion. This is not about the stained virtue of martyrdom itself—but the manipulation of the sacrifice of martyrs. Nor is it about whether their deaths are worthy or virtuous. Instead, it is about whether their deaths are still subversive. If we continue to follow the conventional doctrine of liberation theologies or Marxist thought, we will be stuck in the binary mindset which forces us to stick to a conventional way to liberate. If power relationships are produced flexible and dynamically, our resistance should be as flexible and dynamic as they are. Our resistance should start at the level of our daily life.

Here, some readers may observe the similarity of my micro-political theology to James Scott's idea of *everyday forms of resistance*. In his inspirational work, *Weapons of the Weak: Everyday Forms of Resistance* (1985), Scott points out that resistance emerges between structures and agency and that regarding resistance as something always organized and structural is not common either. He argues that resistance exists in our daily life in the forms of false compliance, ignorance, rumor and gossip, disguises, euphemisms, and even sabotage.[2] These resistive actions are not always visible, collective, organized, or principled. They even accept the basis of dominance rather than negate it. Scott demonstrates this possibility of everyday resistance, which happens in the community of the weak and in the case of those who are too powerless to make a "revolution." But he seems to be pessimistic about whether this kind of "everyday resistance" can really make a change in the end, or whether it is just non-subversive rebellion.

James Scott's form of everyday resistance merely demonstrates to us that not all resistive actions are organized and structural. It shows the possible "alternative" to the Marxist agenda of revolution and social movement. Although everyday resistance is at the micro-level, it differs from my micro-political theology. This is because, rather than considering the opportunity that such resistance may come from individuals and their subjectification, Scott merely shows individual agency within dominant structures. Therefore, in this light, what Scott focuses on is the scale level of resistance rather than the resistance explored in my micro-political theology, which insists that resistance is based on the construction of the self within constantly changing power relationships. Only when the subjects can discern where they are and how they are constructed and orientated can they find their way of disengaging and breaking away from dominance, regardless of the involvement of the scale of resistance. If the decisive issue of resistance is not about the scale, discerning the use of different scales of resistance misses the point. My micro-political theology, therefore, aims to draw attention to the flexibility and dynamic of changing strategies of resistance rather than the scale.

I argue that a balance has to be struck between revolutions and social movements on an organized scale and daily resistance and false compliance on a less visible scale. I believe that neither of them is the best strategy of resistance "for good." We need to deploy different strategies in response to different forms of power relationships. Freedom and persistent resistance come from constantly changing strategies of resistance. And this ability to discern the strategies and to keep disengaging from power relationships is based on the practice of actively constructing the self. Thus, my micro-political theology pays more attention to the practice of discerning the self in relation to power relationships, rather than to a specific proposal of resistive action.

For example, when the oppressors and oppressive structures have produced a new power relationship to control resistance and to contain the subversive power of martyrdom, the resistive strategy should be adapted

2. Scott, *Weapons of the Weak*, 137.

and re-organized based on this newly created relationship. When the oppression aims at erasing the rebellious, the real resistance is to live and to save lives. In this sense, everyday resistance will be useful to allow resistance to be continued. But turning resistance into a "low key" mode—which is *more dispersed* and *less structural*—is not the ultimate goal. It is not just the time of waiting for the next revolution but the way of "organizing" resistance in a non-organizational way. More importantly, the construction of the self in my micro-political theology is to develop the skill of discerning the orientation of power relationships and how to detach from current power relationships. Due to the cultivation of the resistive subjects, we can be more vigilant and more ready to shift our strategies in response to different deployments of power relationships.

The purpose in developing my micro-political theology is not to replace all liberation movements and social movements but to open up our imagination in terms of power resistance—especially when not all liberating actions work out or when the fruits of revolutions and movements do not last. But it would be dangerous for the conclusion to be drawn that we should completely abandon the street strategies taught by Marxism and former liberation theologians and fully turn to focus on our ontological transformation. This is not what I am suggesting in my micro-political theology. Rather, it is based on the reflection that allows us to move on from liberation theologies and that helps us to be ready when liberation movements come to a dead end.

Thanks to Foucault's insights on power relations and subjectification, the understanding of dominance and resistance should be pervasive but not lead to the nihilism of power and resistance. Foucault does not castigate us for participating in liberation, showing us the reality instead that the deployments of power relationships are more complex than we expected. His insight is far more constructive than deconstructive. What I have learned and have come to appreciate from Foucault in the process of constructing my micro-political theology is his *prophetic* voice of scrutinizing power and oppression. Henceforth, we should keep re-organizing our political resistance rather than losing hope when being manipulated by newly produced oppression. Foucault has helped us to anticipate the fact that freedom cannot last long. But he also reminds us that resistance always comes before power relationships.

Bibliography

Abbott, Pamela, et al. *An Introduction to Sociology: Feminist Perspectives*. New York: Routledge, 2006.

Agamben, Giorgio. *Homo Sacer: Sovereign Power and Bare Life*. Translated by Daniel Heller-Roazen. Edited by Daniel Heller-Roazen. Stanford, CA: Stanford University Press, 1998.

———. "L'invenzione Di Un'epidemia." *Quodlibet*, February 26, 2020.

Althaus-Reid, Marcella. *From Feminist Theology to Indecent Theology: Readings on Poverty, Sexual Identity and God*. London: SCM, 2004.

———. "From Liberation Theology to Indecent Theology: The Trouble with Normality in Theology." In *Latin American Liberation Theology: The New Generation*, edited by Ivan Petrella, 20–38. New York: Orbis, 2005.

———. "The Hermeneutics of Transgression." In *Liberation Theologies on Shifting Grounds: A Clash of Socio-Economic and Cultural Paradigms*, edited by G. De Schrijver, 251–71. Leuven: Leuven University Press, 1998.

———. *Indecent Theology: Theological Perversions in Sex, Gender and Politics*. London: Routledge, 2000.

———. "Introduction." In *Liberation Theology and Sexuality*, edited by Marcella Althaus-Reid, 1–4. Reclaiming Liberation Theology. London: SCM, 2009.

———. "'Let Them Talk . . . !' Doing Liberation Theology from Latin American Closets." In *Liberation Theology and Sexuality*, edited by Marcella Althaus-Reid, 5–17. London: Routledge, 2006.

———. *The Queer God*. London: Routledge, 2003.

Althaus-Reid, Marcella, and Lisa Isherwood. *Controversies in Feminist Theology*. Controversies in Contextual Theology Series. London: SCM, 2007.

Althusser, Louis. "Ideology and Ideological State Apparatuses: Notes Towards an Investigation." In *Lenin and Philosophy, and Other Essays*, 85–126. London: Monthly Review, 2001.

Anderson, Pamela Sue. "Feminist Theology as Philosophy of Religion." In *The Cambridge Companion to Feminist Theology*, edited by Susan Frank Parsons, 40–59. Cambridge: University of Cambridge Press, 2002.

Avila P., Rafael. *Worship and Politics*. Maryknoll, NY: Orbis, 1981.

Balibar, Étienne. "Foucault and Marx: The Question of Nominalism." *Michel Foucault, Philosopher* (1992) 38–56.

Banner, Michael. *The Ethics of Everyday Life: Moral Theology, Social Anthropology, and the Imagination of the Human.* Oxford: Oxford University Press, 2014. doi:10.1093/acprof:oso/9780198722069.001.0001.

Beaulieu, Alain. "Towards a Liberal Utopia: The Connection between Foucault's Reporting on the Iranian Revolution and the Ethical Turn." *Philosophy & Social Criticism* 36.7 (2010) 801–18.

Bell, Daniel M. *The Economy of Desire: Christianity and Capitalism in a Postmodern World.* Grand Rapids, MI: Baker Academic, 2012.

———. *Liberation Theology after the End of History: The Refusal to Cease Suffering.* London: Routledge, 2001.

Bellou, Andriana, and Emanuela Cardia. "Occupations after WWII: The Legacy of Rosie the Riveter." *Explorations in Economic History* 62 (2016) 124–42.

Berlin, Isaiah. "Two Concepts of Liberty." In *Liberty*, edited by Henry Hardy, 166–217. Oxford: Oxford University Press, 2002.

Bernauer, James. "Michel Foucault's Ecstatic Thinking." Translated by J. D. Gauthier. In *The Final Foucault*, edited by James Bernauer and David Rasmussen, 45–82. Cambridge: MIT Press, 1987.

———. "The Prisons of Man: An Introduction to Foucault's Negative Theology." *International Philosophical Quarterly* 27.4 (1987) 365–80.

Bernauer, James, and Michael Mahon. "Michel Foucault's Ethical Imagination." In *The Cambridge Companion to Foucault*, edited by Gary Gutting, 149–75. Cambridge: Cambridge University Press, 2005.

Bernauer, James, and Thomas Keenan. "The Works of Michel Foucault 1954–1984." Translated by J. D. Gauthier. In *The Final Foucault*, edited by James Bernauer and David Rasmussen, 119–58. Cambridge: MIT Press, 1987.

Bevans, Stephen B. *Models of Contextual Theology.* Maryknoll, NY: Orbis, 1992.

Blencowe, Claire. *Biopolitical Experience: Foucault, Power and Positive Critique.* New York: Palgrave Macmillan, 2012.

Bonilla-Silva, Eduardo. "Color-Blind Racism in Pandemic Times." *Sociology of Race and Ethnicity* 0.0 (2020). https://journals.sagepub.com/doi/abs/10.1177/233264922 0941024.

———. *White Supremacy and Racism in the Post-Civil Rights Era.* London: Lynne Rienner, 2001.

Brackley, Dean. *The Call to Discernment in Troubled Times: New Perspectives on the Transformative Wisdom of Ignatius of Loyola.* New York: Crossroad, 2004.

Brenner-Idan, Athalya. *The Israelite Woman: Social Role and Literary Type in Biblical Narrative.* London: Bloomsbury, 2015.

Brenner, Neil. "Foucault's New Functionalism." *Theory and Society* 23.5 (1994) 679–709.

Butler, Judith. *Bodies That Matter: On the Discursive Limits of "Sex".* New York: Routledge, 1993.

———. *Gender Trouble: Feminism and the Subversion of Identity.* New York: Routledge, 2006.

———. *Notes toward a Performative Theory of Assembly.* Cambridge: Harvard University Press, 2015.

Büttgen, Philippe. "Foucault's Concept of Confession." *Foucault Studies* 29 (2021) 6–21.

Carr, Anne E. "The New Vision of Feminist Theology." In *Freeing Theology: The Essentials of Theology in Feminist Perspective*, edited by Catherine Mowry LaCugna, 5–29. San Francisco: HarperSanFrancisco, 1993.

Carrette, Jeremy. "'Spiritual Gymnastics': Reflections on Michel Foucault's on the Government of the Living 1980 Collège De France Lectures." *Foucault Studies* 20 (2015) 277–90.

Carrette, Jeremy, and Richard King. *Selling Spirituality: The Silent Takeover of Religion.* London: Routledge, 2004. doi:10.4324/9780203494875.

Carrette, Jeremy R. *Foucault and Religion: Spiritual Corporality and Political Spirituality.* London: Routledge, 2000.

Carrigan, Tim, et al. "Toward a New Sociology of Masculinity." *Theory and Society* 14.5 (1985) 551–604.

Carter, David. *Stonewall: The Riots That Sparked the Gay Revolution.* London: Macmillan, 2004.

Carvalhaes, Claudio. "Oppressed Bodies Don't Have Sex: The Blind Spot of Bodily and Sexual Discourses in the Construction of Subjectivity in Latin American Liberation Theology." In *Indecent Theologians: Marcella Althaus-Reid & the Next Generation of Postcolonial Activism*, edited by Nicolas Panotto, 155–212. Alameda, CA: Borderless, 2016.

Cass, Vivienne C. "Homosexual Identity Formation: A Theoretical Model." *Journal of homosexuality* 4.3 (1979) 219–35.

Cavanaugh, William T. *Torture and Eucharist: Theology, Politics, and the Body of Christ.* Oxford: Blackwell, 1998.

Cavendish, James C. "Christian Base Communities and the Building of Democracy: Brazil and Chile." *Sociology of Religion* 55.2 (1994) 179–95.

Chafe, William H. *Civilities and Civil Rights: Greensboro, North Carolina and the Black Struggle for Freedom.* Oxford: Oxford University Press, 1980.

Chen, Kuan-Hsing. *Asia as Method: Toward Deimperialization.* Durham: Duke University Press, 2010.

Cheng, Patrick S. *From Sin to Amazing Grace: Discovering the Queer Christ.* New York: Seabury, 2012.

———. *Radical Love: An Introduction to Queer Theology.* New York: Seabury, 2011.

Chomsky, Noam. *Government in the Future.* New York: Seven Stories, 2005.

Chopp, Rebecca S. "Latin American Liberation Theology." In *The Modern Theologians: An Introduction to Christian Theology in the Twentieth Century*, edited by David F. Ford, 173–92. Oxford: Blackwell, 1989.

Chou, Rosalind S. *The Myth of the Model Minority: Asian Americans Facing Racism.* Edited by Joe R. Feagin. New York: Routledge, 2016.

Chung, Hyun Kyung. "'Han-Pu-Ri': Doing Theology from Korean Women's Perspective." In *We Dare to Dream: Doing Theology as Asian Women*, edited by Virginia Fabella and Sun Ai Lee Park, 135–46. Maryknoll, NY: Orbis, 1990.

———. *Struggle to Be the Sun Again: Introducing Asian Women's Theology.* Maryknoll, NY: Orbis, 1990.

Clarkson, Jay. "Contesting Masculinity's Makeover: Queer Eye, Consumer Masculinity, and 'Straight-Acting' Gays." *Journal of Communication Inquiry* 29.3 (2005) 235–55.

Clews, Colin. *Gay in the 80s : From Fighting for Our Rights to Fighting for Our Lives.* Gay in the Eighties. Kibworth Beauchamp: Matador, 2017.

Coakley, Sarah. *The New Asceticism: Sexuality, Gender and the Quest for God.* London: Bloomsbury, 2015.

Coleman, Monica A. *Making a Way Out of No Way: A Womanist Theology*. Minneapolis: Fortress, 2008.

The Commission on Theological Concerns of the Christian Conference of Asia, ed. *Minjung Theology: People as the Subjects of History*. Vol. 3. Maryknoll, NY: Orbis, 1983.

Cone, Cecil Wayne. *The Identity Crisis in Black Theology*. Nashville, TN: The African Methodist Episcopal Church, 1974.

Connell, Robert W., and James W. Messerschmidt. "Hegemonic Masculinity: Rethinking the Concept." *Gender & Society* 19.6 (2005) 829–59.

Connolly, William E. "Beyond Good and Evil: The Ethical Sensibility of Michel Foucault." *Political Theory* 21.3 (1993) 365–89.

Cooper, Thia. *Queer and Indecent: An Introduction to the Theology of Marcella Althaus Reid*. London: SCM, 2021.

"Covid-19 Fueling Anti-Asian Racism and Xenophobia Worldwide: National Action Plans Needed to Counter Intolerance." *Human Rights Watch*, May 12, 2020. https://www.hrw.org/news/2020/05/12/covid-19-fueling-anti-asian-racism-and-xenophobia-worldwide.

Crenshaw, James L. *A Whirlpool of Torment: Israelite Traditions of God as an Oppressive Presence*. Philadelphia: Fortress, 1984.

Crenshaw, Kimberlé. "Demarginalizing the Intersection of Race and Sex: A Black Feminist Critique of Antidiscrimination Doctrine, Feminist Theory and Antiracist Politics." *University of Chicago Legal Forum* 1 (1989) 139–67.

Dalla Costa, Mariarosa, and Selma James. *The Power of Women and the Subversion of the Community*. Bristol: Falling Wall, 1975.

Daly, Mary. *Beyond God the Father: Toward a Philosophy of Women's Liberation*. London: Women's Press, 1986.

———. *The Church and the Second Sex*. Boston: Beacon, 1985.

Darity, William A. "Dependency Theory." In *International Encyclopedia of the Social Sciences*, 2. Detroit: Macmillan Reference USA, 2007.

Davidson, Arnold I. "Ethics as Ascetics: Foucault, the History of Ethics, and Ancient Thought." In *The Cambridge Companion to Foucault*, edited by Gary Gutting, 115–40. Cambridge: Cambridge University Press, 2005.

———. *Foucault and His Interlocutors*. A Critical Inquiry Book. Chicago: University of Chicago Press, 1997.

Deleuze, Gilles. *Negotiations, 1972–1990*. New York: Columbia University Press, 1995.

DiAngelo, Robin J. *White Fragility: Why It's So Hard for White People to Talk About Racism*. London: Penguin, 2019.

Doak, Mary. "The Politics of Radical Orthodoxy: A Catholic Critique." *Theological Studies* 68.2 (2007) 368–93.

Douglas, Kelly Brown. *The Black Christ*. Maryknoll, NY: Orbis, 1994.

Durkheim, Émile. *The Division of Labour in Society*. Basingstoke: Macmillan, 1984.

Dyckman, Katherine, et al. *The Spiritual Exercises Reclaimed: Uncovering Liberating Possibilities for Women*. New York: Paulist, 2001.

Elden, Stuart. "A More Marxist Foucault? Reading La Société Punitive." *Historical Materialism* 23.4 (2015) 149–68.

Eliason, Michele J. "Identity Formation for Lesbian, Bisexual, and Gay Persons: Beyond a 'Minoritizing' View." *Journal of Homosexuality* 30.3 (1996) 31–58.

Engels, Friedrich. *The Origin of the Family, Private Property, and the State (of 1884)*. Edited by Tristram Hunt. London: Penguin Classics, 2010.

The Episcopal Church. *The Book of Common Prayer and Administration of the Sacraments and Other Rites and Ceremonies of the Church*. New York: Church Hymnal Corp, 1979.

Foucault, Michel. "About the Beginning of the Hermeneutics of the Self: Two Lectures at Dartmouth." *Political Theory* 21.2 (1993) 198–227.

———. *The Archaeology of Knowledge*. Translated by A. M. Sheridan Smith. New York: Pantheon, 1972.

———. "The Battle for Chastity." Translated by James Bernauer. In *Religion and Culture by Michel Foucault*, edited by Jeremy Carrette, 188–97. Manchester: Manchester University Press, 1999.

———. "The Birth of Biopolitics." Translated by Robert Hurley. In *Ethics: Subjectivity and Truth*, edited by Paul Rabinow, 73–80. London: Penguin, 2000.

———. *Discipline and Punish: The Birth of the Prison*. Translated by Alan Sheridan. 2nd ed. New York: Vintage, 1995.

———. *Dits et écrits*. 4 vols. Paris: Gallimard, 1994.

———. "The Ethic of Care for the Self as a Practice of Freedom." Translated by J. D. Gauthier. In *The Final Foucault*, edited by James Bernauer and David Rasmussen, 1–20. Cambridge: MIT Press, 1987.

———. "The Ethics of the Concern for Self as a Practice of Freedom." Translated by Robert Hurley. In *Ethics: Subjectivity and Truth*, edited by Paul Rabinow, 281–302. London: Penguin, 2000.

———. *The Foucault Reader*. Edited by Paul Rabinow. London: Penguin, 1984.

———. "Friendship as a Way of Life." Translated by Robert Hurley. In *Ethics: Subjectivity and Truth*, edited by Paul Rabinow, 135–40. London: Penguin, 2000.

———. "The Hermeneutic of the Subject." Translated by Robert Hurley. In *Ethics: Subjectivity and Truth*, edited by Paul Rabinow, 93–106. London: Penguin, 2000.

———. *The History of Sexuality, Vol. 1: The Will to Knowledge*. Translated by Robert Hurley. London: Penguin, 1998.

———. *The History of Sexuality, Vol. 2: The Use of Pleasure*. Translated by Robert Hurley. London: Penguin, 1992.

———. *The History of Sexuality, Vol. 3: The Care of the Self*. Translated by Robert Hurley. London: Penguin, 1990.

———. *The History of Sexuality, Vol. 4: Confessions of the Flesh* Translated by Robert Hurley. London Penguin, 2021.

———. "An Interview with Michel Foucault." *History of the Present* 4 (1988) 1–2, 11–13.

———. "Is It Useless to Revolt." Translated by James Bernauer. In *Religion and Culture by Michel Foucault*, edited by Jeremy Carrette, 131–34. Manchester: Manchester University Press, 1999.

———. *L'Origine de L'Herméneutique de Soi: Conferences Prononcées à Dartmouth College, 1980*. Paris: Vrin, 2013.

———. *Madness and Civilization: A History of Insanity in the Age of Reason*. Translated by Richard Howard. New York: Vintage, 1988.

———. "Michel Foucault and Zen: A Stay in a Zen Temple." In *Religion and Culture by Michel Foucault*, edited by Jeremy Carrette, 110–14. Manchester: Manchester University Press, 1999.

———. "Michel Foucault: An Interview by Stephen Riggins." Translated by Robert Hurley. In *Ethics: Subjectivity and Truth*, edited by Paul Rabinow, 121–33. London: Penguin, 2000.

———. "On the Archaeology of the Sciences: Response to the Epistemology Circle." Translated by Robert Hurley. In *Aesthetics, Method and Epistemology*, edited by James D. Faubion, 297–334. London: Penguin, 2000.

———. "On the Genealogy of Ethics: An Overview of Work in Progress." Translated by Robert Hurley. In *Ethics: Subjectivity and Truth*, edited by Paul Rabinow, 253–80. London: Penguin, 2000.

———. *On the Government of the Living: Lectures at the Collège De France, 1979-1980 and Oedipal Knowledge.* Translated by Graham Burchell. Edited by Michel Senellart and Arnold I. Davidson. New York: Palgrave Macmillan, 2012.

———. *The Order of Things.* 1966. Reprint, New York: Vintage, 1994.

———. "Polemics, Politics and Problematization: An Interview with Michel Foucault." Translated by Robert Hurley. In *Ethics: Subjectivity and Truth*, edited by Paul Rabinow, 111–19. London: Penguin, 2000.

———. "Psychiatric Power." Translated by Robert Hurley. In *Ethics: Subjectivity and Truth*, edited by Paul Rabinow, 39–57. London: Penguin, 2000.

———. "The Punitive Society." Translated by Robert Hurley. In *Ethics: Subjectivity and Truth*, edited by Paul Rabinow, 23–38. London: Penguin, 2000.

———. *Remarks on Marx.* 1978. Reprint, New York: Semiotext(e), 1991.

———. "Security, Territory, and Population." Translated by Robert Hurley. In *Ethics: Subjectivity and Truth*, edited by Paul Rabinow, 67–72. London: Penguin, 2000.

———. "Sex, Power and the Politics of Identity." Translated by Robert Hurley. In *Ethics: Subjectivity and Truth*, edited by Paul Rabinow, 163–73. London: Penguin, 2000.

———. "Sexual Choice, Sexual Act." Translated by Robert Hurley. In *Ethics: Subjectivity and Truth*, edited by Paul Rabinow, 141–56. London: Penguin, 2000.

———. "Sexuality and Solitude." Translated by James Bernauer. In *Religion and Culture by Michel Foucault*, edited by Jeremy Carrette, 182–87. Manchester: Manchester University Press, 1999.

———. "The Social Triumph of the Sexual Will." Translated by Robert Hurley. In *Ethics: Subjectivity and Truth*, edited by Paul Rabinow, 157–62. London: Penguin, 2000.

———. *Society Must Be Defended: Lectures at the Collège De France, 1975-76.* Translated by David Macey. Edited by Mauro Bertani and Alessandro Fontana. London: Penguin, 2004.

———. "Subjectivity and Truth." Translated by Robert Hurley. In *Ethics: Subjectivity and Truth*, edited by Paul Rabinow, 87–92. London: Penguin, 2000.

———. "Technologies of the Self." Translated by Robert Hurley. In *Ethics: Subjectivity and Truth*, edited by Paul Rabinow, 223–51. London: Penguin, 2000.

———. "Truth Is in the Future." In *Foucault Live: Collected Interviews, 1961-1984*, edited by Sylvère Lotringer, 298–301. New York: Semiotext(e), 1996.

———. "What Is Enlightenment?" In *The Foucault Reader*, edited by Paul Rabinow, 32–50. London: Penguin, 1984.

Foucault, Michel, and John K. Simon. "Michel Foucault on Attica: An Interview." *Social Justice* 18.3 (45) (1991) 26–34.

Foucault, Michel, et al. "Coronavirus and Philosophers." *European Journal of Psychoanalysis* (2020).

Foucault, Michel, et al. "Iran: The Spirit of a World without Spirit (1979)." Translated by Alan Sheridan. In *Politics, Philosophy, Culture: Interviews and Other Writings 1977–1984*, edited by Lawrence Kritzman, 211–24. New York: Routledge, 1988.

Frank, Miriam, et al. "Rosie the Riveter." *Society* 21.3 (1984) 75–78.

Frank, Walter. *Law and the Gay Rights Story: The Long Search for Equal Justice in a Divided Democracy*. New Brunswick, NJ: Rutgers University Press, 2014.

Fredrickson, George M. *White Supremacy: A Comparative Study in American and South African History*. New York: Oxford University Press, 1981.

Fukuyama, Francis. *The End of History and the Last Man*. London: Penguin, 1992.

"Gender Pay Gap in the UK: 2020." https://www.ons.gov.uk/employmentandlabour market/peopleinwork/earningsandworkinghours/bulletins/genderpaygap intheuk/2020.

Genel, Katia. "The Question of Biopower: Foucault and Agamben." *Rethinking Marxism* 18.1 (2006) 43–62.

Ghamari-Tabrizi, Behrooz. *Foucault in Iran: Islamic Revolution after the Enlightenment*. Minneapolis, MN: University of Minnesota Press, 2016.

Giddens, Anthony. *The Third Way: The Renewal of Social Democracy*. Cambridge: Polity, 1998.

Gill, Robin. *Theology in a Social Context: Sociological Theology, Vol. 1*. Abingdon: Routledge, 2012.

Gluck, Sherna Berger. *Rosie the Riveter Revisited: Women, the War, and Social Change*. Boston: Twayne, 1987.

Gluckman, Amy, and Betsy Reed. "The Gay Marketing Moment." In *Homo Economics: Capitalism, Community, and Lesbian and Gay Life*, 3–10. New York: Routledge, 1997.

Gluckman, Amy, and Betsy Reed, eds. *Homo Economics: Capitalism, Community, and Lesbian and Gay Lif*. New York: Routledge, 1997.

Goldin, Claudia D. "The Role of World War II in the Rise of Women's Employment." *The American Economic Review* 81.4 (1991) 741–56.

Gordon, Colin. "The Christian Art of Being Governed." *Foucault Studies* 20 (2015) 243–65.

Gordon, Colin, et al. "Considerations on Marxism, Phenomenology and Power. Interview with Michel Foucault; Recorded on April 3rd, 1978." *Foucault Studies* 14 (2012) 98–114.

Gottwald, Norman K. *The Bible and Liberation: Political and Social Hermeneutics*. Rev. ed. Maryknoll, NY: Orbis, 1983.

Grant, Jacquelyn. *White Women's Christ and Black Women's Jesus: Feminist Christology and Womanist Response*. Atlanta, GA: Scholars, 1989.

Gutiérrez, Gustavo. "Faith as Freedom: Solidarity with the Alienated and Confidence in the Future." *Horizons* 2.1 (1975) 25–60.

———. *On Job: God-Talk and the Suffering of the Innocent*. Translated by Matthew J. O'Connell. Maryknoll, NY: Orbis, 1987.

———. "The Task and Content of Liberation Theology." Translated by Judith Condor. In *The Cambridge Companion to Liberation Theology*, edited by Christopher Rowland, 19–38. Cambridge: Cambridge University Press, 2007.

———. *The Truth Shall Make You Free: Confrontations*. Translated by Matthew J. O'Connell. Maryknoll, NY: Orbis, 1990.

Haight, Roger. *A Christian Spirituality for Seekers: Reflections on the Spiritual Exercises of Ignatius Loyola.* Maryknoll, NY : Edinburgh: Alban, 2012.

Harcourt, Bernard E. "Foucault's Keystone: Confessions of the Flesh." *Foucault Studies* 29 (2021) 48–70 .

Hardesty, Nancy. *Inclusive Language in the Church.* Atlanta, GA: Westminster John Knox, 1987.

Harding, Sandra. "Introduction: Standpoint Theory as a Site of Political, Philosophic, and Scientific Debate." In *The Feminist Standpoint Theory Reader: Intellectual and Political Controversies*, edited by Sandra Harding, 1–16. New York: Routledge, 2004.

Hart, Kylo-Patrick R. "We're Here, We're Queer—and We're Better Than You: The Representational Superiority of Gay Men to Heterosexuals on Queer Eye for the Straight Guy." *The Journal of Men's Studies* 12.3 (2004) 241–53.

Hartocollis, Anemona. "Harvard Rated Asian-American Applicants Lower on Personality Traits, Suit Says." *The New York Times*, June 15, 2018. https://www.nytimes.com/2018/06/15/us/harvard-asian-enrollment-applicants.html.

Healy, Nicholas M. *Church, World and the Christian Life: Practical-Prophetic Ecclesiology.* Cambridge: Cambridge University Press, 2000.

Hebblethwaite, Margaret. *Finding God in All Things: The Way of St Ignatius.* London: Fount, 1994.

Hilkert, Mary Catherine. "Experience and Tradition: Can the Center Hold?" In *Freeing Theology: The Essentials of Theology in Feminist Perspective*, edited by Catherine Mowry LaCugna, 59–82. San Francisco: HarperSanFrancisco, 1993.

Hogan, Linda. *From Women's Experience to Feminist Theology.* Sheffield: Sheffield Academic, 1995.

Hopkins, Dwight N. *Introducing Black Theology of Liberation.* Black Theology of Liberation. Maryknoll, NY: Orbis, 1999.

Horujy, Sergey S. *Practices of the Self and Spiritual Practices: Michel Foucault and the Eastern Christian Discourse.* Translated by Boris Jakim. Grand Rapids, MI: Eerdmans, 2015.

Huffer, Lynne. *Mad for Foucault: Rethinking the Foundations of Queer Theory.* New York: Columbia University Press, 2010.

Hyun, Jane. *Breaking the Bamboo Ceiling: Career Strategies for Asians.* Glasgow: HarperCollins, 2005.

Ignatius of Loyola. *The Spiritual Exercises of Saint Ignatius: A Translation and Commentary by George E. Ganss.* Translated by George Ganss. Chicago: Loyola, 1992.

Jaschik, Scott. "The Numbers and the Arguments on Asian Admissions." *Inside Higher Education*, August 7, 2017.

Jessop, Bob. "From Micro-Powers to Governmentality: Foucault's Work on Statehood, State Formation, Statecraft and State Power." *Political Geography* 26.1 (2007) 34–40.

Jones, Jeffrey M. "LGBT Identification Rises to 5.6% in Latest U.S. Estimate." In *Gallup*, February 24, 2021. https://news.gallup.com/poll/329708/lgbt-identification-rises-latest-estimate.aspx.

Jordan, Mark D. *Convulsing Bodies: Religion and Resistance in Foucault.* Stanford, CA: Stanford University Press, 2020.

Joseph, Peniel E. *Waiting 'Til the Midnight Hour: A Narrative History of Black Power in America*. New York: Henry Holt, 2007.

Junior, Nyasha. *An Introduction to Womanist Biblical Interpretation*. 1st ed. Louisville, KY: Westminster John Knox, 2015.

Kee, Alistair. *Marx and the Failure of Liberation Theology*. London: SCM, 1990.

Kelliher, Diarmaid. "Solidarity and Sexuality: Lesbians and Gays Support the Miners 1984–5." 77.1 (2014) 240–62.

King, Ursula. *Feminist Theology from the Third World: A Reader*. Maryknoll, NY: Orbis, 1994.

Kwok, Pui-Lan. *Introducing Asian Feminist Theology*. Asian Feminist Theology. Sheffield: Sheffield Academic, 2000.

———. "Theology as a Sexual Act?" *Feminist Theology* 11.2 (2003) 149–56.

LaCugna, Catherine Mowry. "Introduction." In *Freeing Theology: The Essentials of Theology in Feminist Perspective*, edited by Catherine Mowry LaCugna, 1–4. San Francisco: HarperSanFrancisco, 1993.

Lazzarato, Maurizio. "From Biopower to Biopolitics." *Pli: The Warwick Journal of Philosophy* 13.8 (2002) 1–6.

Leezenberg, Michiel. "Foucault and Iran Reconsidered: Revolt, Religion, and Neoliberalism." *Īrān-nāmag* 3.2 (2018) iv–xxviii.

———. "Power and Political Spirituality: Michel Foucault on the Islamic Revolution in Iran." In *Michel Foucault and Theology: The Politics of Religious Experience*, edited by James Bernauer and Jeremy Carrette, 99–116. Surrey: Ashgate, 2004.

Lemke, Thomas. "Foucault, Governmentality, and Critique." *Rethinking Marxism* 14.3 (2002) 49–64.

Loades, Ann. "Introduction." In *Feminist Theology: A Reader*, edited by Ann Loades, 1–12. London: SPCK, 1990.

Lonsdale, David. *Eyes to See, Ears to Hear: An Introduction to Ignatian Spirituality*. Rev. ed. Maryknoll, NY: Orbis, 2000.

Lorde, Audre. "An Open Letter to Mary Daly." In *This Bridge Called My Back: Writings by Radical Women of Color*, edited by Cherríe Moraga and Gloria Anzaldúa, 94–97. Watertown, MA: Persephone, 1981.

Mahmood, Saba. "Feminist Theory, Embodiment, and the Docile Agent: Some Reflections on the Egyptian Islamic Revival." *Cultural Anthropology* 16.2 (2001) 202–36.

———. *Politics of Piety: The Islamic Revival and the Feminist Subject*. Princeton: Princeton University Press, 2005.

Maritain, Jacques. *The Things That Are Not Caesar's*. Translated by J. F. Scanlan. New York: Scribner's, 1931.

Marx, Karl. *The Communist Manifesto (of 1848) Annotated Text*. Edited by Frederic L. Bender. New York: Norton, 1988.

———. *Economic and Philosophic Manuscripts of 1844*. 1st American ed. New York: International, 1964.

McGrath, Alister E. *Christian Theology: An Introduction*. 5th ed. Hoboken: Wiley-Blackwell, 2010.

McGushin, Edward. "Foucault's Theory and Practice of Subjectivity." In *Michel Foucault: Key Concepts*, edited by Dianna Taylor, 127–42. Durham, UK: Taylor & Francis Group, 2014.

McSweeney, John. "Book Review: *Foucault and Theology.*" *Foucault Studies* 2 (2005) 117–44.

Milbank, John. *Theology and Social Theory: Beyond Secular Reason.* 2nd ed. Oxford: Blackwell, 2006.

Mohanty, Chandra Talpade. "Under Western Eyes: Feminist Scholarship and Colonial Discourses." *Boundary 2* (1984) 333–58.

Moltmann, Jürgen. "Political Theology in Ecumenical Contexts." In *Political Theology: Contemporary Challenges and Future Directions,* edited by Michael Welker et al., 1–12. Louisville, KY: Westminster John Knox, 2013.

Moltmann-Wendel, Elisabeth. *I Am My Body: A Theology of Embodiment.* New York: Continuum, 1995.

O'Collins, Gerald, and Daniel Kendall. "Mary Magdalene as Major Witness to Jesus' Resurrection." *Theological Studies* 48.4 (1987) 631–46.

Olssen, Mark. "Foucault and Marxism: Rewriting the Theory of Historical Materialism." *Policy Futures in Education* 2.3–4 (2004) 454–82.

Orr, Gillian. "Bey Can Do It: Beyoncé Re-Enacts Rosie the Riveter's Pose." *Independent,* July 24, 2014. https://www.independent.co.uk/life-style/health-and-families/features/beyonce-poses-rosie-riveter-wartime-poster-girl-who-became-feminist-pin-9624381.html.

Park, Andrew Sung. "Minjung Theology: A Korean Contextual Theology." *The Indian Journal of Theology* 33 (1984) 1–11.

Parsons, Susan Frank. "Feminist Theology as Dogmatic Theology." In *The Cambridge Companion to Feminist Theology,* edited by Susan Frank Parsons, 114–32. Cambridge: University of Cambridge Press, 2002.

Patton, Paul. "Taylor and Foucault on Power and Freedom." *Political Studies* 37.2 (1989) 260–76.

Peñaloza, Lisa. "We're Here, We're Queer, and We're Going Shopping! A Critical Perspective on the Accommodation of Gays and Lesbians in the Us Marketplace." *Journal of Homosexuality* 31.1–2 (1996) 9–41.

Perrigo, Sarah. "Gender Struggles in the British Labour Party from 1979 to 1995." *Party Politics* 1.3 (1995) 407–17.

Petrella, Ivan. *Beyond Liberation Theology: A Polemic.* Reclaiming Liberation Theology. London: SCM, 2008.

———. *Latin American Liberation Theology: The Next Generation.* Maryknoll, NY: Orbis, 2005.

Polanyi, Karl. *The Great Transformation: The Political and Economic Origins of Our Time.* 2nd ed. Boston, MA: Beacon, 2001.

Poster, Mark. *Foucault, Marxism, and History: Mode of Production Versus Mode of Information.* Cambridge: Polity, 1984.

Quero, Hugo Córdova. "Risky Affairs: Marcella Althaus-Reid Indecently Queering Juan Luis Segundo's Hermeneutical Circle Propositions." In *Dancing Theology in Fetish Boots: Essays in Honour of Marcella Althaus Reid,* edited by Lisa Isherwood and Mark D. Jordan, 207–18. London: SCM, 2010.

Rajchman, John. *Michel Foucault: The Freedom of Philosophy.* New York: Columbia University Press, 1985.

Ratzinger, Joseph. "Dogmatic Constitution on Divine Revelation: Origin and Background." *Commentary on the Documents of Vatican II* 3 (1969) 155–66.

Razai, Mohammad S., et al. "Mitigating Ethnic Disparities in Covid-19 and Beyond." *BMJ* 372.8277 (2021). https://www.bmj.com/content/372/bmj.m4921.

Rinaldo, Rachel. *Mobilizing Piety: Islam and Feminism in Indonesia.* Oxford: Oxford University Press, 2013.

Robinson, John A. T. *Honest to God.* London: SCM, 1963.

Robinson, Margaret. "Reading Althaus-Reid: As a Bi Feminist Theo/Methodological Resource." *Journal of Bisexuality* 10 (2010) 108–20.

Rosario, Margaret, et al. "The Coming-Out Process and Its Adaptational and Health-Related Associations among Gay, Lesbian, and Bisexual Youths: Stipulation and Exploration of a Model." *American Journal of Community Psychology* 29.1 (2001) 133–60.

Rotsaert, Mark. "Loving Union with God in Jesus: The Force Behind the Reality of Christian Living." In *The Lord of Friendship : Friendship, Discernment and Mission in Ignatian Spirituality*, edited by Jacques Haers et al., 81–96. Oxford: Way, 2011.

Rowland, Christopher. "Introduction." In *The Cambridge Companion to Liberation Theology*, edited by Christopher Rowland, 1–16. Cambridge: Cambridge University Press, 2007.

Rubin, Gayle. "Thinking Sex: Notes for a Radical Theory of the Politics of Sexuality." In *The Lesbian and Gay Studies Reader*, edited by Henry Abelove et al., 100–133. New York: Routledge, 1993.

Ruether, Rosemary Radford. *Sexism and God-Talk: Toward a Feminist Theology.* Boston: Beacon, 1993.

Said, Edward. "Michel Foucault, 1926–1984." *After Foucault: Humanistic Knowledge, Postmodern Challenges* (1988) 1–11.

Santana, María Cristina. "From Empowerment to Domesticity: The Case of Rosie the Riveter and the Wwii Campaign." *Frontiers in Sociology* 1 (2016) 1–18.

Sawicki, Jana. "Queer Feminism: Cultivating Ethical Practices of Freedom." *Foucault Studies* 16 (2013) 74–87.

Schotten, C. Heike. *Queer Terror: Life, Death, and Desire in the Settler Colony.* Vol. 59. New York: Columbia University Press, 2018.

Schüssler Fiorenza, Elisabeth. "Critical Feminist the*Logy of Liberation: A Decolonizing Political the*Logy." In *Political Theology: Contemporary Challenges and Future Directions*, edited by Michael Welker et al., 37–60. Louisville, KY: Westminster John Knox, 2013.

———. *In Memory of Her: A Feminist Theological Reconstruction of Christian Origins.* New York: Crossroad, 1983.

———. *Rhetoric and Ethic: The Politics of Biblical Studies.* Minneapolis: Fortress, 1999.

Scott, James C. *Weapons of the Weak: Everyday Forms of Peasant Resistance.* New Haven: Yale University Press, 1985.

Sears, Alan. "Queer Anti-Capitalism: What's Left of Lesbian and Gay Liberation?" *Science & Society* 69.1 (2005) 92–112.

Service, Robert. *Comrades! A History of World Communism.* History of World Communism. Cambridge: Harvard University Press, 2007.

Sheldrake, Philip. *Befriending Our Desires.* Collegeville, MN: Liturgical, 2016.

Simons, Jon. "Power, Resistance, and Freedom." In *A Companion to Foucault*, edited by Christopher Falzon et al., 299–319. Malden, MA: Wiley-Blackwell, 2013.

Smith, Christian. *The Emergence of Liberation Theology: Radical Religion and Social Movement Theory.* Chicago: University of Chicago Press, 1991.

Smith-Hefner, Nancy J. "Javanese Women and the Veil in Post-Soeharto Indonesia." *The Journal of Asian Studies* 66.2 (2007) 389–420.

Song, Choan-Seng. *The Tears of Lady Meng: A Parable of People's Political Theology.* Maryknoll, NY: Orbis 1982.

———. *Third-Eye Theology: Theology in Formation in Asian Settings.* Maryknoll, NY: Orbis, 1979.

Stanton, Elizabeth Cady. *The Woman's Bible: A Classic Feminist Perspective.* Mineola, NY: Dover, 2002.

Stauth, Georg. "Revolution in Spiritless Times: An Essay on Michel Foucault's Enquiries into the Iranian Revolution." *International Sociology* 6.3 (1991) 259–80.

Sugirtharajah, R. S. *The Bible and the Third World: Precolonial, Colonial and Postcolonial Encounters.* Cambridge: Cambridge University Press, 2001.

Sung, Jung Mo. "Commodity Fetishism and Critical Metaphysics." In *Socialism in Process,* edited by Justin Heinzekehr and Philip Clayton, 85–98. Anoka: Process Century, 2017.

———. *Desire, Market and Religion.* London: SCM, 2007.

———. "Greed, Desire and Theology." *The Ecumenical Review* 63.3 (2011) 251–62.

———. "The Poor after Liberation Theology." Translated by Francis McDobagh. In *Globalization and the Church of the Poor,* edited by Daniel Franklin E Pilario et al., 65–74. London: SCM, 2015.

———. "Save Us from Cynicism: Religion and Social Class." In *Theology, Religion, and Class: Fresh Engagements after Long Silence,* edited by Joerg Rieger, 43–59. New Approaches to Religion and Power. New York: Palgrave Macmillan US, 2013.

Swinton, John, and Harriett Mowat. *Practical Theology and Qualitative Research.* London: SCM, 2013.

Taylor, Charles. "Foucault on Freedom and Truth." *Political Theory* 12.2 (1984) 152–83.

Taylor, Michael. "With 'Pink Yuan' Ads, China Wakes up to the World's Biggest Gay Economy." *Reuters,* February 21, 2020. https://www.reuters.com/article/us-china-lgbt-advertising-idUSKBN20F01R.

Thistlethwaite, Susan Brooks. "On Becoming a Traitor: The Academic Liberation Theologian and the Future." In *Liberating the Future: God, Mammon and Theology,* edited by Joerg Rieger, 14–26. Minneapolis: Fortress, 1998.

Tran, Jonathan. *Foucault and Theology.* London: T. & T. Clark, 2011.

Trible, Phyllis. 如何和聖經摔跤：從婦女和修辭學的觀點詮釋聖經 [*How to Wrestle with the Bible: From the Perspectives of Women and Rhetoric.*] Taipei: Taiwan Theological Seminary Press, 2010.

———. *Texts of Terror: Literary-Feminist Readings of Biblical Narratives.* Philadelphia: Fortress, 1984.

Turkel, Gerald. "Michel Foucault: Law, Power, and Knowledge." *Journal of Law and Society* 17.2 (1990) 170–93.

Vidales, Raul. "Methodological Issues in Liberation Theology." Translated by John Drury. In *Frontiers of Theology in Latin America,* edited by Rosino Gibellini, 34–57. Maryknoll, NY: Orbis, 1979.

Walker, Alice. *In Search of Our Mothers' Gardens: Womanist Prose.* 1st ed. San Diego: Harcourt Brace Jovanovich, 1983.

Weeks, Jeffrey. *Coming Out: Homosexual Politics in Britain, from the Nineteenth Century to the Present.* Rev. ed. London: Quartet, 1983.

Weitz, Eric D. "Self-Determination: How a German Enlightenment Idea Became the Slogan of National Liberation and a Human Right." *The American Historical Review* 120.2 (2015) 462–96.

"WHOQOL: Measuring Quality of Life." https://www.who.int/tools/whoqol.

Wong, Wai-Ching Angela. *The Poor Woman: A Critical Analysis of Asian Theology and Contemporary Chinese Fiction by Women.* New York: P. Lang, 2002.

Williams, Delores S. "The Color of Feminism: On Speaking the Black Woman's Tongue." *The Journal of Religious Thought* 43.1 (1986) 42–58.

———. *Sisters in the Wilderness: The Challenge of Womanist God-Talk.* Maryknoll, NY: Orbis, 2013.

Williams, Raymond. *Problems in Materialism and Culture: Selected Essays.* New York: Verso, 1980.

Willis, Susan. "Work (Ing) Out." *Cultural Studies* 4.1 (1990) 1–18.

Winnubst, Shannon. "The Queer Thing About Neoliberal Pleasure: A Foucauldian Warning." *Foucault Studies* 14 (2012) 79–97.

Winson, Rebecca. "Sorry Beyoncé, Rosie the Riveter Is No Feminist Icon. Here's Why." In *The Guardian,* July 23, 2014. https://www.theguardian.com/commentisfree/2014/jul/23/beyonce-rosie-the-riveter-feminist-icon.

Worsley, Peter. *Marx and Marxism.* 2nd ed. London: Routledge, 2013.

Printed in Great Britain
by Amazon